MINISTRY AT THE MARGINS

MINISTRY AT THE MARGINS

Strategy and Spirituality
for Mission

Anthony J. Gittins

ORBIS BOOKS

Maryknoll, New York 10545

Second printing, May 2003

Library of Congress Cataloging-in-Publication Data

Gittins, Anthony J., 1943-
  Ministry at the margins : strategy and spirituality for mission /
Anthony J. Gittins.
     p.   cm.
Includes bibliographical references and index.
  ISBN 1-57075-417-9 (pbk.)
  1. Missions—Theory.   I. Title.
  BV2063.G52 2002
  266'.001—dc21
                              2002000850

Dedicated to the members of the
Volunteer Missionary Movement
past, present,
and yet to come.

"I am quite certain that the One who began this good work in you
will see that it is finished when the Day of Jesus Christ comes"
Philippians (1:6)

CONTENTS

ABBREVIATIONS

AG   *Ad Gentes* (Decree on the Church's Missionary Activity), Vatican II document

GS   *Gaudium et Spes* (Pastoral Constitution on the Church in the Modern World), Vatican II document

EN   *Evangelii Nuntiandi*, 1975, Apostolic exhortation of Pope Paul VI (*Evangelization in the Modern World*)

RM   *Redemptoris Missio* (*On The Permanent Validity of the Church's Missionary Mandate*), 1991, encyclical letter of Pope John Paul II

PREFACE

Baptism is a life-changing experience. If you believe that strongly enough, this book may be for you. It is about the challenge of living as if Baptism really matters. Some people may not have given this much thought. Others are very familiar with the phrase "the church is missionary by her nature" (AG 2). This striking assertion is intended to remind Christians that it is necessary to respond to, or *activate,* their Baptism in the very way they live; the phrase is followed by explanation and elaboration:

> God decided to enter into the history of humankind in a new and definitive manner, by sending his own Son in human flesh. Christ said of himself: "The Spirit of the Lord is upon me, because he anointed me; to bring good news to the poor, to heal the broken-hearted, to proclaim to the captive release, and sight to the blind" (Lk 4:8). Now, what was once preached by the Lord ... must be proclaimed and extended to the ends of the earth.
>
> The Lord founded his church as the sacrament of salvation. Hence the church has the obligation to proclaim the faith and salvation which comes from Christ. The mission of the church is carried out by means of that activity through which, in obedience to Christ's command and moved by the grace and love of the Holy Spirit, the church makes itself fully present to all individuals and peoples in order to lead them to the faith, freedom, and peace of Christ by the example of its life and teaching, by the sacraments and other means of grace. The church must walk the road Christ himself walked, a way of poverty and obedience, of service and self-sacrifice even to death.
>
> This task is one and the same everywhere and in all situations, although, because of circumstances, it may not always be exercised in the same way. (AG 3, 5, 6)

This is a fine theological statement. In the past generation, committed Christians from many denominations have come far in ecumenical fellowship as they have responded to its challenge. But it *is* a theological formulation. It leaves a great deal unsaid about *how* the mission should be undertaken in practice.

Christian Baptism calls us to reach out, not to be centered upon our-selves, to undertake to carry the Good News enthusiastically, and to broad-cast it in whatever way we can. There was a time when mission was understood to be an activity of the few and to take place at the remotest corners of the earth. But from the very beginning Christians knew that theirs was a missionary faith and that they were called and commissioned by their Baptism and their Master.[1] Some, of course, went to the ends of the earth, taking *the Great Commission* (Mt 28:16-20) literally. But oth-ers reached out from wherever they were, taking the words of Jesus for their own and believing that the very same Spirit given to Jesus was given to them, and for the very same reasons: *to bring good news to the poor, to proclaim liberty to captives and to the blind new sight, to set the down-trodden free,* and *to proclaim the Lord's year of favor* (Lk 4:18-20).

Mission is an impulsion, a driving onward, a commission to love God and neighbor actively. In a globalized world and a new Christian millen-nium the age-old question is as pertinent as ever: who is my neighbor? Many Christians continue to seek their neighbor across national and con-tinental boundaries; but many more struggle to discover their neighbor much closer to home in the poor and dispossessed, the forgotten and abandoned, the abused and brutalized.

This book attempts to speak to all who take their missionary vocation seriously. It tries to challenge and encourage, to warn and to suggest, to offer thoughts about how we might continue to be more faithful and more Christlike in our approaches to other people. It addresses one of the fundamental paradoxes of our lives: that humanity is the same the world over, yet every single person is unique. It attempts to say something about preparing to encounter the *other* and to recognize a brother or sister. It deliberately repeats many times that *goodwill is not enough*. It tries to supplement good intentions with good preparation and good judgment.

Christian mission must be ecumenical. Together the baptized must pro-claim a common faith and offer a common witness. Together we are the Body of Christ: blemished and in need of healing, but determined and committed nonetheless. Never again can we undertake separately what we are called to do together.

The following pages originated as presentations[2] for an orientation for the Division for Global Mission of the Evangelical Lutheran Church in America (ELCA). Within a few years that orientation was jointly spon-sored by the ELCA and the Presbyterian Church (PCUSA). By the mid-1990s, the Volunteer Missionary Movement, the Episcopal Church, and the Reformed Church of America had joined the orientation, now held twice a year and preparing two hundred candidates annually for cross-cultural mission. Meanwhile some material was also being offered biannu-ally to the Global Ministries Division of the United Church of Christ and the Disciples of Christ in Indianapolis. There have now been fifteen years of increasingly inclusive ecumenical preparation of missionary personnel.

If we are called to be missionary by virtue of Baptism, then mission must be a possibility for all the baptized. But most people do not and cannot travel and live overseas. Therefore mission cannot be dependent on overseas travel. Authentic mission is a movement from the center to the margin: from wherever our center may be to wherever our center is not: from wherever we are to wherever other people are. Mission is centrifugal movement but it is also encounter. When we move to the margins of our own familiar world, we encounter other people. Sometimes the margins are only an arm's length—or a city block or neighborhood—away. So long as we move from the centers and encounter our unfamiliar brothers and sisters in Christ's name and in the name of the gospel, we are followers of The Way and disciples of Christ.

A word on a typographical formatting convention and what it means is necessary at this point. Most text in *Ministry at the Margins* is set in the typeface used in the preface you are now reading. Upon occasion, however, we have set recollections and stories in an indented excerpt style in a different typeface. The first example is to be found below on page 25. It begins "On a public bus in a crowded city in Asia . . ." Such formatting does not indicate a quotation from a printed source but what is sometimes (and somewhat incorrectly) called a "verbatim report" in field education for anthropologists, sociologists, and pastoral ministers and/or their reports to colleagues. The formatting draws attention to the story nature of the verbatim.

Ministry at the Margins is offered to boundary crossers of all kinds. Some may be preparing for a first-time and exciting cross-cultural commitment; others may have criss-crossed the globe already; others again may never have left their own country. It is intended for anyone committed to outreach and inclusion, to forgiveness and reconciliation in the name of Jesus.

This book is about ministry: about small *(minor),* rather insignificant *(mini)* service. A minister is the opposite of a master: not very visible and not self-important, but nevertheless necessary. It is also about margins, edges, and boundaries. Margins are minimally important in themselves, yet they mark boundaries and identify where inside meets outside. Marginal means relatively insignificant, certainly not central.

Mission often takes place at the margins—of society, of nations, of territory, even of agendas. Mission is typically marginal—not mainstream, not consequential, overlooked by those at the centers. Mission is always ministry—humble faithfulness to the example of Jesus, service in the style of the Servant.

Ministry at the Margins is more a handbook than a textbook, more a reference book than an encyclopedia. It is not an academic treatise, and it has few pretensions. It is simply offered to anyone with a hunger and thirst for justice, for God's righteousness, and for the challenge of Christian mission.

Feast of Pentecost
June 3, 2001

PASSING OVER . . .

NORMAL PEOPLE—AND MISSIONARIES

"When are you going to settle down?" You must have heard this a dozen times. It's an often asked question based on a widely shared assumption that sooner or later everyone ought to become more or less permanently planted. Even though the United States and Australia, more than Europe, are built on a history of immigration and expansion, it has often been assumed that when people achieve a measure of success, they will sink permanent roots and become domesticated. Most people from nations blessed with stability and relative plenty seemed content to spend their lives where they were born and raised, or they never imagined alternatives. They simply assumed that this was the normal way to live.

There has always been a counter current, of course. It is rare that human societies are absolutely cut off from the wider world, and there is a natural curiosity that impels some people to venture beyond their familiar domain. Human history is not only the story of contact between cultures but also the tale of the context in which those cultures develop. Nevertheless, we use words like *pioneer, explorer,* or *trailblazer* to identify such people and mark them as unusual or abnormal. Normal people, by implication, are rather more restrained: the homemakers and farmers, solid citizens and patriots.

This book is about people who are not quite normal by conventional judgments. They may be restless or nomadic, and their primary concern is not to settle down. They are missionaries, people energized by a sense of mission, of vocation. They believe, as the second-century *Epistle to Diognetus* put it, that God has assigned them an "important post, . . . and they are not at liberty to desert it."[1]

In 1969 Neil Armstrong landed on the moon, and the idea of (outer) space and distant planets became immediately comprehensible to ordinary men and women. Memories of people from as far afield as Afghanistan and Zimbabwe were indelibly marked with his "giant leap for mankind." In 1970 Boeing introduced the 747, or jumbo jet, and the idea of (inner) space and distant continents was instantly accessible to ordinary men and women. Imaginations of people from San Francisco to Sydney were caught by the inspiration to travel the world. In that twelve-month period the unimaginable cosmos and the vastness of the earth shrank dramatically. Over the past thirty-something years, a generation has grown up with the earth within its grasp, while an older generation now has direct experience of peoples and places that formerly existed only in the pages of *National Geographic*.

As the world has come closer or decreased in size, some of its formerly distant peoples have become larger than life: through telecommunications or travel we can now identify the features of our brothers and sisters anywhere on earth. Now we can choose to look into their eyes and be affected by their lives. Now we have responsibility, where previously our ignorance or lack of involvement might have been absolved by the miles between us. But it is not only people from far away who have come into closer focus; others, so close as to have been overlooked, suddenly become noticeable: abandoned children, incarcerated youth, abused women, the homeless poor. Perhaps there was a time when we could have entered a plea of "not guilty" when faced with litanies of injustice or lists of human needs. That time is long gone. "The poor," whether at our gate or across the ocean, are within reach of today's Christians as never before. As never before, Christian people are accountable for their actions, "for what we have done and what we have failed to do." Recent times have witnessed massive waves of human migration and displacement. Refugees and exiles, unsettled and unwanted people are an indictment to comfortable humanity. And Christians especially are morally implicated in the shaping of the postmodern world.

In recent decades, as the forces of globalization have made the ends of the earth accessible, Christian teaching has reiterated what was in danger of being overlooked: that we have a moral responsibility for each other, that we are indeed our brothers' and sisters' keepers. In a world where the gap between the haves and the have-nots grows ever wider, this is a timely reminder. We are called to examine the boundaries, especially those of comfort, privilege, and security. On the other side of those boundaries, injustice, exploitation and despair thrive. Sometimes we feign not to know this; sometimes we fear to look, perhaps because we are afraid to see and afraid of what it might do to us. But some people do know, do notice, and do want to respond.

But goodwill is not enough. Those whose social conscience is stirred, those who dare to minister on or across the boundaries of their own familiar world, must learn new skills and acquire new knowledge. Perhaps together and in time they will produce wisdom. Talking of boundary-breaking ministry, John Dunne[2] develops twin themes of passing over and coming back. To paraphrase: *the passing over and the coming back are the greatest religious adventure of our time.* Here is a leitmotif for our reflections, and it is worth a closer look:

The passing over
and the coming back
are the greatest
religious
adventure
of our time.

To begin at the end, with the phrase *our time*. There is something peculiar about our present moment, our own contemporary world—*our time*—that is conducive to a religious adventure. Saint Paul said as much two millennia ago, and it is as true now as ever it was, because God is faithful and everlasting: "Now is the favorable time; this is the day of salvation" (2Cor 6:2). But the *Space Age* and the *Internet* are other ways to identify the contemporary moment. We can be on another continent in a matter of hours and virtually anywhere on earth in a matter of days. No longer does it take a year to reach a distant shore and weeks more to penetrate hinterlands. Literally in *our time*—with helicopters, bathyscaphes,[3] and portable oxygen—the earth's remotest regions have become accessible.

Turning now to the first words: *passing over* to distant places is a richly evocative phrase, with strong associations. Perhaps it conjures up the *Passover,* whether the historical event or the annual commemoration of Israel's exodus from Egypt, with its mixture of gratitude and hope. But *pass over* as a verb can also mean to *disregard* or *fail to notice*: we sometimes pass over uncomfortable experiences by refusing to dwell on them or to recall them. There is a third possibility: in American English particularly, to *pass over* is a common euphemism for *to die.* There is an element of death or dying in each boundary-breaking transition and every movement between worlds. Every generous-hearted Christian is called to die in this way as a mark of missionary commitment. If we would save our lives, we must lose them (Mt 16:25); this is not poetry but prose.

Passing over may stimulate a host of memories or associations. John Dunne is suggesting that some form of passing over can be a critical and formative part of our lives. We might reflect on the passing over that describes a missionary life with its ascetic thread and the denial of self it requires.

There is much more: passing over is a constitutive element in an *adventure. Adventure* is not only an exciting word; it might even be unique: it does not seem to have a true synonym—unless we choose *escapade* or *exploit,* one of which connotes recklessness and the other a measure of self-interest. But a true adventure need be neither of these. If we consider words associated, as *adventure* is, with movement or experience, we could produce a list that includes *walk, stroll, vacation, trip,* even *pilgrimage.* Each of these connotes a degree of boundedness or limit, whether in terms of time or of direction. If a friend says she is going for a *walk* or a *stroll* but has not returned by nightfall, something has gone wrong. If you are on *vacation* or a *trip,* you have a fairly clear idea of whether you are at the beginning, in the middle, or at the end of the experience. If you are on *pilgrimage,* you may not exactly know how far remains to travel, but you do have some expectation of the end point.

An *adventure* is quite unlike any of these. Crucially, people do not actually decide to go on an adventure at all: you do not take an adventure; you are taken on an adventure. In the course of an adventure you cannot say whether it is half over or when it will end. You cannot relax or psychologically disengage from an adventure as you can from other forms of experience, because you are not in control and do not know the outcome. An adventure engages you all the time. An adventure is, by definition, associated with risk and uncertainty in a way that other journeys are not.

Whoever hears a call from God and responds to it is thereby commissioned: sent on the *adventure* of a lifetime. This is one of the meanings of *mission.*

Sociologist Georg Simmel spoke of an adventure as something that starts on the very periphery of our life but works its way to life's very center. In a classic essay[4] he characterized an adventure simply as something that makes a profound difference to the whole of a life. It is "a foreign body in our existence which is yet somehow connected with the center; like an island in life which determines its beginning and end according to its own formative powers and not . . . according to those of adjacent territories." An adventure is "defined by its capacity to have necessity and meaning; [there] we abandon ourselves to the world with fewer defenses and reserves than in any other relation."[5]

Simmel described an adventure as "a particular encompassing of the accidentally external by the internally necessary."[6] I understand the "accidentally external" to refer to whatever is contingent, like the geographical location in which the missionary adventure unfolds, and the "internally necessary" to refer to an inner conviction, a sense of vocation or mission. He referred to a "characteristic daring with which [the adventurer] continually leaves the solidities of life" and the certain conviction of an "unknown and unknowable element in his [her] life. For this reason, to the sober person adventurous conduct often seems insanity."[7] Anyone with experience of missionary adventure will know how true this is. Anyone hoping to be caught up in an adventure like this will discover that a spirit of daring, the leaving of life's solidities, and apparent insanity are actually the indispensable fuel that provides the requisite momentum for the adventure.

Returning to John Dunne: he speaks of a particularly *religious* experience or adventure. *Religious* here must include some kind of encounter with the transcendent, the Other, God. People may speak of a variety of experiences as religious—from the first image of the earth from space to the birth of a baby or the music of Mozart—whether or not they are directly associated with formal religious ritual or direct mystical encounters with God. But there is another possibility: that an encounter with other people living in other worlds of meaning may itself be a religious experience. David Augsberger and Dunne suggest that not only can this be a religious experience, it can be superlatively so: *the greatest religious adventure of our time.*

Finally, we consider the whole phrase—*the passing over and the coming back*—since the parts are interdependent. Christian mission is not merely an experience requiring a passing over, whether geographical (from here to there) or ontological (a dying to oneself). It depends for its completeness on a *coming back,* which is much more than a simple return and requires a reengagement with the world and the people we left behind. But missioners, other people, and the world itself will have changed in the interim. So the coming back may be a real challenge.

It is not simply the passing over but the coming back that constitutes the missionary adventure. Many people neither give a thought to the coming back before they pass over nor consider the coming back as an integral part of the adventure itself. But on reflection we can see the two movements as two bookends: between them, the saga of adventure finds its place and context. One reason coming back can be such a challenge is that we simply did not expect it to be an issue. But it can be a positive and creative experience—for those who actually come back, for those they encounter on their return, and for the continuation of mission itself. In order to appreciate the full significance of the coming back, we need to look more closely at the components of the adventure in its total context.

There may be other adventures and other religious experiences in life, but what characterizes the missionary enterprise, namely, *the passing over and the coming back,* is that it is *the greatest religious adventure of our time.* Before we look at the rhythms of the adventure, a word to those whose lives at this moment are not dramatically marked by passing over or coming back. They live close to home—in their native land, in the city of their birth, even in their original neighborhood. Many may not consider the missionary possibilities in their lives. But in the postmodern world, every city is multicultural and every neighborhood is surrounded by invisible barriers separating prosperity from poverty. Anyone who wants to can encounter poor or needy people; anyone who chooses to can pass over and come back. Where there's a will, there's a way. Christian mission is not only for international travelers but for anyone whose life is affected by chapter 25 of Matthew's gospel and by the plight of a hungry, thirsty, sick, imprisoned or abandoned brother or sister.

ADVENTURE IN THREE MOVEMENTS

The adventure of mission can be considered in three parts or movements. Dunne speaks of an odyssey that begins and ends in the Homeland and takes us into what he calls the Wonderland. This insight can be expanded and modified.[8]

FIRST MOVEMENT: THE HOMELAND. The Homeland is wherever our identity was forged and where we sank our cultural roots. Every human baby is the raw material from which a cultural identity will be fashioned. The relationship between nature (genetic endowment) and nurture (cultural conditioning) in human development is complex and difficult to specify. We know that some people born with natural or social handicaps or challenges can become model citizens and that some people born with every imaginable physical and social advantage can become hardened criminals. But even in an age when refugees number in the tens of millions, the Homeland remains the seedbed ("seminary") in which the vast majority of people grow to maturity.

A baby born in Shanghai may become a model Chinese citizen if raised appropriately by adult members of Chinese society. If the same baby is transported to a different homeland and raised by dedicated Italian Americans, she will become a cultural Italian American, even though ethnically she is Chinese. The Homeland is critical for cultural development. If a boy is born in Shanghai and adopted by Chinese parents living in Chicago, he could become a model Chinese American.

Ethnocentrism is an intrinsic feature of human socialization. Every human being tends to be selfish or egocentric, and ethnocentric as well: to see the world and to interpret it as if it revolved around our cultural selves. If a person grows to maturity without a healthy sense of personal, national, and cultural identity, he or she will be unable to function appropriately.[9]

But egocentrism and ethnocentrism are matters of degree: every society expects its members to acquire a measure of sympathy or empathy with other people. This is the ability to resonate with the experiences of others, even to develop an active imagination that would permit vicarious identification with their feelings. Yet this does not thereby reduce or belittle others' feelings. Nor does it imply that we can totally understand—much less experience—those feelings ourselves. But social maturity requires people to acknowledge personal or cultural perspectives different from their own. There are no generic human beings, only specific persons. Yet despite the uniqueness of each person, we can actually come to understand people other than ourselves.

SECOND MOVEMENT: THE WONDERLAND. The Wonderland is a world different from our own: the world of others. The rules of the Homeland do not entirely apply in the Wonderland because different worlds are built on different systems of meaning. But because of our common humanity we may reasonably expect to encounter commonalities even as we encounter differences. The challenge is to know how to interpret both the apparent similarities and the obvious differences we encounter in the Wonderland. Remembering *Alice's Adventures in Wonderland,* we may recall how hard she had to work in order to understand and apply an unfamiliar rationale and to make her way in a seemingly nonsensical world. In every Wonderland people act differently from those in the Homeland. The challenge, for us as for Alice, is to find the appropriate key to open up such worlds of meaning. Simply sitting down and hoping—or crying with frustration—does not help.

Even a broken world can be a Wonderland for the missionary: we encounter traces of wonder in the most painful human circumstances, and we are capable of bringing wonder into the hearts of those we encounter, through the hope we bear. The Wonderland is not a fairyland or place of romance, and sometimes it is the very opposite.

In the following pages we will ponder missionary encounters in the Wonderland. But if we follow Dunne and consider the *coming back* as no less significant than the *passing over,* we need to characterize that third movement. Dunne refers to it as a return to the Homeland, but its true significance may become clearer if we use a different term.

THIRD MOVEMENT: THE NEWFOUNDLAND. Long ago Heraclitus observed that no one can step into the same river twice. In a similar sense, it is impossible for us ever to return home: we are always changing, and home—with family members and friends—is always imperceptibly changing, too.

Returning from the Wonderland, then, we encounter the Newfoundland. And far from ending, our missionary journeys may be only just beginning. Whatever we accomplish in the Wonderland, we do so as outsiders, foreigners, birds of passage. That is not to minimize our possible effectiveness,[10] but it is to distinguish it from what we might accomplish in the Newfoundland. Assuming we have been changed by our boundary-crossing encounters, we return as new or renewed people. Assuming we have been affected by the novelty and challenge of the Wonderland, we return as significantly different people. Meanwhile the events occurring in the Homeland—the changes taking place there—have been incremental and gradually assimilated by the community. The missionary, however, located in the Wonderland but now returned, experiences discontinuity, disjunction, surprise, and perhaps pain at the changes insiders have already assimilated. Some missionaries may feel terrible frustration on their return as they notice in their own homeland, and perhaps for the first time, widespread complacency and even flagrant injustice.

Culture shock usually refers to the impact of a different culture (the Wonderland) on newly arrived and consequently disoriented persons. But such is the human tolerance for novelty, many people encountering an

unfamiliar culture may actually be predisposed to be tolerant and relatively relaxed. When they return to their starting place, however, antici-
pating a return to the familiar and the comfortable, they are not psychologically prepared for adjustments: they imagine they are, quite literally,
coming home. They are not. Their eyes have been opened and their judgments have been modified by their experiences in another culture, and
they are genuinely surprised to discover that the Homeland they antici-
pated really is a Newfoundland. They may find themselves not only struggling to adjust but very critical of persons and situations they previously
tolerated, loved, or took for granted. Culture shock experienced in the
Newfoundland is sometimes referred to as *reverse culture shock,* and it
can be as painful as it is unexpected. Unless able or helped to adjust
appropriately, a returned missionary may be acutely ill at ease and even
offensive to others. But reverse culture shock handled positively may bear
great fruit: returned missionaries may bring to the Newfoundland as many
resources and as much commitment as they ever exported to the Wonderland. Here is the strong voice of a social psychologist:

> One need not sojourn outside one's own country to experience
> culture shock or to undergo a cross-cultural experience. Such tran-
> sitional experiences happen to minority students entering college, to
> parolees from prison, to returning veterans, to married couples who
> divorce, and to those who change roles or occupations in mid-career.
> The frustrations as well as the growth and development inherent in
> such interactions can be experienced in one's own culture. The
> phases, the difficulties involved, and the consequences of such
> experiences, however, are most readily understood in the cross-
> cultural experience where psychological, social, and cultural differ-
> ences are most distinct.[11]

We have much to ponder when we think about Christian mission as *the
greatest religious adventure.* Properly undertaken, it can be life-giving for
many people. But unless it is undertaken with the right spirit, it could
become disastrous. Healthy, enriching, transforming experiences of *passing over* and *coming back* are possible in principle because of the humanity we share with all those who speak different languages and live in
different worlds. But we must be forewarned: unless we are as willing to
be affected and changed by the experience as we hope to affect and change
those we encounter, we should not leave the Homeland.[12] Only when we
step outside our familiar world do we begin to identify personal deficien-
cies we never knew and to discover personal qualities we never expected.
Only when we venture forth do we acquire a set of new perspectives with
which to interpret the Wonderland and in due course to reinterpret the
Newfoundland. *The greatest religious adventure* calls us to a triple personal conversion: to God, to culture, and to other people. This must be
our abiding concern. It is the topic of this book.

Chapter 1

MOVEMENT AND MISSION

Approaching Christian Ministry

A WORLD OF CHANGE

Almost a century ago, when the world was less accessible and people were more sedentary, a famous intellectual[1] flatly asserted that adventures are for the young. That, he said, is because an adventure is "a form of experiencing" and,

> in general, only youth knows this predominance of the process of life over its substance; whereas in old age, when the process begins to slow up and coagulate, substance becomes crucial. The old person usually lives either in a wholly *centralized* fashion, peripheral interests having fallen off and being unconnected with his [her] essential life and its inner necessity; or his [her] center atrophies, and existence runs its course only in isolated petty details, accenting mere externals and accidentals. Neither case makes possible the relation between the outer fate and the inner springs of life in which the adventure consists.[2]

Georg Simmel's studied opinion is touched by gloom, even defeatism. A century later the world is much more accessible, and people seem much more active (television's most popular programs are currently about *Adventure* and *Survival*). The observations surely need modifying now. In 1900 the life expectancy in the United States was forty-six or forty-seven years, and "old age" was not what it is today. When Simmel wrote of the *centralized* lives of the old, he was actually fifty-two, neither lacking in "peripheral interests" nor suffering "atroph[y]," thus not totally closed to adventure. Nor is the egocentrism he referred to limited to the old: young people today are widely criticized for living highly self-centered lives.

The spirit of adventure is surely not the monopoly of youth. The U.S. life expectancy is now seventy-eight or seventy-nine years (a staggering increase of more than 60 percent in a century) and still growing. Millions of "older people" (over forty-six or forty-seven!) are not only young in spirit but highly productive. Yesterday's categories—like yesterday's world—are part of history.

Christian mission is a phrase that evokes myriad images and a confusion of emotions. But the notion itself has always been tinged with adventure and continues to be so. And yet some things *have* changed. If yesterday's missionaries tended to sail away to far distant shores filled with youthful enthusiasm and a willingness to die for the faith and for "pagans," today's missionaries tend to fly away to distant airports filled with mature wisdom and a willingness to live for the faith and for their sisters and brothers.

Moreover, youth itself lasts longer than it used to, and life often *does* begin at forty. Nevertheless, the call to mission continues to attract "youth" (from their twenties all the way up to their fifties) and to excite "older people" (from their seventies all the way down to their thirties). Meanwhile contexts and subjects of mission have continued to evolve. Yesterday's distant or unknown places are today's overlooked or unseen people: homeless men and battered women, victims of crushing poverty and refugees from brutal wars, casualties of domestic violence and statistics of global epidemics. Yet their invisibility does not make them any less our sisters and brothers, whoever and wherever they may be, far distant or merely near distant. Christian mission is as much an adventure as it ever was. It continues to attract both young and old. If the former bring little experience but a lot of heart, the latter may bring less physical stamina but more wisdom.

Understandings of mission have changed, and those who bear the ambiguous name of *missionaries* have certainly changed. Some things, however, remain constant: God's call; the human need for solidarity; and generous people who find life's meaning in having their own lives turned inside out so that hope may be kept alive and the human spirit may not be quenched.

A SENSE OF MISSION

How have understandings of mission changed? How have missionaries changed in consequence? The answer to the second question should become clearer as we proceed, but we can briefly address the first one here.

The International Missionary Council (IMC) in Willingen, Germany, in 1952 famously reworked Karl Barth's idea that mission is an attribute or activity of God before it is a description of Christians. The Second

Vatican Council (1962-1965) famously asserted that "the church on earth is by its very nature missionary."[3] These initiatives together mark a sea change in contemporary mission theology and practice. But though they came (and still come) as a surprise to many people, they are only the reiteration of half-forgotten truths. Even now the Willingen insight has not been adequately absorbed by the Christian community, while the impact of the Vatican II formulation has been mitigated by people who argue that if everyone is a missionary, then no one is a missionary.

The IMC Conference developed the idea that mission derives from the very nature of God: it refers to *God's mission*, the raison d'être of the Trinity itself. David Bosch summarizes beautifully:

> During preceding centuries mission was understood in a variety of ways. Sometimes it was interpreted primarily in soteriological terms: as saving individuals from eternal damnation. Or it was understood in cultural terms: as introducing people from the East and the South to the blessings and privileges of the Christian West. Often it was perceived in ecclesiastical categories: as the expansion of the church (or of a specific denomination). Sometimes it was defined salvation-historically: as the process by which the world—evolutionary or by means of a cataclysmic event—would be transformed into the kingdom of God.[4]

Barth was not the first to describe God in terms of missionary activity. Bonaventure in the thirteenth century had memorably spoken of God as *bonum diffusivum sui*: God *is* diffusive goodness, goodness diffused; the divine outpouring on, and engagement with, the world and humanity are actually descriptive of God's mission. But by 1952, stimulated by two Karls—Barth and Hartenstein—Christian mission had come to be understood as having no life independent of God's sending: God is mission, and "there is church because there is mission, and not vice versa."[5]

Vatican II was asserting not so much that by Baptism everyone actually is missionary: that would be magic or manipulation. Rather, by virtue of Baptism everyone *is called to be, supposed to be, capable of being* missionary: that is the mystery and the marvel. If Roman Catholic Christians after the 1960s, or Protestant and Reform Christians after Willingen (1952), had understood this more clearly, there might now be a mature generation marked by a true missionary spirit. Currently, and despite an encouraging growth of laity in mission, the missionary spirit generally remains quite limited. Many good people still do not understand: *mission means me.*

The common mission of the entire People of God and of each baptized Christian should be seen as an invitation and a mandate. God calls and sends *(co-[m]missions)* the baptized. God offers each one a share of the common responsibility: to proclaim the integrity of the Good News of salvation, the Reign of God, and the church. The church is the visible sign of the Body of Christ historically present in cultures and communities: the *sacrament,* signpost, symbol, or visible message of salvation. The Christian response will vary according to circumstance, but no baptized person is exempt from the call. Therefore people who are not expected to leave their country for long periods are nevertheless called to respond in other appropriate ways. This will demand that they (we) move beyond the comfort or familiarity of home or neighborhood by stretching out and encountering those just beyond. This may take them (us) just around the corner rather than to foreign countries. But wherever Christians go and whatever they do, their baptismal response can still be an authentic expression of Christian mission. If it turns lives inside out rather than outside in and if it results in people carrying God's love in earthen vessels to others in need, then indeed it is such an expression. Christian mission is ultimately the radical activation or flowering of the baptismal call that Christians share with each other and with Jesus Christ, in whom they are united.

These pages are for those who seek to realize the potential of their Baptism. This demands the centrifugal movement of lives, but its authenticity is not simply measured by geography. The movement is explicitly to the other (ethnically, religiously, economically or otherwise disadvantaged or exploited: *the poor*), and it serves to proclaim, explicitly or implicitly, by word or witness, the Good News of Jesus Christ and the promise of the Realm of God. As Gustavo Gutierrez once said provocatively, the aim of mission is "to convince the poor that God loves them."

THE MEANING OF MISSION

Contemplating movement and mission, encounters and experiences, we start with a disturbing line from T.S. Eliot. It has the power to linger in the mind, calling us to greater humility; it has the capacity to focus the attention whenever we embark on a new venture. Eliot ruefully recalls, "We had the experience but missed the meaning."[6]

Sometimes we simply don't pay much attention to an experience, and then it's over and forgotten, leaving no mark on the memory or the soul— like those childhood days when nothing went wrong and we took life for granted. But there are other times when, however hard we try, we simply cannot understand what is happening around us; we are affected by events, perhaps bewildered by circumstances, but clueless about the significance of what is happening. Examples might include the experience of some modern music or drama, or the observance of an unfamiliar ritual. Whether we were conscious of a particular experience or simply failed to notice what was happening around us, we missed whatever meaning it might have carried.

"We had the experience but missed the meaning." We remember Santayana's axiom that whoever fails to learn from the past is condemned to repeat it,[7] yet our lives are often marked by moments of keen regret for failures and oversights. Whatever else we may understand about Christian mission, it surely requires these two things: that our life experience be widened by future new encounters and that we discover meaning in those experiences, past or yet to come. We *can* discover more meaning, not just by deeper introspection but by identifying interpretive keys for unlocking worlds of experience.

You may be on the cusp of a life-forming and life-changing experience. You may be floundering in a sea of bewilderment and confusion. You may be in a more reflective mode, looking back over a richly textured past and trying to interpret particular encounters that seemed significant and yet are incomprehensible. We've all said, "If I knew then what I know now," which shows that knowledge can be cumulative, and that, enriched by experience, it can be forged into durable and true wisdom. As our lives unfold, we *can* become more intentional, increasingly determined, and better equipped to learn from experience.

THE MEANING OF LIFE

Sometimes chaos swirls around us. But we must believe that there is some order, predictability, and meaning in the world. Otherwise depression becomes despair. People-in-groups (concretely *societies,* more abstractly *cultures*) cannot help themselves: they cannot avoid seeking meaning, making meaning, finding meaning. We are meaning-makers par excellence, and not just as private individuals. Our vocation calls us to move from the center of our familiar worlds of meaning and to encounter other people and other worlds. Its purpose is to make us sharers and bearers of hope, to enable us to offer moral support and to engage in a mutually enriching search for the deeper meanings of life. Its outcome is our believing more urgently and more fully that the Jesus of history and the Christ of faith have a relevance and provide a key to open human hearts and offer Godly wisdom and life.

Whoever ministers on the edge of a familiar world is challenged to become an enthusiastic puzzle solver. The human spirit is attracted by problems requiring skill or ingenuity—assuming such problems appear solvable. As tests and selection procedures have shown, missioners[8] display above-average curiosity and tolerance for the unfamiliar. As they step beyond familiar worlds, they face a degree of novelty, both unsettling and exciting, that must be encountered and absorbed, if not immediately grasped or understood. Their puzzle-solving or interpretive skills will be tested beyond previous limits.

Some of us want to fend for ourselves and rely on our own resources.

But we can jump to the wrong conclusions and offend those who could help us most. People from individualistic or ego-focused cultures are particularly prone to this. We may encounter unfamiliar communities, becoming fired by the challenge of the unknown and determined to make sense out of it. But enthusiasm and goodwill can sometimes blind us to our own selectivity and bias. An independent spirit may prevent us from developing relationships of mutuality or interdependence. Without such relationships we will never engage fruitfully with our newly encountered communities. The cultural or cross-cultural puzzles we attempt to solve are not abstractions. They are the stuff of real people's lives. Any significance we discover is not just for our intellectual satisfaction. It is the way we become part of people's lives. The worlds we may never have imagined are not imaginary worlds: people actually live there. When we approach people and their worlds, we must do so with unfeigned interest and genuine respect.

Everyone searches for meaning. But meaning is *encoded* and *contextualized*. Not only must we discover the code therefore; we must carefully interpret the context. Simply observing a game between two teams in the National Football League, or spending a day watching a game of cricket, is an inadequate basis on which to understand these games. Even asking a hundred questions may only produce greater confusion. Unless we first understand that a finite number of rules governs each sport and that the rules of one sport cannot be used to interpret the other, we have not even begun to understand either code or context.

There are rules for sports and rules for societies. Referees and umpires are required for sports, to enforce rules and sanction infringements. But no matter how effective the referee or umpire, rules will always be broken. Sport is a creative pursuit, and the players are strategists who learn to bend or break the rules and to live with—or escape—the penalties. Living in society, like playing sport, requires learning the rules, learning to respect or break them, and learning to play the game.

CULTURAL BAGGAGE

Nobody is completely objective, dispassionate, or open-minded. Wherever we go, we bring with us our not-so-hidden agendas and preferences, our culturally formed interpretations and judgments, our personal tastes and preferences. None of us comes to new situations utterly naïve or entirely open. A measure of successful socialization is that we have learned to adopt a perspective and to make judgments and deductions based on external and internal stimuli. We then defend our perspectives and argue our convictions in the public forum of our daily lives. All this is unremarkable, and often passes unnoticed, until we step out of our own familiar world and into less familiar worlds.

We carry with us preunderstandings: tendencies, biases, and assumptions that we use to make sense of the world. We must identify and unmask them. Then we will realize just how we interpret the world and how culture-bound and limited our interpretations sometimes are. Preunderstandings are like lenses placed between ourselves and the worlds we encounter. Through these lenses, worlds are reflected back to our consciousness. We can identify four typical distorting lenses that are often part of cross-cultural travelers' baggage. As we consider them, we may ask which of them we carry and at what cost.

ETHNOCENTRISM is as common as humanity. It is based on a limited view of reality, made even more limited by ignorance and insecurity. Because it privileges one's own perspective above all others, ethnocentrism inevitably results in negative judgments of the unfamiliar or *the other*. Our own familiar ways, by comparison, are invariably judged the best. Ethnocentrism is sometimes blatant and crudely bigoted, but sometimes more or less hidden for long periods. It may show itself in xenophobia, when the other encroaches on one's own familiar territory and is opposed; it may betray itself in arrogance and intolerance when one moves into other people's worlds. Lager louts—so-called soccer fans but stereotypically beer-swilling, drunken, obnoxious, and violent British youth—bring the game of soccer and the British Isles into disrepute, apparently without remorse. The Ugly American—an expatriate who imposes himself (usually) on the lives of others, showing scant willingness or ability to learn, change, or respect his hosts—would be the transatlantic counterpart.

None of us entirely escapes the tendency to privilege our point of view, to place ourselves at the center of the world. This is inevitable and often unconscious. The challenge is to unmask this potentially virulent disease before it spreads. We must learn to acknowledge and respect other people and their perspectives, even to ask our hosts to remind us whenever we commit egregious sins of ethnocentrism. A certain modesty and appropriate contrition go a long way to eliminate the worst manifestations of ethnocentrism and to ensure that the patience and goodwill of others are not totally exhausted.

People do need to make sense of other worlds of meaning. Initially at least, they will tend to assume that they have the intellectual and moral resources needed for coping with the Wonderland. But this assumption will sooner or later expose their ethnocentrism. So, individually, people must be committed to learning from others and to moderating an unwholesome self-centeredness. (Psychologically or spiritually this is *ego*-centrism; more behaviorally or culturally it is *ethno*-centrism). Otherwise they should be repatriated as soon as possible. This will not solve the problem, but it will remove the problem from where it is doing grievous damage. Any Christian who is not committed to respecting different points of view, to learning from others, and to learning from mistakes is a disgrace.

Ethnocentrism feeds on narrow denominationalism or dogmatic or doctrinaire biblicism. It is difficult to think our thought is wrong, perhaps especially when it is faith-based or denominationally grounded. One of the most poisonous fruits of ethnocentrism is arrogant self-assurance: a person finds unending excuses and justifications while criticizing and condemning other situations and even persons.

This is ethnocentrism. We may notice it in others but deny it in ourselves. Some theological perspectives may actually create a fertile field for virulent ethnocentrism. Do we consider it our business to judge others, to find them deficient, to dictate what they should do, and then to threaten or actually to use punishment? Do we imagine we are authorized to judge others and to interfere with the details of their lives? Do we believe (because of our privileged Christian background or "advanced" culture) we are morally superior to some other people? Do we consider our way of seeing things, our values and beliefs and our actual behavior, superior to other people's? If we are tempted to answer in the affirmative, we are contaminated by ethnocentrism. If we think following Jesus' *demands* that we judge and condemn others, or propose ourselves as paragons of righteousness and exemplars of discipleship, we are in acute need of conversion. Perhaps we forgot the following passage:

> Do not judge, and you will not be judged; because the judgments you give are the judgments you will get, and the amount you measure out is the amount you will be given. Why do you observe the splinter in your brother's eye and never notice the plank in your own? How dare you say to your brother, "Let me take the splinter out of your eye," when all the time there is a plank in your own? Hypocrite! Take the plank out of your own eye first, and then you will see clearly enough to take the splinter out of your brother's eye. (Mt 7:1-5)

Christians who are not deliberately seeking to unmask and undermine their own sinful ethnocentrism are condemning themselves to the damning charge of hypocrisy: there were few worse words in Jesus' vocabulary than that: "Hypocrite!"

ROMANTICISM is the second lens many people wear without apology. Romantics may be more *naïve* than ethnocentric people. But as the polar opposite of ethnocentrism, romanticism can be just as biased and almost as offensive. In a cross-cultural context, romantics adopt a Rousseau-esque approach, imagining they are in the best of all possible worlds. In the face of the overwhelming reality of grinding poverty, the aftermath of barbaric war, widespread famine, or the abuse and mutilation of persons, romantics either are deluded or betray the very people they claim to serve.

There is nothing whatever romantic about disease, poverty, and deprivation or about the plight of the actual victims of these plagues. We have a responsibility to identify the rampant injustice that spawns such sinfulness and to stand with those who suffer its ravages. To refuse to be involved with the needy or with systemic injustice is a particularly shameful kind of selfishness, practiced by many who would like to be considered informed liberals. In today's world it is less and less possible to abdicate responsibility for our exploited brothers and sisters. To look out on the world through rose-tinted spectacles is obscene.

PESSIMISM is a lens that mangles communication and distorts the interpretation of other cultures. It is sometimes part of the cultural baggage transported from the Homeland to the Wonderland. The pessimist cannot see the light and clings to the darkness: failing to identify the positive, the pessimist perceives only the negative. From early reversals or negative experiences in a cross-cultural context, the pessimist typically jumps to the conclusion that nothing will go well, that no one can be trusted, and that he or she (the pessimist) will never be able to understand the people or the surrounding culture. "You'll *never* understand the English [French, Germans, or any outsider group]" is the frustrated cry of the pessimist. The echo is even worse: "The English [French, etc.] don't make any sense." From "I don't understand" to "They don't make sense" is a very short step. Pessimists quickly conclude that it is impossible to discover positive values—or even patterns of meaning—in other cultures and that there is always something to criticize or correct in other people's behavior or belief.

The pessimist might sometimes be perfectly correct: even a stopped clock registers the correct time twice a day. People *do* sometimes act perversely. Some *do* live in a world of their own. Likewise it may be virtually impossible to understand some people (though we should be very slow to draw that conclusion): some believe things—fate or fairies, astrology or interplanetary travel—that seem to defy common sense. Nevertheless, pessimists need to come to terms with some fundamental social facts: cultural systems are built on shared conventions and meanings; not everyone is stupid or irrational; and people *can* learn cultural conventions and meanings. Even some outsiders learn to make sense of other worlds and to respect them, if not to incorporate them into their own lives.

Pessimism is a bacteria-covered lens. The organism develops when a partial view of reality is universalized. One particular thing or a number of things go wrong; therefore (says the pessimist) *everything* must *inevitably* go wrong. Each new challenge is approached and each initiative is undertaken with the expectation of setback or failure. The antidote to pessimism is the refusal to prejudge the future as an extension of the broken hopes of the past, and a conscious search for positive elements in daily encounters and experience.

But this is the very least we can expect of people. Christians, people of faith, must go considerably further. They must be indefatigable bearers of hope wherever they may be. Gustavo Gutierrez once said that there are two kinds of people. The first kind are those who encounter other people or situations and make careful judgments, on the strength of which they then respond, positively or negatively. They would be optimists or pessimists according to how they judge particular situations. The second kind, says Gustavo, are Christians. Because the difference is fundamental, it is worth a second look.

Optimism and pessimism are children of cold reason and detachment from the real world. The theological virtues of faith, hope, and charity are based on neither. Moreover, the Christian response cannot be based merely on what appears intrinsically reasonable already, for the Christian faith brings *something new* to every situation. Christians are bearers of hope—faith, in the future tense—so that although they may be (rationally) pessimistic, Christians may never judge a situation as hopeless and then walk away. Rather, by engaging with the situation, Christians infuse it with the hope they bear. When situations are infused with hope, despair is routed. Christians have reason to be pessimistic about many things, but they cannot give up hope: unlike pessimism, hope can positively transform lives.

RELATIVISM may also find a place in our cultural baggage. Like customized lenses, it comes in many shapes and sizes. It usually refers to any theory arguing that criteria of judgment are relative and vary with individuals and environments. But relativism itself can become absolutized. Then its adherents argue that inevitably and universally there are no criteria for judgment. Relativism thus becomes transformed or deformed into the idea that *nothing anywhere* is worthy or superlative, or even (the romantic opposite) that *everything everywhere* has some merits and some worth. Appropriate relativism, however, requires critical judgment.

In a famous essay, "Anti Anti-relativism," Clifford Geertz says, "I want not to defend relativism . . . but to attack anti-relativism."[9] The warning is apt—for some missionaries no less than for some anthropologists. Here is Geertz as he weaves his verbal web:

> What the relativists want us to worry about is provincialism—the danger that our perceptions will be dulled, our intellects constricted, and our sympathies narrowed by the overlearned and overvalued acceptance of our own society. What the anti-relativists want us to worry about is a kind of spiritual entropy, in which everything is as significant, thus as insignificant, as everything else: anything goes, to each his own, you pays your money and you takes your choice. There may be some genuine nihilists out there, [but] most of the people I meet, read, read about, and indeed I myself, are all-too-committed to something or other: anti-relativism has largely concocted the anxiety it lives from.[10]

A classic illustration of relativism is found in Lewis Carroll's *Through the Looking Glass.* Humpty Dumpty says, "When I use a word, it means just what I choose it to mean." If everyone did this, human communication would be destroyed; when even one person does it, meaning becomes incommunicable—unless the Humpty Dumptys of this world explain carefully what they have actually chosen the word to mean.

Absolute relativism would be the nihilism Geertz refers to: the conviction that nothing anywhere has any value and that there is absolutely no objective basis for truth. This may sometimes seem to be enlightened tolerance of other people's belief or behavior; more often it is a justification for extreme selfishness or total anarchy.

There is a more subtle relativism: call it relative relativism. This would show itself in attempts to grant to other people at least the rationality and good intentions we claim for ourselves, even though we cannot always understand them. Instead of claiming our own belief and behavior as the only legitimate or absolute criterion, such relativism would be a genuine attempt to live and let live: to respect differences, whether broadly cultural or narrowly religious. The missionary zeal of some Christians, however, is sometimes arrogant and ill-mannered: they appear to think they can ride roughshod over other people's lives, reprimanding or correcting them whenever they please. The cultivation of a healthy relativism might be highly appropriate for them: at least it would be a reminder that they are not God. Perhaps they need to remember that command: "Do not judge" (Mt 7:1).

Nobody is perfect, and no culture is flawless. Persons and cultures are capable of, and called to, improvement. Christianity offers the promise of a better life: a life better than mediocre, a life in which sin is overcome by grace and death is swallowed up in victory. Christianity is committed to the *revitalization* of cultures and of people, offering new life for old. But cultures as well as people may be touched by hubris: overweening pride or arrogance. This is antithetical to the Lordship of Christ. Christianity must be very clear about the challenge it poses to people and to cultures. Christianity is committed to the *relativization* of culture. No culture and no person are without sin. Unless cultures and persons bow the knee[11] before Christ, they cannot be redeemed. Missionaries who do not carefully point out the need for the relativization of culture, not simply by rhetoric but by the witness of their lives, are not true followers of Jesus and are perhaps only superficial—or cultural—Christians. We are not called to judge but to witness to the truth.

The *relativization* of culture (or people) without the *revitalization* of culture (or people) is insufficient: it is only imperialistic destruction. And the *revitalization* of society (and person) without the *relativization* of society (and person) is also insufficient: it is only social utopianism. Revitalization and relativization must go hand in hand if the Kingdom or Realm of God ("already and not yet") is to be preached and proclaimed. This is genuine *realized eschatology.*

PARTICIPANT OBSERVATION—and its twin, *observant participa-*

tion—refers to an approach to cross-cultural communication that has been tried, proved, and much criticized. Yet it has survived, becoming modified and even transformed. As a result it now constitutes an approach and a bundle of skills that can be identified and transmitted to others. It grew up largely among social and cultural anthropologists, but it has been used informally and unself-consciously by many missionaries. It might profitably become a much more widely practiced approach to mission.

A participant observer accepts indebtedness, vulnerability, and participant outsidership (much easier said than done, and something we will return to). Participant observation is not easy, and some people will find it much too demanding. It is at times emotionally painful and always intellectually demanding. And yet its successful practice can be life-giving for missionaries and those they hope to serve. Perhaps even more significantly, it is not impossibly difficult and it can be learned, given a suitable temperament and adequate incentives. Nevertheless, it is important to remember that *goodwill is simply not enough* to make cross-cultural living possible. The ability to survive and thrive and to contribute to the well-being of one's hosts is the fruit of grace building on nature. Some aspiring missionaries may discover that they do not have the natural talents required and that for them no amount of effort is sufficient. There need be no shame in such a discovery; but there is no virtue in thinking that sheer determination is enough. Those unsuited to certain types of missional Christianity must be careful not to vent their frustration or incompetence on others.

While every missionary ought to be a participant observer, the fact is that some are not. To live where people speak a foreign language yet not to be committed to learning that language on a daily basis; to reside in an unfamiliar society but to create a home from home and jealously maintain one's own creature comforts; to be surrounded by local hospitality, food, and fabrics yet regularly to eat, dress, and live on goods imported from home: all these betray a serious lack of engagement and participation in another culture. To be self-sufficient when living among and for people of another culture is a grave insult and betrays a culpable lack of authenticity. Whoever does not sense or exhibit any need to be fed, clothed, or housed or to receive gifts or services is not in relationship. No strong links can be forged with such people. To be independent and show no vulnerability is to fly in the face of the gospel, which calls us to interdependence and the honest acknowledgment and sharing of our needs as we share our resources.

Participant observers acknowledge their need for the local people, for services and information, for hospitality, and for relationships. They believe the way to understand other people is to experience their ways: of training their children to learn and speak, of rewarding and punishing their members, of treating their dead and addressing their Maker. Participant observers believe it is possible, though difficult, for outsiders to make significant progress in the interpretation of another culture. They *know* Japanese people can communicate with Germans, and Norwegians with Nigerians, even while accepting George Bernard Shaw's incisive point that England and America are "two countries divided by a common language." Participant observers accept that cross-cultural living is delicate but entirely possible, just as they know people can learn to walk or swim without always being conscious of their own feet or arms. Participant observers respect the virtue of patience as much as the power of observation, and graciousness as much as participation.

By adding observant participation to participant observation,[12] a person strives to understand other people as they understand themselves. Such an undertaking requires the cultivation of empathy and the accumulation of insight. It may not be entirely possible for some, but it is absolutely demanded of all. The question for us might be this: should missionaries try to be participant observers, and if so, how might they undertake that task and at what cost?

A FINAL MOVEMENT?

So much for the simple mechanics of passing over and coming back. So much for the easy references to our preunderstandings, and the baggage or lenses we all carry. There is a final movement, which can neither be reduced to nor separated from the others: the continuous and never-ending movement of our hearts to others and our lives to God. The missionary call really does not start only when we first notice it: like gentle music that wakes us, it was going on while we slept. The missionary call does not cease when we return from the Wonderland: there is simply no end to mission. So we need to embrace the steadfastness of God's never-ending Covenant call and resolve to participate in our never-ending conversion-response.

Reflecting on the profound implications of all of this (of the charge to put our hands to the plow and not to look back and of the promise of Jesus the Christ to be with us all days), we can take heart once more from the words of John Dunne, words we borrowed at the outset. He concludes his own reflections thus:

> What seems to be occurring is a phenomenon we might call "passing over," passing over from one culture to another, from one way of life to another, from one religion to another. Passing over is a shifting of standpoint, a going over to the standpoint of another culture, another way of life, another religion. It is followed by an equal and opposite process we might call "coming back," coming back with new insight to one's own culture, one's own way of life, one's own religion.

One has to pass over, to shift standpoints, in order to enter into the life of Jesus, even if one is a Christian, and then one has to come back, to shift standpoints again, to return to one's own life.[13]

But this adventure, this passing over and coming back, is expensive. It costs, as T.S. Eliot put it so well, "not less than everything." No one who passes over and comes back can escape unscathed. Indeed, following Augsberger, who quotes Paul Clasper:

To "pass over" is to enter a new world; to "come back" is to return a different person. One is bound to look at one's own world with fresh eyes and with fresh questions once the journey . . . has been taken. . . . It is easy to see why a narrow, fearful sect-mentality always urges a careful restriction of personal contacts. One can be "contaminated" by alien perspectives! . . . If we want to "remain the same" it is best not to venture out.[14]

And yet . . . for those who do respond to the missionary call of Baptism, it is not so simplistic: they are not free *not to* venture, to risk, and to encounter others in friendship and in faith. Their vocation demands it, their God demands it, and the people they will one day befriend demand it.

Chapter 2

MEANING AND COMMUNICATION

Living with Integrity

INTRODUCING MEANING

Let's agree that we want to avoid crude ethnocentrism and romanticism. Let's also accept that we have an abundance of goodwill. Still, we must acknowledge that no one can *fully* enter another culture any more than anyone can fully enter the unique world of another individual. Human beings are the same the world over, but they are also uniquely different. How can we possibly prepare ourselves for other worlds and their puzzles and for the challenge of communicating the gospel intelligibly?

Meaning—the end, purpose, or significance of reality—is intimately related to language. A recent survey counted 13,500 "distinct and different languages" in the world.[1] This staggering statistic tells us something about the range and variety of meaning to be found in our small and fragile planet. And not one single society considers itself to be acting meaninglessly on a regular basis.[2]

If meaning were a purely individual matter, communication would be impossible. If meaning were a purely private issue, human language would never have evolved. More than six billion people with a universal propensity for language is dramatic proof of the social nature of language. Wherever communication takes place, meaning is shared, negotiated, exchanged—even developed or forged. When mother and baby engage in what some consider meaningless babbles and gurgles, their "babytalk" is clearly effective and meaningful: it is reciprocal, generative, and ongoing. Communication itself requires a mutually satisfying exchange of signs, symbols, carriers of meaning; and meaning is shared when mutually held signals and values are effectively exchanged. Without some mutuality of signals and values, people simply cannot communicate and meaning cannot be shared. There are serious implications here for all would-be communicators, particularly for those who bring Good News.

Geertz remarks that the primary function of every culture is meaning-making, and claims that the primary function of anthropology is the decoding or interpretation of cultures (this last phrase is the title of one of his most famous books). He is identified as an *interpretivist*. Here is a helpful lens through which to view any culture, though it is neither the only one possible nor the best in every circumstance:[3] interpretivism is vulnerable to the charge that it soon becomes too subjective. Nevertheless, it will be the main approach in these pages. Let us think of culture as "a pattern of meanings embodied in symbols."[4] Symbols are things, material or nonmaterial, employed to represent something else. Language is a symbol system, but so are gestures, postures, and various sorts of objects.

Meaning is found wherever there are social groups; human society cannot survive without shared meaning.[5] But meaning alone is insufficient for sustained social life. If a group judges certain beliefs or behavior unacceptable (meaningful or comprehensible but not approved), it must be able to punish deviants. Thus it defends and maintains its boundaries and its own standards: its world of meaning. Meaning is like a living organ within the social body; it may flourish, change, even corrupt, because there are deviant cultures and dysfunctional societies. It would be naïve to think that every society represents the best of all possible worlds, but just as naïve to imagine that cross-cultural communication is a simple matter of translation.

If something becomes irrelevant or is rejected, it has lost its meaning for a particular person or group. Would-be participant observers must be able to discover how people understand or give meaning to various realities. Then they can compare them to other people's meanings, near or far away. The dictionary defines meaning as "the shared interpretations of individuals in groups, as applied to external phenomena." So it is very important that missionaries know how to interpret another world of meaning and to identify its inhabitants; otherwise any intended dialogue is no better than monologue, and one person's good sense will appear gibberish to another. As Saint Paul said so well, "If I am ignorant of what the sounds mean, I am a barbarian to the person who is speaking, and he is a barbarian to me" (1Cor 14:11). True communication requires mutual intelligibility, and mutual intelligibility must be developed and tested over time.

Though different people and different groups inhabit different worlds of meaning, these are not always absolutely separate worlds. They may overlap, so that a person can—more or less—manage in another world. Even Americans, Australians, and the British (not to mention English, Irish, Welsh, and Scots) can negotiate their language differences and reach a measure of mutual intelligibility.

But if worlds of meaning are socially constructed,[6] they have their own integrity and coherence. Issues like deviance, irrationality or meaning-lessness, and judgments of who is normal, rational, or comprehensible: these will have been addressed by insiders long before any outsiders arrive. An outsider has little authority to declare on the subject, however tempting that may be. Any unassimilated outsider[7] is beyond the world of meaning or the meaning-sharing group and sometimes likely to speak what appears nonsense to insiders. As outsiders, it is our responsibility to learn what wisdom circulates among insiders rather than to assume that local people have none. (Then we might try to imagine what sense local people might possibly make of us or some of our behavior.) In that way we will at least be working toward a respectful understanding, rather than judging others and condemning everything in their world that differs from anything in our own.

How would we react if a stranger entered our home and proceeded to tell us exactly what is wrong with us and our behavior? At best such high-handedness would appear insensitive, comical, or irrelevant; at worst, wildly inappropriate if not downright offensive. If well-intentioned missionaries dictate to other people what they should and should not do, we ought to know that our words will sound ungracious or offensive. This is no basis on which to build mutuality and trust. Outsiders have no business to make demands, and some missionaries' expectations are, from the perspective of the insiders, impracticable or outrageous if not morally impossible. Christian missionaries, as well as civil society, psychiatrists, and the judiciary, have often decided unilaterally who is deviant—and punished them. If their sanctions are strong and effective, they may think they are justified. But time will tell. Today many missionaries and others are more measured in their approaches and a good deal less certain about their successes.

> On a public bus in a crowded city in Asia, I was amazed by the sounds, smells and sights, and fascinated by everything around me. Sitting in front of me was a man I did not notice until he leaned out of the open window and very deliberately spat—or rather allowed gravity to carry his saliva to the ground. I was only mildly irritated by this behavior, until he repeated it a few moments later. Then every few minutes he leaned out of the window. My first reaction [that he was uncouth] was replaced by a second [that he was mentally disturbed]. Finally, reflecting that this was an Islamic state with many ascetics, I concluded that the man was performing a relatively unobtrusive religious act: he was fasting, and not even swallowing his own saliva. I do not know if I was correct, but certainly my opinion of the man changed.

Meaning attaches to the most ordinary things, but meaning does not always travel as easily as the jumbo jets that carry us to other worlds. It has to be located in its own context and carefully translated into another.

INTRODUCING RATIONALITY

Not everything that is meaningful is necessarily rational, and whoever ventures to the margins and beyond will be stretched on the rack of rationality. One person's rationality may be another person's craziness.

We may respect other worlds of meaning and even be willing to question our own. We may explore how our world is constructed and maintained and even criticize its inconsistencies. We may be sensitive to the effects of our encounter with others and even determined that it should not turn into an invasion. But still we must look beyond meaning and consider the problem of rationality.

We may agree that other people attribute meaning to life, yet still find them irrational. Our mental institutions are full of such people: many seem to make meaning, yet society calls them irrational or mad. Mental illness, as the West understands it, is arguably the outcome (sometimes at least) of a set of irrelevant but strongly supported and sanctioned ideas, foisted by the "sane" on the "insane." Perhaps the deepest reality is that those widely understood to be sane are a little crazed and many of those diagnosed insane are rarely a threat to themselves or each other but only to the medical professionals. Perhaps no one is absolutely normal. People from parts of the so-called developing world sometimes have a much greater tolerance for—and are much less threatened by—their less socially aware and productive members than people from the mighty West. And people with mental illness have been treated in a variety of ways across cultures and through history.[8] There are valuable lessons for us here, applicable to our preparation for marginal[9] ministry.

The line between rationality and irrationality or madness is not always easily drawn. *The principle of contradiction* states that it is not possible for something both to be and not to be at the same time: X is either A or non-A. Our (Aristotelian) logic may persuade us that a person cannot simultaneously be in two places. Our (Western) experience or common sense may convince us that a person cannot turn into an animal and back into a human being. Yet Aristotle has not said the only or the last word; and Western experience and common sense are contextual rather than universal.[10]

Hindu logic is fourfold or even sevenfold. The former (X is either A or non-A; neither A nor non-A; nor both A and non-A; nor neither A nor non-A) is both a symbolic logic and a logic of cognition that can achieve a precise and unambiguous formulation of universal statements without using the "for all" formula.[11]

And how shall we understand perfectly lucid people utterly convinced of the reality of witches (people who can move out of their bodies and wreak havoc while appearing to be sleeping peacefully in their beds)? What shall we make of apparently sane people who believe *(know)* that they have seen Mary, the mother of Jesus? How shall we judge a respected elder who says matter-of-factly that he can become an elephant?[12] Must we repudiate these people's reality or judge them irrational? And what about other people who listen to our declarations that Jesus rose from the grave, that Mary was a virgin mother, or that there is such a thing as Everlasting Life?

If you see a man lying in a hammock, clutching his belly and claiming to experience the symptoms of pregnancy—and if the rest of the group agrees with this interpretation—do you conclude that he is mad or disturbed, faking or rational? And if you lived with people whose men deliberately created nosebleeds on a regular basis, or cut their penises with a sharp instrument and bled copiously, would you judge this to be irrational behavior? Both of these—and many, many more—are institutionalized, systematic, culturally integrated behaviors, which are not deviant and which *do* make sense. But they do not necessarily make sense in the context of a boardroom or on Broadway, and they may not be found in our seminaries or parishes. Context is all in such matters.[13]

We are all capable of acting unsystematically or irrationally, but *no survivable group acts irrationally for long;* the cost is, quite simply, death. Groups that survive for any length of time are *basically* and *generally* rational, systematic, predictable, and orderly. Groups that have survived for many generations have thereby acquired a cultural identity. Still, dead cultures litter the sands of time, and societies that *persistently* promote or tolerate irrational, ungrounded, or unrealistic behavior will ultimately die.

Rationality is related to the communication of ideas and the organization of behavior. It has a near-objective status; it is not a purely subjective matter. To "live in a world of one's own" is to be lacking social integration and communication skills. People so classified might be judged to be irrational. Autism is a condition—due perhaps to the body's inability to metabolize certain metals—in which a person's world is totally centered on the self, lacks external points of reference, and is unreachable by others. But rationality indicates social life, and social life bespeaks rationality. So it should be possible for people to discover and acknowledge rationality, even though not primarily their own. Perhaps then we can accept that there are other worlds and other societies than our own and that other people (apparently different from ourselves in terms of rationality) are not irrational *just because they act or think differently from us.* We might even suspend our judgment when their behavior or belief seems meaningless. And it might actually be possible for us to accept that their worlds of meaning are viable and worthy worlds, containing the key to *alternative forms* of rationality.[14] All of this may be quite demanding; some of it might challenge our own assumptions and theology.

Meaning and rationality are crucial to any definition of culture. Every culture carries the weight of meaning that its members collectively give it.

New members receive meaning from their culture through early education or socialization. If something is meaningless to a person, it can hardly be part of that person's culture. (In a pluralistic culture a statement like that can be contested because different worlds overlap and coexist. But in smaller, more tightly bounded cultures, it is almost axiomatic. What *could* a microscope mean among traditional Kalahari Bushmen? What meaning could a refrigerator or air conditioner have for a Netsilik Eskimo?)

Outsiders will appear irrelevant unless they allow themselves to be situated in the actual world of the people they come to serve.[15] Yet incoming visitors, operating from different paradigms, naturally assume that their own frames of reference are the correct if not the only acceptable ones. They will gradually discover other frames of reference. Sadly, some visitors only judge their hosts negatively and treat them as irrational or sinful. This quickly leads to alienation and to the visitors being treated as irksome and irrelevant. Local people have their own frames of reference that serve their own needs and purposes more or less well. They are not necessarily conscious of those frames, any more than we are of ours. But new ideas from outside can only be assimilated through the insiders' lenses or paradigms. If outsiders' ideas do not make sense, they will inevitably be judged meaningless or even irrational. To complicate matters further, insiders may interpret outsiders' actions or words in ways quite unintended by the outsiders and sometimes never even known by them. Thus each side comes to misunderstand the other. Cross-cultural communication is a delicate business, and people need to work diligently for real understanding. Strangers are not the only ones who need to make sense of what they encounter, however. Only if both parties are working toward mutual understanding will relationships gradually develop.

The agents of mission must encounter people at the level of the heart and spirit. But if Christianity is perceived as irrelevant, what hope is there of touching hearts or spirits? Ultimately, if the local people honestly reject the missionary message, must not the missionary, out of respect for individuals and consciences, withdraw graciously?[16] Force (whether threatened or employed) and fear (however provoked) are characteristic of what is usually called proselytism. They are always immoral, never justified.

Not only are people quite conservative where meaning is concerned: shifts in meaning create shifting worlds. But when people move between worlds, they may be quite manipulative and insensitive to other worlds of meaning. This can demean local people by judging them stupid, hardhearted, or immoral. We all know stories of ambassadors of Christ whose idea of modesty is so strict that it cannot tolerate nakedness, even in private or in bed.[17] They criticize local people, provide League of Decency clothing for local women, and allow only "modest" women in the church. Such interpretations and responses simply do not fit with local people's frames of reference. They may be at a loss to understand how such outsiders can possibly be rational creatures. Local people sometimes do adapt to missionary expectations, of course, not because they are seen as reasonable but because conformity can be turned to their own advantage. At other times they conform because of fear or force. This is no basis on which to build a gospel of freedom and love.

TRANSLATING THE GOSPEL

Most missionaries will not be sidetracked into micromanaging other people's lives. But where does one draw the line? What is detail and what is essence? Emissaries of the gospel will understandably feel that some aspects of the gospel message are not trivial and are indeed nonnegotiable for any would-be Christians. The Jews were perplexed and scandalized by the "hard sayings" of Jesus, but he did not soften them. The gospel should not be compromised, but it must be comprehensible. The Christian life should not be presented as easy, but it must be presented as morally possible. And the challenges of the gospel can only be issued through the medium of effective cross-cultural communication and comprehension. We saw that mercy and pity were regarded by some of the ancients as pathological emotions, not worthy of rational people;[18] yet they are intrinsic to the Christian message. St. Paul preached those very virtues, presenting a serious challenge to his listeners, who regarded themselves as highly civilized people. But despite the difficulties of the *kerygma* and the scandal of the Cross, the challenge was presented, comprehended, and accepted by some. This is the model for us today.

Change happens and grace abounds. Yet grace must build on human nature and the culture in which it is expressed. If the missionary enterprise is not to fail abysmally and if people are not to be disappointed and distressed, a firm grounding in knowledge of human nature and culture and an understanding of meaning in cross-cultural situations are required. The gospel *is* intended to change people, but through the grace of God freely accepted by enculturated (socialized) people. So what is the preferred kind of change? And what kind of change is creative and liberating rather than enforced and enslaving? Good intentions not only pave the road to hell; historically, they have often been the kiss of death for cultures and have dreadfully compromised the Christian mission. Good intentions are no justification for a patronizing, doctrinaire, elitist attitude; they are no substitute for good preparation.[19]

Christianity must find appropriate ways and suitable categories for transmitting the Good News. If it cannot be understood, it will never become meaningful, and unless it is meaningful, it can never be assimilated in a way that can produce *metanoia*, or life-giving transformation, for local people. In their zeal to spread what they believe to be Good News, some missionaries have tried to make other people more and more like themselves, not only in a narrowly religious way but in a rather crudely cultural way. But as Lamin Sanneh so brilliantly argued, individual missionaries were actually not all that important. People took what made sense to them or what they could apply to their lives; and their (cultural) genius—and the grace of God—produced responses that missionaries could never have foreseen and were quite incapable of controlling.[20]

Good theology teaches that God wants each person to be more fully alive, more fully human, and more fully responsive, not in our image—whoever we are—but in God's. Yet missionary Christians who resist the temptation to direct the pace or shape of change in other people's lives sometimes feel unclear about what they should be doing. It can be very difficult to let God be God and not to try and seize initiatives.

As instruments of the gospel and of God, we carry Good News in the earthen vessels of our own lives and the fragile containers of our own theological formulations. We do want to let God be God, but we also take ourselves rather seriously as instruments: we want to carry over or transmit—to translate—the message. But as the axiom reminds us, every translation is a betrayal, something is always lost in translation, and the message is always modified or impoverished as it passes from one to another. *Traditor traductor:* the translator is a traitor; translation is betrayal. So is it not true that if we try to transmit the gospel into other cultural contexts, it must inevitably be at the price of impoverishment or compromise? If so, it would place an insupportable burden on us.

If we only take a negative view, we might miss some important facts: not all change is for the worse; and much that remains *unchanged* (unattended to or uncared for) actually does go bad. Change *is* sometimes for the better, and translation *can* bring clarification. We say in English that a person is "at death's door," which is vivid and informative. But to make a *formal* translation into French would destroy its meaning. But the French have already given some thought to being close to death: their phrase, *à deux doigts de la mort* (literally, "at two fingers from death") is just as vivid and informative. It is a *dynamic* equivalent of the English phrase. To be "two fingers away from death" is perfectly clear. So we should consider not only what might be *lost* in translation but what may be *found* in translation. This would allow us to approach different cultures-in-context on a more positive basis and to begin to construct local theologies.[21]

Here is an example of what may be found in translation:

> On a trek in Africa, I reached a village. As I climbed the hill, I saw the old chief, sitting outside his hut. He was blind, and as I greeted him, he asked my name. I told him it was *kpele waa* (literally, "big beard"; that is what people called me). He was *Nabi Yagba*, and I repeated his name to myself until I remembered it.
>
> Six months later, as I reached his village again, I could see him from afar, sitting outside his hut. "*Nabi Yagba!*" I called; he asked me

who I was. I knew he must have recognized my voice, and I said, not *kpele waa*, but *nya mia* ("it's me"). "Ah," he said in recognition, "*kpele waa; ta mia*" ("big beard; so it is").

Until then I had not realized that my response *(nya mia)* meant literally "I am (the one)." I knew it implied that he would recognize me by the sound of my voice. What I had never realized before was that *nya mia* is virtually identical to *EGO EIMI, I Am Who I Am*. In recognizing the parallelism, I also realized for the first time that Moses, like *Nabi Yagba,* must *already* have known the identity of the person whose voice spoke on Mount Sinai: God was saying, "It's me!" And Moses now knew explicitly what he had long known implicitly.

Some profound truths can be found in translation, just as translation can become betrayal if done carelessly or without respect or knowledge. Browbeating local people into bringing their drums into church in an attempt to inculturate the liturgy may be embarrassing for them and in the end disappointing for us. Perhaps people do *not* want to be persuaded to retrieve "cultural" behaviors they consider outmoded or inappropriate; perhaps they are aspiring to other values. Perhaps our simpleminded attempt to translate local drums into liturgical instruments is just that: simpleminded. Uninformed missionaries may antagonize their parishioners and then wonder why the people are not cooperating. Authentic translation of the faith—into ideas, words, and gestures, or doctrine or liturgy—is a complex and subtle issue that can only be approached through careful and mutual communication.

A translator's rule of thumb applies to those who carry the gospel message to others: to translate from English to French requires knowledge of *both* languages. So often people attempt cross-cultural translation with virtually no knowledge of one of the cultures. An oft recounted example illustrates the likely outcome. Someone, evidently not fully conversant with English, translated Matthew 26:41, which in English is rendered, "The spirit is willing but the flesh is weak." The translator tried bravely but failed. Because he completely missed the context, his literal rendering—"The wine is agreeable but the meat stinks"—both lost *and* gained something in translation.

Translation *is* possible, but it is always risky and costly. The practical and crucial question for us this: how can gospel values in general, and not only the actual words of Scripture, be translated adequately, appropriately, creatively, but above all meaningfully?

BELIEF AND BEHAVIOR

At the beginning of any journey, the act of getting started—the movement from inertia to steady momentum—is often more difficult and demands more energy than maintaining speed. *How* do we get started in understanding other people? *How* do we generate the energy needed to move us into other worlds? Let us identify some of the issues involved. As we ponder their significance, we may be preparing ourselves for our encounters.

The first issue is the relationship between belief and behavior. Belief underpins behavior: it is the soil from which behavior springs. Ideally, behavior expresses belief and belief generates behavior, so the study of one should illuminate the other. People don't behave without reason. People do not hold beliefs totally unconnected to their actual world. If there were no connection between belief, behavior, and the real world, lives would soon lose their meaning. A healthy, integrated existence cannot tolerate much meaninglessness or irrelevance. If people's existence is filled with irrelevance, life becomes drudgery and enthusiasm vanishes. Where behavior is enforced, unhealthy reactions or sheer formalism will result; and if irrelevant behavior is not enforced, it will sooner or later disappear.

But there is more to consider as we attempt to interpret behavior. Imagine watching a person putting a tooth under a pillow (behavior); you ask why; you receive an answer (belief), either directly or from a third party. But in order for you to draw any valid conclusions about the belief behind the observed behavior, you must pay attention to the agent, the informant, and the context; so much hangs on this. If a six-year-old girl is putting the tooth under the pillow, that may be significant; but what if it is the archbishop of Chicago? Likewise, if the informant is your five-year-old nephew, that might have some bearing on the meaning of what is going on. And if the informant is a shaman in a Mongolian village or a diviner in the Sudan, the whole drama takes on a totally different meaning. Context is crucial. Only when a specific context is understood can meaning be gleaned from behavior. Yet so often we wander into unfamiliar contexts, trying to interpret behavior but with no understanding of context and no awareness of its significance. Context changes meaning.

We can make people change their behavior, or we may intimidate them with threats of punishment or even damnation. But it is only possible to change people's beliefs or alter their worlds of meaning with patience, forbearance, understanding, and the passage of time. Even then, our ideas and values must be perceived as relevant and internalized by those we encounter; the fact that we ourselves are convinced is not sufficient.

Whoever tries to understand other people's beliefs and behavior must first place them in their total context. This requires painstaking and informed work. Even when we think we have specified the context, we discover there is rarely a perfect fit between people's beliefs and behavior. Nor is it easy to discover just what a single person—let alone "the English" or "the Maasai"—believes. Do we simply ask individuals and then believe what they say? Even our questions are loaded, biased in terms of what *we* think appropriate and relevant. Our style of questioning often allows people to respond in ways they hope will please us. Even when two people agree on something, that does not prove they both accept or believe in the same way.

We may assume that if people have beliefs, they will be able to formulate them. But beliefs are not like possessions. For most people, belief is not codified. Historically, people have rarely thought in terms of "having beliefs." A Hindu or a Buddhist or an adherent of any number of religions does not need a set of beliefs that can be articulated in a formal way.[22] Judaism sets much greater store by how one behaves than by what one believes formally. Religion is much more than belief; it is coordinated social action. We all know people who *say* they believe certain things but whose behavior totally belies what they say.[23] Scripture is full of examples of the lack of fit between what people say and what they do. Official church statements make the same point. Here is one:

> The split between the faith which many profess, and their daily lives, deserves to be counted among the more serious errors of our age. . . . Let there be no false opposition between professional and social activities on the one part, and religious life on the other.[24]

There will always be some tension between culture and gospel. The gospel message will always challenge people's behavior and belief. Here is the *Lausanne Covenant*:

> Culture must always be tested and judged by Scripture (Mk 7:8,9,13). Because men and women are God's creatures, some of their culture is rich in beauty and goodness. Because they are fallen, all of it is tainted with sin and some of it is demonic. The gospel does not presuppose the superiority of any culture to another, but evaluates all cultures according to its own criteria of truth and righteousness, and insists on moral absolutes in every culture (1Cor 9:19-23). Missions have all too frequently exported with the gospel an alien culture and churches have sometimes been in bondage to culture rather than to Scripture. . . . Churches must seek to transform and enrich culture, all for the glory of God.[25]

As we move toward an understanding of others, we should note some important issues. First, belief(s) and behavior are neither completely detached nor perfectly matched. Second, the belief underpinning behavior is not always easily accessible. Third, what people believe does have some consistency and is not a random or discrete set of opinions or convictions; therefore we can legitimately speak of clusters of belief and behavior, or *belief systems*. It is sometimes easier to see and understand clusters or systems rather than individual entities because the total context can be more easily identified; but it is always a challenge.

Belief systems may not be available in leather-bound display copies or formulated in creeds. But that is not to say they do not exist. Some—not all[26]—beliefs may be reconstructed by careful observers. But nobody should ever assume—or, worse, assert—that "these people have no beliefs (no religion, no morality)." That would be an indictment of the speaker.[27] Regrettably, people have passed such judgments, and many had the authority (certainly the power) to reinforce their prejudices and harm other people. We must be sensitive and tread carefully as we trespass on others' lives.

Why *should* beliefs be codified? In the absence of writing, all really relevant information can be stored in several effective ways. There is great subtlety of learning to be found in cultures without writing systems (*oral* cultures; not *illiterate,* since that very word is negative or privative, therefore prejudicial). From our own literate and computerized vantage points we may overlook our own forgetfulness. Many of us have terrible memories. Unlike oral people, we have lost the ability to store prodigious amounts of information in memory and through orally transmitted stories and folk wisdom.

Communities of people (as distinct from isolated individuals) have adequate knowledge of their values and beliefs. Those values and beliefs will be interrelated (hence belief systems). A belief system is "a scheme into which people are born (or sometimes construct), which helps to make sense of their experience and to order the universe."[28]

To order the universe: that is critically important. If people do *not* have a belief system, their universe will begin to fragment. Many people in today's pluralistic world already feel alienated and unmoored, adrift and confused, without certainties or clear values. On the other hand (to romantics at least), small-scale societies seem more able to engage their members and prevent alienation or anomie (lawlessness or meaninglessness). Traditional peoples worry that a wider world will impinge and create rapid and uncontrollable social change, breeding social ills of many kinds. But social change is not incompatible with the transmission of values or belief systems. The social function of belief systems is to create and maintain meaning and order in the universe.

A question for cross-cultural travelers is this: what happens to belief systems under pressure from the forces of social change? A second is this: how can missionaries support relatively stable worlds of meaning and simultaneously allow them to expand to assimilate the novelty and challenge of the gospel?

In the face of internal or external threats to social and religious stability, societies defend their barriers and boundaries to maintain what is within and repel what is without. Not only in small-scale societies are unwelcome encroachments from outside resisted; we all know situations in which religious and other groups behave in exactly the same way. Missionaries have often been raised in worlds with strong and resistant boundaries. We are sometimes as resistant to change and as sure of our value systems as are the people into whose worlds we walk (or fly, thus creating even greater confusion).

Belief systems are not like social clubs or credit cards: you cannot belong to several or multiply your collection more or less at will. Emile Durkheim spoke of beliefs as *obligatory:* they preexist us, and most of us are not really free to drop or add to them at will. Language provides a helpful analogy. Few of us are truly bilingual (and even those who are raised bilingually show marked traces of imperfections in *both* languages when compared with their monolingual peers). We adopt and acquire the language of our group. We go through life with the language that helped create our first enduring world. Indeed it is the only language there is until we move out of the group or until the group is infiltrated. In today's world most people know that other societies and other languages exist, but this was not always so. Only a few centuries ago—and in rural Europe and many other places even today—people spoke one language, lived in one enclosed world, subscribed to one belief system, and gave little thought to the nature of belief or the multiplicity of worlds.[29]

Many communities continue to resist external pressures, and a few remain virtually homogeneous. Homogeneous communities tend to be isolated (islands or rain forest communities) or to create isolation (Amish communities or monasteries). Yet the world *is,* if not a global village, then a global metropolis or slum, and several belief systems can and do coexist, much to the confusion of the inhabitants. The existence of alternative or conflicting belief systems in a particular society is a crucial variable for determining the *openness* or *closedness* of a society, of its readiness for, or resistance to, change. People who cross boundaries hoping to serve particular communities should note how *open* or *closed* those communities already are, and assess their own potential relevance accordingly.[30]

If belief is not to be found full-blown on every lip or in sacred writings, it may be alive and well in ritual and ceremony. Ritual is a form of symbolic action that redefines and re-creates boundaries; ceremonial maintains and strengthens them. An initiation ceremony—circumcision or sacramental Confirmation—may be seen as a ritual, and a Sunday liturgy among believers as a ceremonial. But these things may be interpreted incorrectly or misconstrued; and the distinction between ritual and ceremonial is only a rule of thumb. Only by examining and learning to interpret symbolic behavior *in context* do we learn about people and about the belief systems within which these actions are embedded. Ritual and ceremonial both try to say the unsayable or to do the undoable; and they employ symbolic action, not ignorant practical action.

Belief systems are not figments of the imagination. People who act systematically do so as an extension (or sometimes in deliberate violation) of a belief system. But belief systems underpin behavior, and the meaning of behavior cannot be reduced to the hunches of outsiders. The mere fact that some people's behavior makes little or no sense to the outsider is not a valid reason for concluding that it is intrinsically meaningless. Intelligent people sometimes assume they are the final judges of what makes sense or is meaningful or rational. This is as dangerous as it is arrogant.

BELIEF, LANGUAGE, CONVERSION

It is almost impossible to understand belief systems at first hand unless we know the language. A cultural heritage is transmitted through language.[31] Through language people can communicate abstract notions, allusions, values, and expectations. But equally important is this: the very way people come to understand what *is,* what is true or real, depends very heavily on language. Language is an essential medium through which successive generations come to know what to believe and how to behave, and also what not to believe and how not to behave. Language is not just a vehicle for communicating ideas; the very nature of reality is mediated through language. In a profound sense thought itself and ratiocination (the activity of thinking) are determined by language. So it would be difficult for us even to imagine the world as it exists and is perceived by three different people, all monolingual, one of whom speaks English, another Welsh, and a third Mende (a West African language). Do they live in the same world? Do they think the same things or in the same way? More important still for those who cross boundaries in the name of Jesus Christ: can the untrained English speaker presume to understand *witchcraft;* the Welsh speaker *spirit possession,* or the Mende speaker *consumer capitalism?*

Why is this so important? Because the Good News of Jesus invites people to a conversion that includes a modification of their belief and behavior. Because conversion must not be a moral impossibility for people. Because, for conversion to be possible, people must understand the Good News through their own language and patterns of thinking. And because the Good News requires preachers capable of effective two-way communication. All this is important because without deep commitment to learning another culture we will not understand other people's beliefs and behavior. Whoever wills the end must also will the means. Unless we are deeply engaged with the actual lives of the people among whom we minister, we are not deeply committed to being bearers of a life-giving gospel.

Our primary topic is belief and behavior, but we must emphasize the broader importance of language, systems of belief, and context. What right do we have even to assume that people are *free* to switch beliefs? The implications are serious.[32]

To recapitulate: belief and behavior are organically related; the fruit of belief is the behavior it produces; people's behavior reflects their underlying belief. In a perfect world there would be a perfect fit or a true consistency between belief and behavior. But we do not live in a perfect world, and there will always be some discrepancy between them, in ourselves or in other people. Christians share a set of beliefs—minimally the Creed of the Apostles, Nicea, or Constantinople. Adherence to those beliefs ought to produce Christian behavior as its fruit. If the beliefs are wholesome and life-giving, the fruit should be likewise.

People who are not Christian are not without beliefs, formalized or not. Adherence to cultural beliefs ought to bear fruit in cultural behavior. If the beliefs are wholesome and life-giving, their fruit will be, too. A bad tree does not produce good fruit, and a good tree does not produce bad fruit. But like everyone else, Christians are heirs to sin. In all those God created there is good and bad, grace and sin: life-giving fruit and deadly fruit. One missionary task is to help improve the fruit in other cultures.

Here is a maxim: *Quidquid recipitur ad modum recipientis recipitur* ("Whatever is received, is received according to [the capacity of] the receiver"). A giver, a donor, cannot absolutely determine how a gift will be received or used. But in order to minimize abuse or maximize appropriate use, the donor should explain the nature and use of the proposed gift. What does this mean for the gift of the Good News of Jesus?

The gospel challenges people to turn and be converted. But cultures create social contexts with their own significance, worlds of meaning with their own rationale, and ways of behaving with their own justification. So, as each particular culture is called to be converted to the gospel, it is called to assimilate another belief system, another way of living: in short, another culture. Many cultural values are already quite consistent with gospel values: hospitality, reciprocity, or respect for elders. Conversion to the gospel will then be a matter of developing and extending one's cultural heritage. But since sin is also at work in every culture, the gospel will constitute a real challenge and perhaps even a scandal to every culture it encounters. People must be enabled both to reflect on their own cultural legacy and to understand the meaning of the gospel legacy. Those who bring the gospel must search for points of engagement between the Good News of Jesus and people's yearning for truth, integrity, and redemption.[33]

The gospel message, like every human culture, is contextualized or embedded: there is no naked gospel any more than there are disembodied societies. Language is the soil in which the gospel becomes a living Word, and the medium through which people of every culture internalize the world, express their deepest aspirations, and discuss their common problems. The gospel must be translated not only into the language but into the life of every people it encounters, and every people encountered by the gospel must translate the lives of its members (their belief and behavior systems) into the language of gospel love and gospel justice. This is why missionaries' understanding of people's language—the language of their lives no less than their verbal repertoire—is critical to the effective transmission of the Good News. This is why a people's understanding of the gospel—its promise and its hope no less than its books and verses—is critical to the effective Christianization of its culture. Behavior, belief, meaning, rationality, and language: interdependent components or threads of people's lives. Whoever presumes to communicate the Good News must understand that effective communication requires a grasp of each and of all these.

THE PROBLEM OF BIAS

How can we prepare ourselves attitudinally for another world and its puzzles and for the challenge of communicating the gospel intelligibly? We began with that question. We have seen several possibilities and considered some contours of our encounters. But one issue will not easily be resolved. It must be unmasked so that we cannot avoid it: our own bias or prejudice.

Bias has many shapes and sizes and names. Ethnocentrism has many faces: racism, sexism, clericalism, elitism, intellectualism, and more. We might distinguish *personal* and *cultural* bias, both of which need to be minimized by constant self-questioning and an openness to receive and interpret feedback from others. The less honest we are with ourselves, culpable and vulnerable human beings, the more prejudiced we will become as we try to cover up and appear in control. Missionaries of a certain style are particularly prone not only to interpret others through their own familiar categories (a common form of self-defense) but to allow this attitude to become fixed, judgmental, and very un-Christlike. Learning to become vulnerable after years of learning the opposite can be tedious and painful. But unless we are vulnerable, real communication is hardly possible; people tend to be intimidated by overbearing figures. Our own bias (leading us to behave self-righteously or to deny our faults and failings while pointing out those of others) must be identified and addressed if we are to be credible bearers of the gospel. The promise, the hope, the forgiveness, and the redemption brought by Jesus are for us as much as for those we encounter. We, no less than they, are needy and unworthy. Unless we are striving to remove the bias in our own eye, we have no business to be pointing to the limitations in other people's vision.

Perhaps we can glimpse ourselves through the mirror of these two quotations:

As long as the idea [that the nineteenth century world was the pinnacle of human achievement] dominated, it was very hard to see the greatness in other cultures. [Even] in our own century it was still taken for granted by most people that an enormous distance separated the "primitive" from ourselves and primitive religion from ours. We can no longer believe in a gulf. But the "true equality" varies with who describes it. An old bias has been overcome, but certain ethnocentricities, or rather "culturocentricities," remain. We cannot say that now the universality of [humanity] has been established.[34]

That is a quote from a historian of religions. Here is a quote from an anthropologist:

To see ourselves as others see us can be eye-opening. To see others as sharing a nature with ourselves is the merest decency. But it is from the far more difficult achievement of seeing ourselves amongst others as a local example of the forms human life has locally taken, a case among cases, a world among worlds, that largeness of mind, without which objectivity is self-congratulation and tolerance a sham, comes.[35]

Bias, unchecked and aggressive, is ugly; but there may be virtue in some bias, whether personal or cultural. Total lack of bias, if it were possible, would make us less than human because apathetic and passionless. Total lack of bias might lead to rampant relativism, a philosophy of "Anything goes," "One thing is as good as the next." This is not what Jesus stood for. It should not be what his followers stand for. Some bias or partiality is a legitimate part of Christianity or any other culture. It is helpful if it reminds us of a hierarchy of values, judgments, and truths. But like any appetite or capacity, it must not get out of control. It must never be used at the expense of another person.

We share a common humanity but each one of us is different. We cannot reduce another person to ourselves, feel another's feelings, or think another's thoughts. Given the constraints of culture, language, and bias, the wonder is that we can communicate at all. But we know that we can, however tentatively. Nevertheless, we must not too quickly assume that we understand others completely or that they understand us as we would like. Still, the transmission and translation of the gospel build on the possibility of cross-cultural communication. With appropriate care we can assist the process. Here we have considered some of the challenge, some of the promise.

SENSE AND NONSENSE

Understanding Other People

===

INTRODUCTION

Good news that makes no sense is not good news. We have all watched people reading foreign newspapers in familiar or unfamiliar scripts. Unless we understand Arabic, we can make absolutely no sense of what is perfectly meaningful to millions of Arabic speakers. If we have a little French or Latin, we may be able to make some sense of a Spanish newspaper; but we know from experience that to understand some of the words is not at all to understand the meaning.

Those who bear the Good News of Jesus Christ must not only be able to interpret other cultures; they must be able to transmit a message that makes sense to other people. It is not sufficient if something makes sense to the one who speaks, if it leaves the hearer mystified: without mutual understanding there *is* no communication, no dialogue.

RULE-GOVERNED CREATIVITY

Here are three monumentally important social facts. We owe them to Ferdinand de Saussure (1857-1913), the Swiss pioneer of structural linguistics:

1. Every day people create streams of speech so creatively that many are actually unique: they have never been *uttered* before in exactly that form. Speaking is not just a matter of stringing together familiar phrases.
2. Every listener is constantly absorbing and interpreting streams of speech that have never been *heard* before in exactly that form. Understanding is not simply the recognition of previous strings of words.

3. Language is amazingly creative, and the possible combinations of words are virtually infinite; but every language has a structure that can be *discovered* and *described*, even though most speakers are hardly aware of it.

Noam Chomsky (1927-) extended Saussure's revolution and reduced contemporary English to about 150 rules[1] for creating, assessing, and judging whether *utterances* (the technical word for a speech sequence) are grammatical, acceptable, and meaningful—or not. He demonstrated that some things may be grammatical but meaningless while others may be ungrammatical but acceptable, even meaningful. The implications for theology and ministry are staggering.

The possibilities opened up by twentieth-century structural linguistics are enormous, for missionaries no less than anthropologists or linguists. If we can discern rules underlying language, what about behavior? If we can determine whether particular examples of language are acceptable, meaningful, and grammatical, can we say anything about the ethics of behavior?

Human speech is expressed in myriad languages, each reducible to its own grammar. Can we construct an analogy between speech and morality? Can we visualize a moral universe with several, or even many, moral systems (like different grammars)? Would this be incompatible with a single gospel truth and a single right way of living? And if there *were* only one legitimate moral and doctrinal language, whose should it be and how should it be transmitted? What a scramble there would be among missionaries of many tongues and traditions to propose their own version. This has already happened, of course: in two thousand years of Christianity, the "one true faith" is not expressed in a single voice or a common speech but in a babel of voices, more than there are languages in the world today.[2]

Even if we could imagine and agree on a single, universal moral and doctrinal grammar, our problems are not over. Chomsky formulated the brilliantly grammatical but quite *meaningless* sentence "Colorless green ideas sleep furiously" to demonstrate the limitations of grammars lacking built-in meaning evaluators. Such (semantic) components would check grammatical constructs against the real world of meaning. The translation we already noted—"The wine is agreeable but the meat stinks"—is another utterance that seems perfectly grammatical yet somehow fails to convey an intended meaning.

Christians may sincerely attempt to preach a single, consistent, universal gospel; but every Christian appropriates and transmits the message in a slightly different way, and every hearer assimilates a message in his or her own fashion. The twin burdens of proclaiming authentic Good News and assuring orthodoxy in the receivers can be very heavy. But the danger of uttering what appears grammatically correct (orthodox) to the speaker but is incomprehensible or meaningless to the hearer must not be under-estimated. We may wish to be understood, just as we may wish to provide nourishing food; but if we speak unintelligibly or provide dehydrated rations to people without water, our goodwill is in vain.

LEARNING THE RULES

Shared meaning depends on common context and mode of communication. Two chess players are in *communication* when they play. Though they use the same set of rules, each of them plays differently, strategically and tactically (in terms of ends and means). Plans are made and constantly adapted according to one's opponent's actual play but also according to one's own perceptions and interpretations, intuitions and guesses, skills and limitations throughout the game. Communication is *not just* a matter of two people using the same rules. This is why chess, with its myriad moves and endless possibilities, is so compellingly interesting.

> At this point let me say that I do not play chess. I know the basic rules but have little understanding of strategies or game plans, and not a grain of imagination where chess is concerned. Still, I can speak of chess as comprehensible because it is rule-governed and because the rules are rather easy to grasp. Although I could never make some of the moves I observe, I can understand some of them even with my primitive knowledge. So I can gradually come to understand more of the meaning of chess and of chess players.
>
> But to the aficionado, chess is endlessly interesting precisely *because* it permits creativity—and even a kind of rule breaking—to the smart or unscrupulous. Given time and motivation, novices can not only simply learn the rules but actually relax enough to relish the cut and thrust of competition. Chess, like many other games of skill or forms of communication, can be learnt at any age; but like them too, it is best learned and practiced from an early age.

One point cannot be overemphasized. People neither *intuit* nor make up rules; rules have to be *learned*. People who have never learned the rules of cricket might sit for the full five days of an International match and still not understand the purpose, the outcome, the tactics, or the drama. Those who do not know the rules of chess could watch it for a lifetime and still not understand the range of possibilities from which a player can choose a move. People who have not been taught the subtleties of American football will never understand the lyricism of the professional commentator. The temptation to interpret a game we do not know, by means of the rules of an apparently similar game we do know, is almost irresistible. It must be resisted.

On a flight in New Zealand (an avid cricketing nation), I was reading an article on Don Bradman, the incomparable Australian cricketer. The article was illustrated with photographs and statistics of the great man. An American woman, seated adjacent to me, volunteered the information—with equal measures of curiosity and distaste—that she had never understood cricket, and asked if I would kindly explain it to her. To try to explain cooking or genetic engineering would have been as easy in the circumstances.

Unfortunately, I tried to share my enthusiasm for cricket. But the context (a crowded plane on a short flight) was inappropriate, and we had no common universe of discourse. Attempting to speak in terms she might have understood, I started to explain cricket in terms of baseball. But not only do I struggle to discover in baseball the subtlety I find in cricket; this woman was as innocent of baseball savvy as she was of cricket. I tried; I failed. I failed to explain the rudiments, much less the magic and the mystery of the game I most enjoy. Cricket is just not "like baseball": cricket is cricket and may always remain inscrutable to noncricketers. (Nor is baseball "like cricket": baseball is baseball.)

We cannot and must not attempt to reduce one culture and its rules to another. So how can the examples of chess or linguistics, baseball or cricket help us as we encounter other cultures and their people? There are myriad games, rule-governed yet full of creative possibilities, and there are many cultures. Cultural life is no more random than chess or cricket, and no less rule-governed. But rules can be *discovered* and *described*, though with serious effort. But we *must* discover and learn the rules; otherwise we will never understand and will constantly misinterpret. Rules out of context will not work, any more than the grammatical rules for Bulgarian will allow us to speak good Italian. Rules from the wrong context will be disastrously misleading.[3]

BREAKING THE RULES

If rules never changed and if nobody ever broke them, we would have a *steady-state* system that would soon become very tedious. But neither games nor languages work like that for long. Certainly cultures and people do not, despite numerous efforts to make them do so. The Academie Française has fought a losing battle to preserve the purity of the French language; but languages are living systems, and change cannot be forever controlled or mandated.

When we consider social institutions like the state or the church, we see the tension between lawmakers or law preservers, on the one hand, and law keepers or law breakers, on the other. The process of change may be painful, but change does and must come, for where there is no change, there is no life. Societies, languages, and people that do not change die.

People who live in *traditional* societies do not perceive social change as a good or a desirable thing, and the whole social effort is directed to claiming and re-creating the past and preserving stability in belief and behavior. Yet despite people's perceptions, even traditional societies change, from stone axes to steel knives, from gourds to plastics, from loincloths to Levi's; and soon there are headache pills and radios, Nestlé's baby formula and laptops, Mercedes trucks and machine guns.

There are also more traumatic ways to break the rules. The very presence of mission or other outside agencies provides a range of previously unavailable opportunities and alternatives. Once these exist, people begin to remake their choices. Sometimes the choices are manifest in the repudiation or the overthrow of what is not wanted. But outsiders who encounter other cultures and people need to discover what the people themselves perceive as deviant, objectionable, or intolerable—as well as normal, attractive, or desirable; otherwise we will be totally confused about where the underlying rules are and what is deviant rather than chaotic. Societies have a built-in tolerance (more or less) of rule breakers, as well as a theoretical breaking point that, once reached, signals the breach between the *ethos* and the *worldview*. But rule breaking may be a necessary procedure for drawing attention to coming change.

One traditional missionary approach was the "clean sweep," which attempted to eradicate everything within a target culture in order to replace it with something new. The assumption was that cultures were unequivocally bad.[4] But if you deliberately undermine, belittle, or attempt to eradicate cultures or ways of living, there is nothing left for the Good News to be grafted onto. Demoralized and disillusioned people can hardly turn around to those who have made them so, and accept them with trust and hope. If you forbid me to speak my language when I do not know yours, how will I ever learn it and how can we possibly communicate?

Do missionaries attempt to change people? A simple affirmative answer is insufficient. It fails to appreciate the difficulties created for the people affected by change. Worse, it overlooks the subtle problems of communication that must be resolved if change is to be morally defensible. A simple negative answer is just as bad. It fails to appreciate the seductive possibilities the missionary presence brings with it and the confusion such presence can sow in the lives of those affected by it. Missionaries *are* agents of change, both intentionally and accidentally. But we must treat people with great respect lest we compromise the gospel we preach and harm the lives of those we intend to heal. The question should be reformulated: *how* might missionaries approach the delicate and fraught issue of change—social, theological, and pastoral?

MODELS AND MUDDLES

If it is possible to interpret other people's behavior after the fact, is there any way of doing so before it happens? It might be very helpful to think we could predict the behavior of others and understand its rationale, but we must also acknowledge human freedom and unpredictability lest we reduce people to machines and become totally muddled by our models from linguistics or game theory.

We may not predict any particular piece of behavior with accuracy because people differ among themselves, change their minds, and sometimes act whimsically. Still, we can approach others, expecting their behavior to be meaningful; we can hope to interpret events as they occur; and we can expect to be able to comprehend what they actually do. Our linguistic or game analogy helps us here: we know that we can judge whether a response to our statement or a move on the chessboard is legitimate, fair, or meaningful—or illegal, improper, or meaningless. If we are in conversation or playing chess and our partner responds to us in gibberish or eats the pawn, we *know* something odd or deviant is happening. Our knowledge is part of the same body of knowledge that tells us how a person might or even should act. So we can claim to be able—to a significant degree—to predict other people's responses.

Linguists develop *generative models*[5] with which to produce consistently meaningful examples of various languages and to exclude deviant forms. But generative linguistics looks at each language on its own terms or in the context of its own integrity. It does not establish one language as supreme and others as inferior. Missionaries who do other than this will fail to identify the grace in every culture; by only identifying the sin they betray themselves. If God is in every culture before missionaries arrive, every culture has the *semina verbi,* seeds of the Word.

Every utterance presupposes a language, every game presupposes rules, every *ethos* presupposes a *worldview,* and every piece of social behavior presupposes an underlying social structure. Every Christian who encounters another culture or an unfamiliar world of meaning must become a cultural and semantic puzzle-solver because every language and game, every ethos and piece of behavior is *coded.* Since we do not set off on our missionary journeys with all the codes, we are challenged to discover them. Jesus advised his disciples (actually commanded them):

> Ask, and it will be given to you; search, and you will find; knock, and the door will be opened to you. For the one who asks always receives; the one who searches always finds; the one who knocks will always have the door opened. (Mt 7:7-8)

We should take these words literally and remember their implications: people who ask are people who acknowledge they do not have the answers; people who search are those who are lost or some distance from their destination; and people who knock are not at home but outside someone else's home or at least without a key to their own. By contrast, those with all the answers, those who know exactly where they are and who are at the center of their chosen world, will not need or choose to ask, search, or knock. People who do not admit ignorance, undertake risk, or ever venture out will pay little heed to Jesus' command.

SENSE, NONSENSE, NON-SENSE

Here is an exercise to pass the time, stimulate the imagination, or perhaps create frustration, depending on temperament. The latter point is important: we all have breaking points, and some of us have little tolerance for puzzles. But if we spend some time with the exercise, we may discover something important about ourselves and about our capacity to encounter an unfamiliar culture and to learn something about its rule-governed creativity.

On the "nonsense" page below you will encounter various arrangements of letters enclosed within a variety of shapes. Look at it, and see if you can *think of the whole page as a massive overdose of stimuli—like those bombarding you as you step off an airplane for the first time in another world, another cultural context.* Look at the table, and follow these simple instructions:

1. If possible, work at this with another person or in a small group.
2. Time yourself, and spend three minutes with the list. Do not think of it primarily as language, but imagine it as input that greets your senses—sight, smell, taste, touch, and hearing—as you step off the plane. Pay attention to your response as you try to absorb the page. Notice how your eyes and mind are working and responding. Are you aware of *where* you are looking. Are you "reading" the page systematically, or are your eyes darting all over? Are three minutes a long time, a very long time, or just an instant?
3. Try to express how you *feel* during these three minutes (*stupid, frustrated, superior, intelligent, angry, relaxed*) and your actual *thinking process (logical, scattered, systematic, engaged, disengaged, stimulated).* As you do this, you may notice that in the course of three minutes, or depending on what parts of the page you were encountering, you may have felt a range of emotions and thought in a number of different styles. This is good to share with your small group.
4. Try to identify what caused you to move through the page. Did you want to get to the end before the three minutes elapsed? Did you

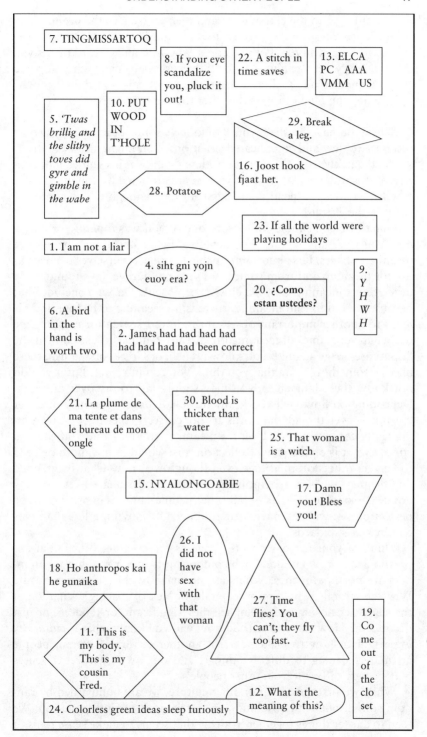

7. TINGMISSARTOQ

8. If your eye scandalize you, pluck it out!

22. A stitch in time saves

13. ELCA PC   AAA VMM   US

5. *'Twas brillig and the slithy toves did gyre and gimble in the wabe*

10. PUT WOOD IN T'HOLE

29. Break a leg.

16. Joost hook fjaat het.

28. Potatoe

23. If all the world were playing holidays

1. I am not a liar

4. siht gni yojn euoy era?

20. ¿Como estan ustedes?

9. Y H W H

6. A bird in the hand is worth two

2. James had had had had had had had had been correct

21. La plume de ma tente et dans le bureau de mon ongle

30. Blood is thicker than water

25. That woman is a witch.

15. NYALONGOABIE

17. Damn you! Bless you!

18. Ho anthropos kai he gunaika

26. I did not have sex with that woman

11. This is my body. This is my cousin Fred.

27. Time flies? You can't; they fly too fast.

19. Come out of the closet

24. Colorless green ideas sleep furiously

12. What is the meaning of this?

want to get to the end quickly and then go back to the beginning in order to interpret the page *as a whole* and *in context?* Did you stay with things you *thought you could interpret,* and discard things you thought were meaningless—or things you personally felt you could not understand (such as a language you knew you didn't know)? Again, you might discuss this after the three minutes.

When you have finished, you should have some idea about your own response to new and complicated situations. You might also have disassociated quickly from the exercise, feeling that it was insignificant or contrived. It is useful to know whether you are attracted by conundrums or whether you can suspend your judgment long enough to enter into the spirit of the exercise.

One thing you should find: every one of you was *looking for meaning.* You were not actually instructed to do so. But human beings are meaning-makers. It is almost impossible to *prevent* ourselves from looking for meaning and from sometimes sensing that we have found it. At other times meaning may be elusive or absent. Do we conclude that because we fail to find meaning, there is no meaning to be found? This leads to another important observation: in our search for meaning we use whatever frames of meaning are already familiar to us. Look at the "nonsense" page again. If you know French, or Greek, or Spanish, there may be something there that you think you can interpret. But if you do not know these languages, you may simply fail to discover meaning. Depending on how well you know those languages, you may discover meaning—even though the words are not correctly spelled or even grammatically correct. As you look for meaning, you may find you want to *correct* what is on the page. Reflect on this: why do we want to or need to correct other formulations, even though we know what is intended and the message is clear? Applying this to our missionary lives, we may notice personal tendencies to put other people's houses in order or to be perfectionists: we may have little tolerance for anything less than perfect by our standards.

Think of your responses to the page as representing your initial impressions of a new culture. Each component is numbered, but the numbers are not in sequence. What do you make of this? Is it significant? What about italics, bold print, capitals, or lack of spacing? What about the shapes enclosing each item: are they significant, or random, or just decorative? How can you tell? So how will you know what is *culturally* important or how to make sense of another culture? Different people attribute meaning to different things, and our own interpretive lenses may be very different from other people's.

When we first encounter another culture, we are bombarded by random stimuli but with absolutely no instructions for interpretation. We tend to cluster things together in a way that seems to make sense to us. It is easier to do this than to ask questions every step of the way. But inevitably, some of the clusters or categories we create provisionally are different from the way local people categorize their world. Alternatively, our initial categorization of reality will harden, and we come to believe that our categorization is real, objective, factual, or absolute.

When we first encounter God in another culture, will we place God in a context that includes spirits, polytheistic beliefs, vengeance, and explanations for evil? Or will we locate God in a cluster that includes humanity, the physical world, benign concern, and faithfulness? How do we know how other people understand God and the world? And what about marriage? Do we consider it a religious reality or as economic or perhaps political behavior? All of us tend to chop up external reality and create categories that help us think about the world and address life's unfolding experience. Different cultural groups may actually encounter or perceive reality differently. What is *really* real among the Dyak people of Borneo may be rather different from perceived reality among Cambridge professors. But whether people are Dyaks or dons, they consider their interpretations of reality appropriate and the meanings they attribute to the world as the *correct* meanings. Cross-cultural travelers may be disturbed when they encounter other people's reality; but they can learn and grow. Some, however, cling to the notion that their reality, meaning, interpretation, and truth is the *only* reality, meaning, interpretation, and truth; they find cross-cultural living intolerable or make it intolerable for others.

In 1972 Njala Komboya was a large African village of perhaps a thousand people. Far from any big city and without electricity or transportation, it was effectively isolated. One morning I was called to visit a sick man. He was lying on a straw mattress and surrounded by family members who evidently thought he was dying. He was twenty-nine years old.

He motioned to everyone except myself to leave. He was very agitated. He wanted to tell me his story before he died, and as a Christian he wanted the sacrament of Reconciliation.

He was walking from the village to his plot of land one day when he came upon a group of witches eating a meal of human flesh. He was terrified and tried to escape, but they saw him and forced him to eat. He was revolted but he had no choice. But once he had eaten, he was complicit in the witches' evil. They ordered him to provide the next human meal.

Reluctantly he planned to kill a neighbor whom he did not much like, though he certainly did not hate the man. But the neighbor had protective antiwitchcraft medicine, and it paralyzed the would-be killer. His family had found him at dawn that morning, lying paralyzed between his own hut and that of his intended victim. He knew he was going to die.

When he finished his tale, I consoled him, blessed him, and gave him absolution. He immediately calmed down, so quickly that I was astonished. His breathing slowed, his eyes shut, his body relaxed, and he fell asleep. In fifteen minutes he was dead.

Where shall we start with an attempted explanation? Was this delusion or devil worship, autosuggestion or madness? And what was *really* real here? A full explanation would take us too far afield. But readers should ponder this experience: notice how you try to interpret it, how selective you are with the facts as presented, how willing you are to take the young man's story seriously. And if you discovered that when all this had happened, the young man had been in bed, having a nightmare, and that the previous day he had been hit by the heavy branch of a falling tree, what difference would that information make?[6]

Let us accept that we seek meaning and we interpret in terms of the interpretive lenses we ourselves wear. Now we can return to the "nonsense" page.

As you first look at the nonsense page, try to imagine that you have just arrived in another culture. We are told that initial encounter with a completely new reality subjects us to half a million sensory stimuli *per day*. But this is far too many stimuli for us to absorb, and consequently we begin to filter or *tune out* many of the things we see or hear, taste or smell or feel. Effectively then, we simply do not notice what is actually there. But we do not tune out randomly: there is method in our sanity. What we exclude or overlook tends to be what we do not understand or cannot comprehend. To say that we compartmentalize our knowledge and experience is to say that whatever knowledge and experience we *lack* will either be put in a pre-existing compartment, or will be filtered out, simply because there is no compartment to put it in. Of course we can create new compartments, just as we can learn new languages or techniques: but there are limits, and some of us are more limited than others, whether because of intelligence, age, or temperament.

* * *

Now, look more closely at the page, be conscious of your responses and reactions. Try to identify whatever you think you understand. Then notice what you looked at and discarded. Is there *anything* on the page that you would be prepared to accept as utterly meaningless. Why?

Some items have a surface meaning, but beneath that you may note a different meaning. Every language is laced with metaphor, simile, and other figures of speech; words alone do not fully yield meaning. And every language has idioms—strings of words or sayings whose meaning is quite unpredictable from the meaning of the individual elements. What does the English phrase "to kick the bucket" mean? It all depends on the context. But knowing the context may not be sufficient: we also need to know whether and how the meaning is context-dependent. Until we know that "to kick the bucket" may have nothing to do with buckets and a lot to do with death, we could never predict the meaning of the phrase, even though we have a stack of degrees.

Look at the "nonsense" page again, and try and track your own mental processes. Below are some observations. They are not exhaustive; meaning depends on many factors, and some legitimate meanings may remain hidden. You can compare your own interpretations with mine. But notice how social location is a significant factor in each person's interpretations. Perhaps you can identify your own interpretive or hermeneutical lenses and then reflect on or, better, discuss their significance.

1. *I am not a liar.* Superficially, a simple assertion of the speaker's veracity and an implicit request for people's trust. But Richard Nixon spoke those exact words. Does that affect their meaning? "Famous words" have a special contextual meaning. But if they are the words of a liar, what do they really mean?

2. *James had had had had had had had had been correct.* Did you bypass this perfectly grammatical and meaningful sentence? Imagine James is learning the past tenses of the verb *to have:* the simple past *(had)* and the pluperfect *(had had).* But *had had had* is not a legitimate English past tense. Imagine that James had written—or, as we say informally, James had had—the incorrect sequence *had had had.* He should have written the pluperfect, *had had.* In other words (and using *had* for *put* or *written*), James had had *had had had; had had* had been correct. What appears unequivocally meaningless can be a carrier of meaning. (If you work on this and punctuate it, you can make it make sense.)

3. There is no number 3. Why should there be? What difference does it make? Were you looking for a number 3? Why? Sometimes we look for something in a culture but it isn't there.

4. *siht gni yojn euoy era?* This looks suspiciously unlike a real language. It is not a stream of letters but is broken into segments (significant? meaningful?). Depending on how persistent or perverse you are, you may immediately see how to "translate" it: disregard the breaks, invert the sequence, and produce *areyouenjoyingthis?*—or "Are you enjoying this?" If so, did you impose meaning, or was it actually there? Can you tell? What are the cross-cultural implications?

5. *'Twas brillig and the slithy toves did gyre and gimble in the wabe.* Italics are used here. Did you notice? We monitor or censor what we perceive, unconsciously trying to make sense of everything. Sometimes we may exclude an important component of meaning. If you recognize this as *Jabberwocky,* Lewis Carroll's "nonsense poem," you have brought something from your pre-existing knowledge to the interpretation. Did you feel a tinge of superiority? What about the meaning? Actually it does not mean anything, yet it is not meaning-

less. It is intended to be meaningful to anyone with the imagination to "fill in" the content of words like *slithy* or *wabe*. Carroll used the English grammatical and syntactic structures but did not stick to the English lexicon. But we can easily distinguish various parts of speech: noun *(toves)* or verb *(gyre)* or adjective *(slithy)*, even though we know they are not actual words. But small children do not know that. As they learn the language, they gradually learn to distinguish real and unreal words: but their imagination soars when they hear *Jabberwocky*, which they find wonderfully evocative, spooky, and exciting. They *invest* the words with meaning.

6. *A bird in the hand is worth two.* How can you tell what this might mean unless you already know that it is incomplete? If you do know this, you know how to complete it. But there is more to it: this is a figure of speech, a proverb or wisdom saying. It carries condensed meaning and applies to circumstances that have nothing at all to do with birds or bushes. Cultural immersion should expose us to this kind of verbal wisdom, but it may be years before we come upon it, and it cannot be guessed at. But there is also wisdom in daily life; we may never see beneath the literal, missing many layers of social meaning and significance.

7. *TINGMISSARTOQ*. Word or sentence? What shall we make of this? In the mid-1930s a U.S.A.F. Sirius airplane overflew the Northwest Territories of Canada and the startled Inuit people far below. They had never seen such a thing, and someone pointed and said something like "What's that odd piece of flying stuff up there?" *Tingmissartoq* (however written) came to be the Inuit word for airplane.

8. *If your eye scandalize you, pluck it out.* Meaning depends on knowledge of context and on criteria for literal or metaphorical interpretation. Literally, and decontextualized, the phrase carries meaning, but the context (Mt 5:29) modifies the meaning radically. I once met a man in a locked psychiatric ward. He was there because, tempted by immoral thoughts, this good Christian had plucked out his eyes and almost bled to death. For him, the meaning was clear.

9. *YHWH*. (Again, think not only of these actual letters; think that you are bombarded by stimuli as you arrive in an unfamiliar culture. Think of the possible layers of meaning that need to be unpacked.) Here we have the *tetragrammaton* (four letters) representing the name of God, Yahweh. But God's name should not be uttered. And written Hebrew omits the vowels. But this is not Hebrew: the letters are English. On the "nonsense" page they are written vertically instead of horizontally. So, to interpret **YHWH** in its fullest meaning, you need several pieces of information and must discard what is irrelevant (the vertical presentation of the letters). This example illustrates the complex-

ity of interpretation; people may see the same thing but understand it in very different ways. So it is with culture.

10. *PUT WOOD IN T'HOLE.* It is easy enough to *translate* this by disregarding the capital letters and reading it as "Put the wood in the hole." But what does it *mean?* It is a local form of English still found in northern England. Thousands of years ago, in the Neolithic Age, people would have lived in caves or enclaves. If they protected themselves against wild animals while they were asleep, they would have needed to secure the entrance. "Put wood in t'hole" refers to securing the entranceway, perhaps with a tree branch or piece of wood. Today, if a person comes into a cold room without closing the door, someone might shout, "Were you born in a barn?"—or, "Put wood in t'hole!" But not everyone would understand.

11. *This is my body. This is my cousin Fred.* Each phrase is comprehensible, but together they are quite problematic. The first is, almost literally, a consecrated phrase; the second, utterly banal. Some people feel quite uncomfortable in saying the two phrases together: the sacred and the profane should not come so close. If we encounter such a juxtaposition in other cultures, it may be quite shocking.

12. *What is the meaning of this?* This is circular language: it means what it means. We can understand the meaning of the words yet must ask what they mean in the circumstances. The meaningful is simultaneously almost meaningless. Examples occur in culture: a dance may be simply a dance.

13. *ELCA PC AAA VMM US.* Acronyms can make sense individually, but a cluster of acronyms might lead us to think they are somehow related. Thus, if *VMM* "means" Volunteer Missionary Movement, then perhaps *ELCA* "means" Evangelical Lutheran Church of America. From there it is only too easy to jump to conclusions and, attempt to interpret the others in terms of the first two. Thus, *PC* might mean Presbyterian Church—but what of *AAA* and *US?* There is simply no way to interpret any or all of these from the available information. But being compulsive puzzle solvers, some of us will not be content with that; we will try to make all the acronyms yield to an interpretation, thus actually *imposing* meaning. We will encounter many similar things in other cultures; we must be careful how we group them and how quick we are to think we know what they mean.

14. There does not appear to be a number 14. What could this mean? Culturally we might encounter analogous situations: this can be very frustrating to some people.

15. *NYALONGOABIE.* This sequence may appear meaningless or random. In Sierra Leone, West Africa, *nya longo a bie* is anything but meaningless: it means "I *[nya]* love *[longo a]* you *[bie]*." But among

the Mende it has different connotations, depending upon who says it, to whom, and in what circumstances: *longo a* can mean "love, want, desire." Meaning can be almost infinitely subtle.

16. *Joost hook fjaat het.* If you think this is Dutch, you jumped to the wrong conclusion for the right reasons! It looks like Dutch (except to those who know Dutch). But it is entirely fabricated (double Dutch). It means nothing. I made it up as *something without meaning.* Is it possible that some things look culturally meaningful (at least to the outsider) but are actually meaningless? Anthropologists used to speak about remnants, and the consensus was that there are no cultural remnants. I am not so sure. (What is the meaning today, of lapels or buttonholes or cuff buttons on men's jackets?) We must be careful not to *overinterpret.*

17. *Damn you! Bless you!* Separately each phrase has meaning. But somehow they seem wrong together. Some people complain if the first word is spelled or spoken. Others would say that mutually exclusive phrases lose their meaning. Culturally we may encounter things we feel to be out of place because they do not belong together. This leaves us with a difficult job of cultural puzzle solving.

18. *Ho anthropos kai he gunaika.* This may be Greek to me, but a Greek speaker could not understand it unless he or she were familiar with the Latin alphabet: it uses English letters. And though it might actually mean something ("The man and the woman") to someone who knows Greek and English, it is grammatically incorrect. Culturally speaking, some things may not be *grammatically correct* but they may still be *meaningful* or *acceptable* to all but the purist. But culturally, too, some things may be interpretable only to specialists of various kinds. A medicine man, diviner, or shaman might be able to interpret in ways that ordinary people cannot. Some people may interpret Greek in English orthography, even though many Greek people cannot. Think about this. It is rather complex but significant.

19. *Come out of the closet.* Any English speaker can identify these words and produce a meaningful phrase. The fact that they are arranged vertically (on the "nonsense" page) may add to the image by evoking a closet. But *interpretation* depends on context. If a child is playing hide-and-go-seek, this phrase may be taken literally; if the context is an invitation to an adult to disclose a sexual orientation, the phrase must be interpreted metaphorically. Simply to be a speaker of English is not of itself sufficient to interpret the sentence. How can we interpret cross-cultural ambiguity unless we are deeply immersed in the culture?

20. *¿Como estan ustedes?* The initial question mark may be interpreted either as an error or as a convention to indicate Spanish language use. If the latter, the phrase could be translated as "how are you

[pl.]?" Someone with very little Spanish might be able to interpret this correctly. (But see number 21.)

21. *La plume de ma tente et dans le bureau de mon ongle.* At first blush, or if we were to hear it rather than to see it written, this could be *interpreted* literally as "The pen of my aunt is in the desk of my uncle." But it does not actually say that. There are spelling mistakes and incorrect grammar. But those who do not know French would not notice that. And anyone with a working knowledge of French would compensate for the errors and interpret the presumed intention of the writer: another aspect of interpretation. If the writer, however, were a schoolboy and the reader were a teacher, the teacher would not accept what was written. It may be well intentioned, but it does not actually say what it attempts to say. Yet we would not want to be too pedantic. Pedantic missionaries are offensive.

22. *A stitch in time saves.* Like number 6, this carries some meaning and can be made to yield meaning. But whoever knows the phrase "A stitch in time saves nine" knows this is incomplete. But more: the completed phrase can apply to situations unrelated to sewing or embroidery. Language can use particular words to say or to mean something quite different from their literal meaning. To understand a culture is to understand its metaphorical meanings. As Geertz once said, until you can laugh at jokes in another culture you do not yet understand the language.

23. *If all the world were playing holidays.* This is an incomplete conditional phrase. So, though the words are meaningful, we cannot interpret much at all. The writer's intention cannot be guessed at. To know these are Shakespeare's words may help: in *Henry IV Part One* we find "If all the world were playing holidays, / to sport would be as tedious as to work." Even then, not everyone understands it. The words alone, and even the composite phrases, need an interpretive key that is beyond the reach of many people. So it is with culture.

24. *Colorless green ideas sleep furiously.* This famous and intentionally meaningless, though quite grammatical, phrase was coined by Chomsky to demonstrate that not everything that obeys the rules of English grammar makes sense. For those who undertake cross-cultural ministry, it may serve as a sobering reminder: some of the orthodox propositions of our faith, when translated "grammatically" into other languages, may leave people completely in the dark about what they could possibly mean. Could our ministry be "grammatical" but "meaningless"?

25. *That woman is a witch.* Again, context is all. I heard this said in West Africa, where it was meant quite literally and was so understood by almost everyone. Elsewhere it might be intended metaphorically, but the intention of the speaker is not always as translatable as the words

themselves. (See number 11 for ambiguity and other problems of transmission of meaning.)

26. *I did not have sex with that woman.* On its face value, a simple denial. At a more contextual level, a famous statement by a famous person in relation to a famous scandal. But, for all the emphasis of the denial, the meaning transmitted was in fact false. This is an example of the barefaced lie. How are we to interpret statements in other cultures when some of them may actually be statements of untruth?

27. *Time flies? You can't; they fly too fast.* Here is a complex but perfectly meaningful group of words. To make sense of it, regard the word *flies* as a noun rather than a verb. Then imagine someone with a stopwatch, trying to time flies as they pass by. It is a bizarre but meaningful notion. Is it possible to time flies? No, because they fly too fast. In cultures, too, we may encounter the bizarre and learn about polysemy—the many layers of meaning attached to words and ideas.

28. *Potatoe.* This was one of Vice-President Dan Quayle's more embarrassing mistakes because he was correcting a schoolchild who had spelled *potato* correctly. Without the context, it is simply a misspelling. But even a misspelling can carry meaning. Do missionaries have a tendency to "correct" everyone else?

29. *Break a leg.* To those in the theatrical profession these are words of encouragement, equivalent to "Good luck!" But the profession is notoriously superstitious, and wishing someone good luck would be sure to bring bad luck; so this is a reverse good wish. Some think the phrase is an oblique reference to the great Sarah Bernhardt, who "had but one leg, and it would be good luck to be like her." But no one knows. Cultural meaning can be as subtle as this.

30. *Blood is thicker than water.* Finally an example of *social change,* or change in language use or meaning. "Blood is thicker than water" is a phrase that carries metaphorical meaning, about the bonds of family being stronger than those between strangers. Water evaporates, leaving no mark; not so blood. But the phrase took on a completely new and horrifying meaning during the genocide in Rwanda. In a nominally Christian country it was used to mean that Baptism (water) was not as significant as ethnic differences (blood). Baptism might call all people to belong to one family, but differences of "blood" truly distinguished people and justified killing them.

All these sayings, statements, words, or jumbles of letters may or may not carry meaning. But we can hardly resist looking and trying to interpret, even with something as trivial as the "nonsense" page. And we can be much more serious and determined—and hopelessly wrong—in another cultural world. Using this "nonsense" page as an analogy with culture, we may reflect profitably on the subtleties of meaning as well as the excitement or frustration encountered by those who search for meaning. Some of us lack the stamina to pursue the struggle for interpretation, while others may jump to premature conclusions—and even condemnations. Not every conclusion is worth jumping to.

Here are ten summary points and questions about meaning and culture. They can be a reflection or conversation piece for those committed to understanding other people's words. Words or ideas that seem particularly important are italicized.

1. It is almost impossible to refrain from interpreting the world. As we do, we may actually impose meaning and overinterpret, especially when working alone. But *insiders* already understand the context or world of meaning that *outsiders*—at least initially—cannot. With help, outsiders may come to *expose* or *discover* meaning. The best way to do this is by *dialogue*. Unless we engage others in our search for meaning, we will make very serious errors. But *true dialogue changes both parties.*   ***Am I prepared for this?***

2. When we are tired, frustrated, or sick, we may become careless in our search for meaning. We may even give up. Then it is very tempting to *conclude that things are meaningless,* and just as tempting to *conclude that people are stupid.*
          Can I imagine myself in such a situation?

3. Things make sense to me when they fit my sense-making grid, my world of meaning. They make little or no sense to me when, for some reason, there is a lack of fit. But what makes sense to me does not necessarily make sense to everyone. And *some things that make no sense to me are not necessarily meaningless.*
          How do I react when something makes no sense to me?

4. People commonly operate socially in meaning-making or meaning-sharing groups. They do not normally make up meaning. Whenever it has become settled, *a group's world of meaning is quite conservative, resisting change.*
          What does this suggest to a sensitive cross-cultural missionary?

5. Not everything makes sense to everyone. Perhaps it never can, given our different worlds of meaning and our uniqueness as individuals. Is this regrettable? *Does the missionary enterprise stand or fall on the possibility of a uniform universal understanding?*
          Have I considered this question seriously?

6. It *is* possible to slip or step outside a familiar world of meaning. We would not fall into a vacuum but into another person's or group's world of meaning. Remember Alice, the Mad Hatter's tea party, and the Queen of Hearts? *It is possible to survive in another world of meaning.*   **How do I rate my own chances?**

7. Outside my own frame of reference I am vulnerable and ignorant. That is uncomfortable and perhaps painful. How will I cope? Vulnerable people sometimes curl up, or lash out. But *some people learn to risk, trust, and ask for help.*

     What would I do?

8. A missionary must adopt a stance toward others. Are we inclined to accept other people's ideas and wisdom, or do we want to give them the benefit of our own? When our meanings and views do not match our hosts' and when our certainties are not theirs, *will we be trusting or suspicious, gracious or judgmental, patient or intolerant?*

     Do I have any real idea of how I might react?

9. Can a missionary approach another culture open-mindedly, willing and able to accept the meanings held by local people? Or do missionaries claim their beliefs (meanings, interpretations) as the only correct ones? If the latter, can local people make sense of, and respond to, the novelty of missionary explanations? And if they truly espouse dialogue, *might missionaries need to change the way they understand the world, and God, in people's lives?*

     Am I willing to be changed?

10. The creation and maintenance of meaning is critical to human functioning. Given that worlds of meaning are both internally coherent and intrinsically precarious, in venturing to encounter other worlds of meaning and other people's lives, *what does a prospective missionary need to know, to learn, and to remember?*

     Am I aware of the immense challenge of the missionary enterprise?

Language is finite and exists within real communities, and so with culture and meaning. The missionary task is enormous. We may *learn about a culture* or set of meanings from third parties, but we can only truly *learn a culture* and learn meaning from direct experience. Each person carries the responsibility for creating and sharing, learning and experiencing, bungling and cherishing communication and meaning; these do not just happen or exist in culture, like palm trees or mud huts. José Comblin tries to put some of this into words:

> It is the Church [who, precisely?] that receives the words expressed
> by Jesus in human form as signs of God's word and message. It is the

Church that tries to find the words capable of touching human hearts. In short, it is the Church that performs the constant task of mediation and translation. Real transmission of God's word entails a constant re-invention of the message so that it will accurately express the substance of the divine word to human beings. The message does not exist on its own as some fixed, prefabricated discourse, as some standing monument of the past, as a textbook for recitation. The message is a "wayfaring" one, calling for translation at every moment.[7]

Communication is a two-way process. What Comblin says is only part of the truth. The other part is that the message must be *received,* and received *comprehensibly.* For this to happen, those who preach the Good News must also take pains to understand the language and ways of thinking of those who will receive it.

Comblin rightly says that the church transmits the message of Jesus; but the church ultimately means people. Evangelization is indeed what the church does, but its shape and effects depend on the cumulative work and witness of individuals. As used in this book, evangelization should be understood at its simplist and most etymological level: the announcing of the Good News of Jesus in a comprehensible way, in the hopes of its being welcomed. And this depends on its being understood. If it is announced appropriately, its relevance will be discernible by the recipients. But it may not be perceived as relevant. That might be due to the inadequacy of the messengers or the perceived untimeliness of the message. Evangelization does not automatically guarantee the wholehearted acceptance of the message; it works with the gratuitous grace of God to produce a response in the hearers.

Adequate evangelization requires the building of relationships. Relationships define the church as a community of believers. They are part of the broad context in which conversion of heart takes place: the community itself. If evangelization and the fostering of interdependence do not march together, the results will be dire. Either proselytization masquerading as evangelization will produce the poison of coercion and imperialism, or too casual an approach will lead to superficiality or uncritical relativism. Instead, we need a clear presentation of the scandal of the Cross and a clear invitation to serious moral responsibility. Evangelization produces fruit when certain relationships are strong. First, the relationship between God's grace and the living word: neither acts as magic, but together they transform. And second, as we have seen, relationships between people require the sure foundations of effective communication and proficient translation.

We tread on dangerous ground here, but as missionaries we *must* seek to understand other worlds of meaning and contexts other than our own, where people's judgment of what is real or true differs considerably from ours. We must look squarely at such contexts and discover the rules and the rationality by which they operate. Otherwise *we* act irrationally in assuming our communications will and should be understood or in naïvely believing that we are engaging in real dialogue.

We have seen how the rules governing belief and behavior can be identified and how they may be broken. Missionaries must be sensitive to how and when rules are broken, but they must also work to understand this: unwritten but very real rules do indeed exist.

We claim to be earthen vessels bearing a life-giving gospel. We say we want to do what is most wholesome and liberating for other people. First we must identify the actual hopes and dreams, the fears and nightmares of the people we encounter. Then we must discern how the Good News is relevant to the actual situations in which those people live. Only then can we propose ways in which the people may benefit from the Good News. And ultimately we must allow people the freedom to accept or reject.

MERGING AGENDAS

Looking for Relevance

SEEKING COMMON GROUND

We are developing several themes: human cultures are complex worlds of meaning; it is difficult but possible to encounter unfamiliar worlds of meaning; and each culture or world of meaning is more or less resistant to others. Unless we identify themes like these, we may approach other people far too naïvely. Since this book is not only about anthropology but about mission theology and spirituality, we must link them more explicitly to the Christian agenda.

Christian theology defends believers' right and duty to offer the Good News of Jesus to whoever has not heard or not yet absorbed it. This implies that the Good News *can* in principle be effectively translated into the circumstances of other peoples' lives. It is a huge implication, but translation is not a magical transfer of information. Messengers must be able to assess the effectiveness of their communication and determine whether anything critical is lost in translation.

This chapter considers how the agendas of missionaries and of those they encounter might converge or indeed pass each other by. It will caution that if missionaries impose on local people, they will compromise people's freedom and may mutilate the message itself. If force or fear are components of the missionary agenda, we will call them by their true name: sins.

Stepping into another world as a visitor is like walking self-consciously into a room full of people. The newcomer is the only one who does not know what is happening, and does not share the context or perspectives of the insiders. When missionaries step into other worlds, they are at some disadvantage. Can outsiders and insiders establish common ground?

ETHOS AND WORLDVIEW

As we self-consciously enter other people's lives, we need tools, we need language, and we need to find meaning. A good place to begin is by discovering the difference between people's actual experiences and their deepest hopes.

If people everywhere were totally content and had satisfactory answers to all their questions, the gospel would have little relevance to their lives: in such an idyllic world there would be little excitement about outsiders' Good News. This is why, in secularized societies seduced by the promise of progress, the gospel is far less relevant than it once was. But there is no society where most people have no concerns or unanswered questions. People may be more or less able to manage, but they never stop asking the question *why* because unexpected things happen and life is not always predictable or controllable.

Ethos and *worldview* offer a helpful distinction.[1] The *ethos* is the palpable experience of life as it is lived: the tone, spirit, or character of a particular culture. When you walk into a prison, a mosque, or a marketplace, the ethos is the typical "feel" or *ambiance:* it embraces the characteristic smells and sounds and sights. More generally, the ethos is *the way things actually are*. The ethos of a cathedral may be very different from that of a football stadium, but the ethos of Chartres cathedral is also very different from that of Coventry cathedral. The ethos of different places can be compared.

Worldview (from the German *Weltanschauung*), sometimes defined as the way a particular culture understands the world, is also glossed as *philosophy of life*. But *worldview* can refer to people's perception of an underlying system or reality: as *the way things should be* if everything were running smoothly.

If ethos is *the way things actually are,* worldview is *the way things ought to be*. "We are all in the gutter, but some of us are looking at the stars," said Oscar Wilde. If "the gutter" is the ethos for some people, then "the stars" represent their worldview: people who live in the gutter can still hope for the stars. Yet not everyone is actually looking at the stars—or even believes they continue to shine: for some, the ethos is all there is because their worldview has collapsed. They live for nothing and hope for nothing. This leads to despair. Fatalism is the hopelessness that rushes into the void where a worldview once stood: a sense of absolute powerlessness overtakes those whose *ethos* has become terminally stifling and awful.

An oppressive ethos can be temporarily tolerated so long as people have something to hope for. Likewise, an ideal world, or worldview, can be threatened by the experience of a nightmarish ethos. Prisons, mosques, or marketplaces are not always as they might be: prisoners sometimes riot, mosques are sometimes blown up, and marketplaces are sometimes devoid of fresh food. But people know how these things *should be* and *could be*. The worldview is the picture we have of the way things should be and could be if everything were running perfectly.[2]

So long as people have a worldview—though their lives are in turmoil and others are breaking the law or committing sin (the ethos is never perfect)—the world is not total pandemonium. But if chaos takes over completely, the worldview has been destroyed: there are no remaining points of reference and the disarray is permanent. Then something more widespread than individual fatalism is at hand: then social and cultural death is at the door.

Wherever belief and action are not in phase, there is tension: lawlessness, anomie, hypocrisy, or sin. If there are effective sanctions and law enforcement, such situations can be remedied. But when a real revolution occurs—civil, scientific, or religious—belief and action that were formerly conjoined become separated: what was once significant is now *meaningless* or *irrelevant,* and previous sanctions are no longer effective or maintained. Human history is a history of revolutions and changing or competing worldviews. Change is sometimes traumatic but not always disastrous. Modifications of worldview are sometimes necessary for human development.

What if certain societies are not geared for progress and do not perceive change as a good thing? What if change *is* catastrophic and people move from a world of meaning to a world of meaninglessness in a few years or a generation? What if their points of reference are uprooted or obscured and their ethos cannot be reconciled with their worldview? Such questions face enormous numbers of people today. No wonder their actual behavior seems to be inconsistent with their professed beliefs. No wonder former beliefs seem to collapse under the pressure of rapid social change.

The Christian worldview is very different from any actual ethos. Christians proclaim continuing existence after death—a place of rest and bliss for the just. Missionaries assert that God is relevant and vitally committed to every person. We say the *basileia,* the *Kingdom,* the *Realm of God,* is already breaking through, already palpable in today's world. Missionaries acknowledge this paradox: that the *basiliea,* while *already* to be felt, is nevertheless *not yet* in place—And this is precisely where the gospel of Jesus is relevant: it explains *how* God's Realm can be promoted and *how* every *ethos* can be transformed. We announce that the Good News helps promote a more Godly *worldview,* where every tear will be wiped away and where justice and peace can be found.

TOWARD COMMON AGENDAS

Since every society seeks to narrow the gap between actuality and possibility (ethos and worldview), the missionary message should be widely relevant. But if we attempt to impose a worldview without first determining the points of contact between the questions other people ask and the answers Christianity proposes or between Christianity's questions and different cultures' answers, there will be a lack of connection between the two. Unless the agendas of Christianity and local people converge, they will run on parallel tracks and may be mutually irrelevant.

I have argued that cultures, like grammars, are rule-governed. If we want to make sense cross-culturally, we must understand cultural grammars and semantics. This can also be stated theologically. A passage in *Evangelii Nuntiandi* (the 1975 exhortation of Pope Paul VI) deserves not only to be quoted but to become a yardstick for all would-be missionaries:

> Evangelization loses much of its force and effectiveness if it does not take into consideration the actual people to whom it is addressed, if it does not use their language, their signs and symbols, if it does not answer the questions they ask, and if it does not have an impact on their concrete life. But on the other hand evangelization risks losing its power and disappearing altogether if one empties or adulterates its content under the pretext of translating it. (EN 63)

This very basic statement respects the integrity both of the gospel and of cultures. But unless it is taken very seriously indeed, it is only rhetoric. Evangelization—and evangelizers—*must* take into consideration actual people, use their language, their signs and symbols; answer the questions they ask, and have an impact on their concrete life: we must encounter and affect a people's *ethos* and the *worldview* that underpins it. If Christianity were to take people this seriously, there would be a greater convergence of agendas. Some people would become interested in a message they find relevant to their lives, and some would find Christianity's rationale persuasive. But others would not, for even a relevant gospel may not always evoke a radical Christian response: the rich young man went away sad even though he was attracted by Jesus and by his words (Mk 10:22).

People receive according to their capacity to receive, and they discover for themselves what is relevant. Therefore missionaries—consistent with the observation of Paul VI that the content must not be emptied or adulterated—must not simply proclaim a message: they must understand what other people deem relevant to their actual lives and why.

SOCIALIZATION

Outsiders are initially marginal, and insiders do not know strangers' agendas. So, since local people (insiders) cannot get on the agenda of missionaries, we should try assiduously to identify their agenda. Only then can we hope to become relevant to the lives of those we claim to serve. Only then might we actually get on their agenda. Every culture, every enduring social group has institutionalized programs of *socialization* by which the older generation transmits its wisdom and the younger generation learns how people ought to live. Socialization is a process for turning the raw material of society (babies) into the finished product (mature adults).

> The continuation of a form of culture implies mechanisms of socialization and knowledge transmission, procedures for displaying the range of accepted meanings and representation, methods of ratifying acceptable innovations and giving them the stamp of legitimacy. All of these must be kept operative by the members of the culture themselves, if its concepts and representations are to be kept in existence. Where there is a continuing form of culture there must be sources of cognitive authority and control.[3]

If we learn how people are socialized and identify cultural agendas, we may discover whether and where there may be a place for us. Missionary irrelevance would be a tragic waste of human energy, and missionaries cannot expect to be blessed by God unless their good intentions and dedicated works actually benefit their brothers and sisters.[4]

SOCIALIZATION IN GENERAL

We are social animals; we do not exist purely as individuals, nor do we respond—whether to the gospel or to other cultural choices—purely as autonomous individuals. People belong to social groups or societies, and social pressure is significant in human lives. A dangerous and counterproductive missionary strategy would be to appeal to people simply as independent individuals. This may have relatively little effect, or it can result in isolating individual converts from the community on whom they depend—with very serious consequences.

Reflecting on human diversity, we are struck by both the uniqueness of each person *in some sense* and yet a common, universal humanity. We are a single human species: we *can* understand each other, behavior *is* meaningful, people *do* act rationally, and mutual intelligibility *is* possible. If it were not so, the proclamation of the gospel—not to mention its cross-cultural comprehensibility—would be impossible.

The uniqueness of everyone within a common humanity is an important, problematic, and extremely challenging idea. We are individuated and unique, but we do not individually or uniquely modify our environment, create our language, or formalize our belief systems. We are all born into a preexisting world in which we inherit and acquire beliefs and language. Yet we are not sponges but active agents. During our socialization each of us acquires generically human but specifically personal and cultural qualities. These will mark our subsequent relationships and significantly determine our capacity to change.[5]

Once we have matured as members of society and assimilated social rules and expectations, we become relatively ethnocentric: we see, judge, and act from our cultural perspective. If group or territorial boundaries are strong and tightly maintained we will have little or no awareness of alternatives. Some societies appear extremely open, boundaryless, and accommodating to outsiders, but adult members of human groups are relatively settled in certain ways. We cannot easily think our thought is wrong. We may acknowledge error in individual cases, yet the patterns of our thinking are not easily changed;[6] and the idea that our epistemological system itself may be "wrong" is something most of us simply cannot entertain.

Such notions (that human societies operate with shared and *obligatory* conventions; that people are born into a preexisting, enduring world; that it is quite difficult to think our ways of thinking are wrong) will be crucially important as we explore the social impact of evangelization. We should come to understand more readily the reactions we meet as well as the problems we create as we invade other people's worlds of meaning. But in order to think through the implications of evangelization, we must step back and approach the whole issue of social life, not from familiar perspectives and with comfortable answers to the questions that *we* deem appropriate but in a much more tentative and open way.[7]

Humanization is the process of making human, and *socialization* relates to particular elements in this process. Children have to be trained, to be *made* human, to become assimilated to the society that preexisted them. They must learn to identify their society and its boundaries, and how it relates to a wider world: to history, current events, and the future. They must discover their own place: their freedom, limitations, and the constraints that are part of their existence. They must understand the sanctions that govern them, and discover meaning in their lives.

Every society addresses such issues long before missionaries arrive. The more we missionaries examine local socialization processes, the more we will identify compatibility or friction between gospel and culture. We will foresee harmony—or dissonance—between the socialization demanded by Christian conversion and that already characteristic of each social group. Without such sensitivity, the gospel will not be assimilated and conversion will not be facilitated—though something may be foisted on people and their response may be counterfeit conversion.

Socialization *individuates* members of social groups: the baby becomes a child and gradually an adult, full member of society. But each society— through its own traditions, sanctions, accumulated wisdom, and public priorities—is responsible for socialization, so there is enormous cross-cultural variety in style and emphasis. If groups in their ethnic, social, or religious diversity are to be perpetuated, reproduction is not enough; new members must be assimilated and trained to meet the group's needs. *Reality* itself is *socially constructed,* built up gradually in the consciousness and experience of its members, by the socialization processes they experience. Children are selectively taught what is real, relevant, and right. So they must know what is not real, irrelevant, and wrong. An example might help:

> In Western society, children who have nightmares are comforted by parents and told not to worry because "it was only a dream." They learn that what is *not real* cannot hurt. They learn that what *seems real* is not always so and that dreams are not *really real.* Jungian analysts might take exception to such a simplistic view, arguing that dreams help in the social reconstruction of reality. But among the Hausa of Nigeria, children are taught that dreams are indeed *really real* and far more meaningful than any other experiences. Hausa children who wake while dreaming are never told, "It was only a dream," but helped to internalize it and learn its important lessons. In adulthood the interpretation of dreams will help them negotiate life itself.
>
> Or think of God: some people are socialized without any reference to God as part of the real world, others positively to discount God's existence, and others again to outgrow such credulity, as they outgrow belief in Santa Claus. When socialization is complete, it will have formed people's understanding of reality itself.
>
> Or driving. Some people are taught to drive on the left, and for them such behavior is natural and correct. But others are taught to drive on the right and do so with the same obedience and the same acceptance of the naturalness and correctness of their behavior. Socialization in both cases establishes conformity and standardization of behavior: it creates a predictable and enduring world.
>
> Everything works well—until our ideas about dreams or God, or driving a car encounter conflicting ideas and alternative worlds . . .

Through socialization we come to see, hear, and do what our group tells us to. Sometimes we simply do *not* see, hear, or do other things because they are not relevant. What we are trained to perceive becomes the real. Whatever else may exist either passes unnoticed or is judged unreal. Reality is mediated to us in two main ways: by training and by language. We should look more closely at training: socialization. It must always be understood in context, but we can make some general comments. Every child must negotiate two important stages: *internalization* and *generalization.*[8]

Internalization

By *internalization* a particular external world is grasped and made meaningful. Children come to understand certain social expectations, and they learn to behave appropriately. Transport a child from London to the Arctic Circle, and the child will be overwhelmed and alienated. But lead the child by the hand into his or her own familiar bedroom, and the child will identify and name a host of things. *This* bedroom is a meaningful world; the Arctic is threatening and meaningless. But reverse the process, and an Inuit or Saami child will scream at the suburban bedroom yet gurgle in his or her familiar environment.

During internalization a child assimilates *recipe knowledge*: how to get from the bedroom to the kitchen or from the igloo to the tundra. Recipe knowledge is simply contextual *(how to)* knowledge: how to dress, eat, or attract help. Whoever internalizes knowledge can act on the world, observe the world's reaction, and modify behavior accordingly. A child becomes assimilated into a preexisting world and takes the first tentative steps to independence. Without internalization and recipe knowledge, the individual, whether Xhosa or Christian, Macedonian or missionary, is alienated or lost.

Generalization

Generalization is the capacity to do or avoid doing things *because they should or should not be done* rather than because "mommy" or "grandpa" says so. The process may be like this: first a child learns *"Mommy does not like you to bite your sister"*; later he or she will generalize to *"I should not bite my sister,"* and later still to *"People should not bite sisters."* When finally the child knows that *"people do not bite people,"* the sequence is complete. Other processes relate to personal hygiene, eating habits, and so on, which vary cross-culturally. But without the ability to generalize, the child remains immature and socialization is incomplete.

We distinguish the *generalization of norms* from the *generalization of others*. The former is achieved when one moves from the specific to the general and from the individual to the totality (from "I must not steal this" to "stealing is not allowed"). The latter has occurred when one moves from *Mommy* to *people* and from *is* to *ought*. A child develops a separation and a freedom from a specific parent or a specific *other* and makes generalizations that cover an ever-widening number of others, generalizations that would be deemed essential for mature Christianity.

Failure to generalize and internalize produces serious problems for individuals and groups. In the West the breakdown of the extended and the nuclear family (due, among other things, to urban renewal, relocation, divorce, and the biological revolution) has contributed to a high crime rate, especially among juveniles. Many youngsters exhibit a striking incompleteness of socialization. The inability to internalize and generalize helps explain recidivism or backsliding. We are left with some serious questions: what is the value of (severe) punishment; how may specifically Christian education and socialization assist people?

Significant others

Socialization requires three different categories of people. *Significant others* are pivotal, socially acknowledged as responsible for socializing others. Typically they are one's parents. But parents may die or disappear, and some may be too young or irresponsible, so surrogates may be appointed. Nonparents may stand in the place of a parent *(in loco parentis)*. Social change in the West has radically affected our understanding of who counts as significant others and what rights and responsibilities are involved. We note their critical importance here and explore their authority.

Significant others have authority to train, to reward and punish, in accordance with the social norms. *Authority* is the socially acknowledged right to control, command, or determine; *power* refers simply to the physical capacity to act. You may have *power* to poke someone's eye out, but you do not have authority. In small communities children are subject to the authority of all who stand *in loco parentis,* in the same (structural) place as a parent. To be out of sight of a parent is by no means to be safe from parental sanctions: a neighbor upholds parental expectations, reports wayward behavior to parents, and sometimes punishes misdemeanors directly. In more individualized societies such social control no longer exists, and at significant cost to the socialization of their members.

The threat or actual use of punishment (or reward) is a feature of socialization, and significant others have legal authority to exercise appropriate sanctions (physical or other punishments). But the best and most effective significant others are those who invoke *moral* and not only legal authority. Moral authority operates when someone shows respect for the person who wields it, and because of this respect, rather than from fear of punishment, modifies behavior.

> When I was about seventeen and thought myself quite grown up, I did something wrong. Though I have no recollection of the details, my memory of the significance has not dimmed after forty years. I recall my father—whom I respected above everyone else—looking at me sadly and with evident disapproval in his voice. Very quietly, and looking me in the eyes, he said, "Son, I'm very disappointed in you." That was all: no shouting, no threats, no punishment. But I knew I had hurt my father and diminished myself. My regret was all the more keen because of his disappointment in me. Here was a man of quiet dignity and moral authority; the impact of his disappointment was profound.

Legitimators

Sometimes appeal must be made to legal authority. The second category of people who contribute to socialization control legal sanctions:

they are *legitimators*. A police officer upholds the law; a judge enforces it. Both, and others in different societies, have particular status or legitimate authority to call people to accountability and to punish wrongdoers.

A legitimator may enforce the law through fear or threat or by appeal to legal authority. Many people will conform because they fear the consequences. Legitimators have a necessary social role. But imagine a legitimator who exercises moral rather than simply legal authority: a kindly police officer, a respected teacher, a gentle pastor. Imagine people who keep the rules not simply from fear of punishment but because they respect the moral dignity of legal authorities. We have all encountered employers or clergy, even police, who rarely invoke their legal authority. An authoritarian attitude of "You'd better do that or I'll . . ." is very different from one of "Please would you . . .?" The first implies legal sanctions and particular punishment; the second appeals to one's sense of righteousness.

Adjacent generations (parent/child) are frequently marked by tension and the use of legal sanctions ("You're grounded; go to your room," and so on). But alternate generations (grandparent/grandchild) are often characterized by warmth and the presence of moral authority: there is less need for a grandparent to discipline a child, since that is the primary responsibility of parents. In fact, warm and comfortable relations develop largely *because* grandparents are not primarily disciplinarians but indulge their grandchildren. Missionaries might ponder the possibilities here.

Peers

Peers comprise the same age cohort as oneself. Sometimes only same-sex cohorts count as *true peers*, and sometimes the *peer group* is mobilized formally and has particular responsibilities. The Boy Scouts and Girl Scouts are peer groups whose members are bonded together in loyalty and socialized within those peer groups as they pass through the ranks. Socialization, however, is relatively informal and optional: people are not required to join the movement. But in some societies the socialization process uses the peer group explicitly. One thinks of Maasai age grades, where the peer group is tightly bonded during the course of initiation, so that one's age-mates become the most significant people in one's life, even more important than parents or spouse. *Peer pressure* is the power of one's cohort to demand support and conformity to expectations. Peer-group authority is not strictly legal or backed by legal sanctions but is a kind of moral authority.[9] The peer group exerts moral pressure, and this is often strong enough to produce atypical behavior. Whether one stands fast against a rushing lion or takes flight, smashes a car windshield or runs away, may depend on the moral authority of one's peers: it is not due to fear of legal sanctions, nor is it purely spontaneous.

So much, then, for authority, whether legal or moral, and for pivotal people in societies, whether significant others, legitimators, or peers. Missionaries at the margins need to understand how and where authority is distributed. But since the distribution of authority is intimately connected to socialization processes, we must discover whether and how we might become relevant authority holders with realistic expectations of being listened to and affecting other people's lives.

SOCIALIZATION IN PARTICULAR

Primary socialization

Primary socialization relates to the *generalization* of *norms* and of *others*. It is complete when they are firmly embedded in consciousness, when the child has created its first enduring world. "The use of reason" identifies when primary socialization is achieved, for it indicates a child's ability to generalize and to accept responsibility: to differentiate between right and wrong. But *each* society makes its judgments about these things, and the lines between them are drawn differently across cultures. Children who have completed primary socialization are not uniform, but in their own particular world they can make responsible moral decisions and are called to accountability.

Secondary socialization

If one has negotiated the rapids of primary socialization and sailed on into a broad river of culture fed by the streams and tributaries of meaning, the course is still not complete. Rivers are characterized by flooding and spate, eddies and narrows. Likewise change, reappraisal, rebellion, experimentation, and the testing of sanctions are the characteristic hazards and challenges of human lives. A child may distinguish right and wrong *as laid down by significant others*. The child may respond to imperatives *when upheld by legitimators and enforced by sanctions*. But as an adult he or she will not always be shadowed by those significant others, not to mention the sanctions. How will this person respond then?

Secondary socialization overlaps primary socialization. An individual now transforms and applies the lessons of primary socialization, achieving a personal synthesis of behavior patterns and a response to life's realities, and perfecting the skills of *internalization* and *generalization*. As people grow, becoming responsible and independent, they no longer obey rules simply because of the authority or presence of others: unfamiliar situations arise, extenuating circumstances occur, and self-interest modifies many responses.

An adult incapable of making decisions or responding to new situations is unfree or immature. So youth must experiment, vacillate, change, and build up experiences on which to draw as new situations are encountered. During secondary socialization—adolescence and beyond—people discover imperatives and possibilities. Where multiple alternatives present themselves, judgment and choice must be exercised, while a lack of alternatives should produce uniformity of response. Secondary socialization requires numerous different cultural contexts: age grades, peer groups, schools, seminaries, and rites of passage. All help to move the individual from child to adult.

Resocialization

To live is to change, and we respond to a changing world in different ways. Even when secondary socialization has transformed us from morally discriminating children to responsible adults, there is still room for modification or transformation. *Resocialization* applies to imperceptible changes or more dramatic transformations that characterize us as we move beyond secondary socialization. Without such a term we might think of people as static, programmed, and predictable. In a sense, resocialization is a never-ending process. For people of faith, another word for it is conversion.

MERGING AGENDAS

Many missionaries recognize the force of socialization, at least implicitly or negatively. They frequently confess their inability to call people to Christian conversion once they have become adults. But missionaries also know that they can accomplish little of any consequence among the children and adolescents unless it is underwritten by people with authority—chiefs, elders, parents, or peers.

We should be urged to build on local socialization, but that demands considerable knowledge of the language and effective cultural analysis, and these are beyond the scope of many. But there is another reason for widespread failure to engage with local lives and agendas, and it is not sociological but theological.

We have not always judged indigenous cultures or socialization processes suitable ground in which to plant the gospel. Cultures have been viewed with suspicion, as utterly corrupted by sin or seriously deficient and therefore incapable of receiving the gospel. Other societies and people have not always been considered worthy ground for the gospel: hence the notion of *pre-evangelization*, implying that people are not ready for the real thing. Sometimes adults have been neglected, even condemned, for resisting Christian truth while missionaries have focused on the children. The assumption[10] is that if the children are educated and evangelized, they will become a generation of Christians that will raise subsequent generations in the true faith. The assumption is naïve. It is based on the notion that existing cultures can be uprooted or overlaid, and it greatly underestimates the influence of the adults.

The classical *clean sweep* describes the attempted destruction of tradition, custom, ritual, and material culture—all that missionaries considered inferior, immoral, or incompatible with Christianity. People labeled "animists" were told they were deluded, yet the missionaries who denied the very existence of spirits not only devoted inordinate energy to destroying them but simultaneously accused people of trafficking with the devil! Such *demonization* gave mixed messages.[11] Not many missionaries seem to have noticed the inconsistency, but many embraced the principle of the clean sweep as the only way to clear the cultural ground for the planting of the gospel.

Nor was culture the only thing devalued: people were sometimes treated like blank slates to be written on at will. The image of a *tabula rasa* is not familiar to a cyber generation: it refers to a clay tablet on which impressions or letters could be inscribed, after which it could be scraped flat to be written on again. This image was applied to people, whose minds were thought to exist in a pristine state before being inscribed by culture—or being scraped clean to be written on afresh. In either case, people were treated inappropriately. And because they were *not* blank slates, they did not passively receive or assimilate the gospel in the way its communicators expected.

We must not exaggerate: some missionaries were highly respectful of people and aspects of their cultures, especially in the early centuries. Nevertheless, the notoriously slippery word *culture* came to be used as a singular and evaluative term and was applied by (European) missionaries exclusively to themselves and their worlds. The idea that God was somehow to be found in every culture was not a theological axiom; on the contrary, the image of a missionary bearing the light of Christ into the pagan darkness was elaborated to portray the missionary as actually bringing God to Godless people. Such attitudes seriously impeded the progress of evangelization. Ironically, they also serve to illustrate the enduring strength of the socialization processes of the missionaries who espoused them.

What of the adults? They may have been judged too set in their ways to become Christians, but they did not disappear. They were still the agents of socialization. The children still had to answer to them and not only to innovating missionaries. Adults exercised the sanctions: they could punish and reward. If this did not always produce a confrontation, it often produced something worse: the germination of a public and a private morality, the former on display for the benefit of the missionary but the latter operating behind the scenes. Bad syncretism or dual religious systems[12] flourished because the education or socialization proposed and undertaken by missionaries was not the only socialization occurring. Missionaries might open schools and provide education, only to find that classroom evangelism was not endorsed by the parents; out of school the cultural processes of socialization continued. What had been learned in the daytime was at least partially unlearned in the evening.

If agendas are to merge, then (short of conquest or tyranny) the major players in the respective cultures—*significant others, legitimators,* and *peers*—must become relevant to each other. If outsiders or strangers forego brute strength or naked *power,* they must nevertheless accumulate some *authority* or remain irrelevant. To claim *legal* authority might be premature and counterproductive, identifying them with colonial or imperial administrations. *Moral authority* is ultimately far more powerful and persuasive but cannot be enforced. It requires both the exercise of authority and its acceptance: without some approval by authority holders, outsiders remain peripheral. They must be legitimated but they cannot legitimate themselves. Those who achieve legitimation become part of the agenda of the people; but many missionaries fail to be legitimated. Despite hard work and sterling efforts they find themselves, like Sisyphus, working mightily but to no avail. This is not accidental, though the reasons are not always understood. Some missionaries persevere doggedly, out of a misguided sense of faithfulness to God, instead of discovering the cause of their frustration and determining how they might actually become relevant.

> In West Africa I used to walk almost everywhere. Reaching a village after a long, hard trek, I wanted only to rest and drink water. Most villages had few or no Christians, and many village chiefs were less than enthusiastic about my coming. I only went to villages in response to people's invitation so I knew there was some interest. Basic courtesy prompted me to pay my respects to the village chief, and indeed I did so. But not always.
>
> Sometimes I felt exhausted, and sometimes I sensed the apathy of the chief. So I rationalized each situation. Eventually I realized that unless the chief felt comfortable with my visit, whether or not he was personally interested in Christianity, the local response would quite soon peter out and I would be forced to go elsewhere: I was simply not relevant. *But I could have been* if the chief had endorsed my presence. Wherever the chief did endorse my presence, there I was relevant. As I discovered, chiefs were generally more than happy to do so, so long as their authority had not been undermined or slighted.

CONSTRUCTING AGENDAS, CONVERGING AGENDAS

People's agendas—their important socioreligious issues—are concrete and particular. Here is a thought experiment. Consider rural Africa or

South America, Asia or Australia, and distinguish, for simplicity's sake, just three kinds of settlement: forest or jungle; savannah or open land; and lakeside or oceanside. In each case the local people's agenda relates to the land, the settlement, and the people's actual experiences. Those who live in forest or jungle have little sense of the vastness of the universe and may rarely see the horizon. They live within a local microcosm, and their concerns are localized. The Supreme Being may seem very far away, while local spirits abound and people's devotions relate to them. If life is hard and infant mortality high, the important agenda items will relate to the maintenance of the community itself. People will be very concerned about human life and its preservation.

By contrast, if people live on open land where life is easier and infant mortality lower, the agenda may focus on matters of food gathering or crops, or perhaps peaceful coexistence with neighbors. People may perceive themselves to be living in a big, expansive world: a macrocosm rather than a microcosm. As worlds expand, people may develop ideas of a Supreme Being to whom they can relate in some way. The more relevant the Supreme Being becomes, the less relevant are local spirits.

Third, consider people who live by water: a lake or the ocean. Their agenda will relate to fish and fishing, or sailing and commerce. Because they can see the bowl of the sky and the horizon, they might become attuned to the movements of the stars as they stand before the heavens' immensity. Their microcosm is open to the macrocosm, and their own world is relativized by the vastness of space.

Actual worlds cry out for interpretation: people ask the significance of this mountain or that vast ocean, of the dense and secretive forest or the limitless expanse of water. They need to probe the meaning of events that mark their lives: why this crop failed, why that child died, why some evildoers prosper and some selfless souls suffer. They compare themselves with others: Why do other people do *that?* Why are other people more or less happy, competent, or successful? Their agenda reflects the very stuff of their lives. People from different worlds have different agendas.

Missionaries are from other worlds. Our agendas are relevant to our actual lives: we, too, are concerned about health and stability, integrity and justice. Some fundamental human questions will be common to ourselves and the people we encounter, but not all. Our respective priorities may be very different. But Christianity claims to address questions relevant to *everyone,* and we surely want to assist with the well-being of those we serve.

Two important questions arise: how will we discover the convergence between the questions people ask and the answers we bring; and what style will we adopt as we try to ensure that we leave a lasting and truly Christian impression of ourselves?

We can develop questions that concern people in their own circumstances, because at a fundamental level their questions are the common human questions. But since the formulation and ordering of questions are likely to differ between us, so we must elicit local questions instead of simply offering our own contextualized answers. Otherwise we will remain irrelevant. Since people learn from legitimators, significant others, and peers, we missionaries must determine who we want to be, who we can and cannot be, and whom people perceive us to be.

Some people, raised in liberal democracies in the so-called First World, are wary of social hierarchies and committed to building equality. Laudable though this undoubtedly is, not all societies are open to egalitarian relationships, particularly if dictated by outsiders. Outsiders are not immediately significant and not expected to take initiatives that belong to insiders. But insiders may operate within a stratified and hierarchical society. The last thing incoming missionaries should do is insult or alienate their hosts. However much missionaries might want to be *peers* and to be treated as such, we are not and cannot be, at least for a very long time. To force ourselves on others, no matter how well-meaning we may be, is unrealistic. We are *not* peers; nor can we hope to become relevant or part of the local agenda if we insist on becoming peers or treating others as such.

This leaves missionaries with two possibilities: becoming *legitimators* or *significant others*. Those who cling to the coattails of diplomatic privilege or colonialism may exercise some legitimate authority and be able to invoke the associated sanctions. But they will never win people's hearts. They may regard themselves as significant persons in their own culture and convince themselves that they are *significant others* in the society where they minister. True significant others have moral, as well as legal, authority, however. Exercise of legal authority alone cannot call people to conversion. But missionaries cannot *claim* moral authority. Only if they are *granted* it, can they capture people's hearts and engage with their agendas. The only way to achieve moral authority is the way of Jesus, the way of service; it requires laying down one's life, and it demands *kenosis,* disclaiming the trappings of legitimacy and authority that many crave. Missionaries who merely become *legitimators* operate like police officers or teachers; those invested with the moral authority of *significant others* are recognized as relevant, noble, worth listening to—even worth following.

PASTORAL FLEXIBILITY AND INFORMAL SOCIALIZATION

Missionaries have sometimes treated people of other cultures as uniform when virtue would have admitted that a pastoral plan for one area might be quite inappropriate for another. But often Christians in mission perpetuated pastoral plans imported from other times or places. Missionaries must pay close attention to the dynamics of socialization operative in particular cultures at particular times, in order to formulate more dynamic and relevant pastoral approaches. These respect the uniqueness of individuals and cultures. They would facilitate real inculturation—authentic indigenization, translation, and incarnation—of the living word of God across time and space, a word already spoken "at various times in the past, and in various different ways, [and] in our own time" (Heb 1:1-2).

A rule of thumb may be flexibility and adaptability, not a fixed or predetermined approach. Yet who can implement such plans if an elaborate missionary bureaucracy is already in place? What are the alternatives?

Where missionaries attempted to isolate and indoctrinate the children, adults soon identified Christianity itself with children rather than adults. Christianity was seen as rather harmless and perhaps even good, but something children would grow out of once they became mature and reflective. When children left school and became marriageable—specifically, sexually active—many seemed an embarrassment to the missionaries, ceasing to be active church members and communicants until they were widowed or dying.

The alternative is for the institutions of socialization and knowledge brokering to be understood and respected by missionaries and for formal education to support and build on them rather than attempt to supplant them. Western, literate missionaries may overvalue formal education and overlook the much more pervasive informal education that is an essential component of all socialization. Socialization is a continuous process mediated through practical training and social bonding and sharing. The schooling that missionaries consider indispensable often appears relatively insignificant or only narrowly relevant to the perceived priorities of oral people. Because it is a language of the macrocosm rather than the language of the home, such education could hardly be assimilated like the values of the people.

THREE DANGEROUS HALF-TRUTHS

It would be intolerable for us to assume that because evangelization—as we understand it and from our own socioreligious context—makes sense and is legitimate (even obligatory), we are thereby justified in proceeding to another community on our own terms, disrupting it with the "dangerous knowledge" of the gospel, and then leaving the responsibility entirely with the people. To fail to respond to socialization processes in other cultures is tantamount to saying one or other of the following half-truths:

1. *There is little real difference between a Zulu and an American, a Bantu and a Briton.* This opinion may seem universalistic and lib-

eral. But we can reveal its true colors: instead of imagining that a Zulu can pass easily as an American, or a Bantu as a Briton, imagine yourself—American, Briton, or whatever—deposited in South Africa or Zimbabwe, lacking any knowledge of the local language, isolated and confused. Then it becomes obvious just how monumental are the differences between oneself and another. It becomes clear that one person's socialization is of limited applicability or appropriateness in an unfamiliar situation. Zulus and Americans, Bantus and Britons have a right to be evangelized not through foreign programs but through processes that are familiar and meaningful to them.

2. *There is only one way to approach other people, for evangelization or anything else.* This is cruder and more easily unmasked. Yet missionaries have often forgotten it in their haste or zeal or insecurity. We may sympathize with one who adopts a certain posture and assumes it to be always and uniquely valid. But that would be quite inappropriate and inexcusable for a missionary. We may leave home and culture in faithfulness to the Great Commission, but we must always treat others as subjects, not as objects. This means *listening* to and *receiving* the blueprint through which they understand the world. *That* is their existential reality. *That* is the point from which they will be called to respond to the gospel. To overlook or repudiate this is to depart from the way of Jesus, who came to seek and find people and to address them in the context of their own lives. Only if we meet people on their turf—epistemological or geographical—can we communicate. The burden is on us, not initially on them, to be respectful, comprehensible, and relevant.

3. *"The gospel" is more important than people.* Some say with St. Paul, "Woe to me if I do not preach the gospel." Some think that if they preach the gospel (as if it were that simple!), people should take it or leave it, and if they leave it, they are in bad faith. But Jesus came to bring abundant life and never failed to address persons, emphasizing the priority of people over things, laws, and even the Sabbath. We cannot foist our interpretation of the gospel on people without reference to their actual lives. We dare not pass judgment on those who do not respond to our expectations, the more so if we hardly understand their own perceptions and interpretations of our message. A law that cannot be obeyed loses its moral force. Have we failed to notice that some missionary demands are morally impossible? Have we taken steps to improve the situation? Sometimes perhaps; but threats and sanctions are inappropriate and unjust. Unless we understand the prevailing social and moral conditions, we will be unable to facilitate life-giving change in collaboration with local communities. Without such change and collaboration, the gospel will become an oppressive load (see Lk 11:46) that we try to impose, rather than a liberating word of life and love.

SEVEN CONCLUSIONS

First, the gospel might have been much more effectively inculturated (offered to, and accepted by, societies). If it had, the universal church would look very different locally, and many missionaries would have been freed to seek other challenges. There is great need for first evangelization (preaching the gospel where it has never been preached). But many missionaries are tied to routine jobs in local churches still dependent on expatriates after more than a century. Collaboration is wonderful, but dependency that prevents self-reliance is a sin and a shame.

Second, Christian evangelization has not always succeeded in bringing one generation to the faith and then seeing it pass the faith to the next generation. The wisdom and integrity of parents and grandparents have been resources often overlooked or wasted by Christian churches as they preached a gospel of love and respect.

If, third, we can identify our own socialization processes, we may understand how things might have been different. As we consider our openness to, or fear of, strangers, we can draw lessons about our own conservatism or radicality, our certainties and doubts, and some of our motivations. We will become sensitive to the range of social processes—normal or pathological—that have made people the world over similar or different. We will never forget that people are different as well as similar, unique as well as comparable. We will never impose our preconceived solutions on other people's problems or other people's worlds. We will remember that people *must* use the elements of culture—relationships, rules, sanctions—that already exist; they *must* synthesize these into a personalized, coherent, and socially acceptable whole. We might then admit that the perhaps unfamiliar "Grace builds on culture" is as axiomatic as the more familiar "Grace builds on nature." Both nature and culture may need to be challenged and perfected; neither should be overlooked, demeaned, or destroyed.[13]

Fourth, imbued with the Spirit of Jesus, we will pray to be freed from the temptation to judge our own worldview, responses, and initiatives as the only possible or valid ones. We will strive to respect the integrity of others and the reality of their cultures and experiences. We will honestly try to understand other people's formative socialization processes. We will painfully learn that it is not only others who are odd, unpredictable, sometimes secretive, ambivalent, and occasionally unreliable; we can be all these things, too. We will pray to rejoice in these confusing realities as we continue the pilgrimage. Our pilgrimage points us to the vernacular— local ways, indigenous languages, new worlds of meaning, and the honest hearts of people—where the Reign of God is not without witnesses.

Fifth, language is crucially important in socialization; someone without language is virtually unsocializable. Not that mutes cannot be responsible people; many have language even though they lack speech. The wild boy of Aveyron represents the individual who is intractable until and unless tamed by language.[14] This raises a central issue for missionaries: how do *we* measure up as language learners? Without language can we ever become socialized into the society where we minister? If we cannot piece together the enduring world of the other and if we fail to understand the difference between right and wrong *as perceived within the society,* can we ever be trusted by the people, or must we remain peripheral and they uncommitted? I do not argue for a cosy relativism or forgetfulness of personal standards, but I question how we can call and challenge people without some personal experience of their experience, and how we can hope to make sense to them if they make no sense to us.

Sixth, if we have not experienced the primary socialization of those we encounter, how can we forge the links necessary for partnership? If we acquire the language, we may begin to construct reality as native speakers do, at least slowly; but we must also acquire the culture. To learn languages bookishly is to overlook the natural interaction through which people assimilate spoken language during socialization. Unless we intersect with local socialization processes, we will never be comprehensible to them. They and their socialization predated us. We must find a convergence lest evangelization be marked by tragic divergence. This is a lifetime's agenda, yet few of us remain with our hosts for a lifetime.

Seventh, evangelization is not simply the encounter between "the gospel" and "culture"; it is a dynamic interaction of values and traditions and morality, implicating real people living in particular circumstances. Authentic and successful evangelization must be sensitive to these realities. Could we ever think that "the gospel" as mediated by Swiss Calvinist missionaries of the 1880s to a highly centralized kingdom in Muslim Cameroons would have been preached or perceived in the same way as "the gospel" as mediated by Irish Roman Catholic missionaries of the 1950s to the heavily "Christianized" Igbo people of Nigeria? If not, what wisdom do we need to carry with us?

PROCLAIMING GOOD NEWS

Translating the Gospel

THE PROBLEM OF LANGUAGE

Like the proverbial elephant in the living room, language is an ever-present component of culture and therefore of evangelization. But some people do not want to talk about language because they are afraid to. They fear the prospect of learning a new and probably difficult language; perhaps they fear failure itself. There is also a relatively recent factor that affects language and mission significantly: the prevalence of short-term mission service. Some people expect to complete their mission service before they could ever become proficient in the local language. What should they do? It is a serious issue and raises some fundamental questions.

A related issue is rarely addressed because many people have never even considered it. It is the matter of language *use*. People from highly literate cultures sometimes consider other people as *illiterate*. Their objective may then be to offer those people the benefits of literacy. Some will argue that learning a minority language is unnecessary and that it is actually better for local people if the missionary uses a world language such as English, Spanish, or French as much as possible.

A further concern is the place and function of language in society: how it is absorbed and expressed in its speakers' lives and how it shapes understanding and experience.

With these three issues in mind, we address the elephant in the living room: language.

LANGUAGE AND CULTURE

Language study and practice are intrinsic to mission. Mission is impossible without communication, and Christianity purports to be Good

News in any language. Missionaries have produced some of the finest scholarship in language studies, from philology to semantics, from grammatology to comparative linguistics, from the creation of new scripts to the phonetic notation of unwritten languages. The legacy of missionaries is incalculable.

When the topic of language and mission arises, every missionary has something to say, some conviction to impart, some justification to invoke, some position to defend, some fellow missionary to judge. Rarely are people dispassionate about language.

Language is a vehicle and human thinking is its passenger. Attitudes to the one affect attitudes to the other. Sometimes the striking uniqueness of an untranslatable word or phrase leads to borrowing, and a foreign word becomes part of one's language: pajamas, potato, naïve, klutz, khaki— how could we manage without them? But we not only need words for foreign imports; sometimes we encounter things in other worlds, and our own language fails before never-before-experienced sights or sounds. Learning new words helps us feel less alien in foreign worlds.

We *try* to maintain communication across the chasms that separate languages and their worlds, but sometimes we fail. Sometimes we forget that communication should be a two-way street if it is to facilitate rather than to obscure understanding. It requires some reciprocity. And that is very demanding.

REALITY AND RELEVANCE

Different people notice different things and draw different conclusions about the world. Socialization tends to standardize the perspectives of people with a common culture, but it cannot succeed absolutely; people are not clones. Where there are wide cultural differences, perspectives and judgments are often far apart. This is not only due to people's powers of observation. It is also a question of relevance. We have examined this but need to elaborate a little.

From earliest socialization people are selecting and rejecting from myriad possibilities as they refashion a world according to their developing priorities and sense of relevance. Relevance fashions lives. There is a corollary: fickle people, unable to discover relevance, inhabit a world without a hub, shorn of meaning and lacking focus.

Relevance is culturally determined. Some people find relevance in fish, rain, or crops, while others depend on electricity, computers, or beer. One culture justifies a way of action that another finds bizarre or offensive (scarification or liposuction). Societies select from a wide range of possibilities.

Take speech sounds: every language uses roughly fifty of three hundred possible speech sounds. Every language has some sounds in common with every other language, but no two languages use precisely the same set of linguistically significant speech sounds (phonemes). The implications are important. Some sounds that are relevant to a Xhosa or Tamil speaker are similar to those relevant to an English speaker, and some are not. Within an Arabic-speaking community, the phonology of Arabic is in no way odd. But to an outsider in an Arabic-speaking community, some sounds are not only unfamiliar (and previously irrelevant) but extremely difficult to produce or recognize.

If Vietnamese people settle in the United States after learning Vietnamese, they always retain some sound patterns and articulations of Vietnamese, even when speaking English. Each of us assimilates clusters of relevance, whether in sound, taste, custom, or virtue. We carry them with us, and they cannot be entirely repudiated even when we are separated from our original legitimating community.

Now we can apply this to matters of *religious* relevance: religious attitudes, belief, rituals, sanctions are all embedded in the social fabric. As people are socialized, they absorb religious understandings of what is relevant, of what is intrinsic to their identity. These can only be repudiated at enormous cost to individual and social integrity.

If notions of relevance are as nonnegotiable as the language people speak, what are the implications for ourselves, and how might we hope to bring the Good News of Jesus Christ? We may be quite clear about what is relevant to us, and we might imagine our message is equally relevant for others. But people in other cultures are not empty slates, and they have their own history and criteria of relevance. So we might ponder the following. First: other people generally feel at home in their own culture as we do in ours. Second: it is difficult for one person to feel emotionally and intellectually comfortable in another culture. And third: people's measures of relevance are relatively resistant to external influence.

If relevance is culturally determined and culture is mediated primarily through language, we will only appreciate how people determine what is relevant and cling to it when we have the key to their understanding: language. Unless our marginal ministry is driven by a genuine respect for other people's values, we will never persuade them of the relevance of our own. Without mutuality there will be no exchange of a living word. We may succeed in colonizing people; we may get them to pass our examinations; we may present them with a moral system; but we will not bring into their world and lives a humanizing and liberating and relevant extension of the Reign of God.

LANGUAGE AND THOUGHT

Does language shape thought? Is thinking enslaved by the language of the thinker? Is there a simple answer? Edward Sapir (1884-1939) and

Benjamin Lee Whorf (1897-1941) were fascinated by the way language shapes cultural experience. Whorf suggested that thought is virtually determined by language: *we can only think what our language allows us to think*. Whorf was no fool but an expert in the structural study of some Native American languages. He understood the problems and limits of translation and translatability. His expertise can help us identify some crucial missionary questions:

- Can our ways of thinking ever change substantially? If not, what about other people's ways of thinking?
- Does the notion of Christian conversion imply that people should substantially change their ways of thinking?
- What happens when we try to interpret, assess, or think things in the way people from other cultures or with other languages do?
- Can we appreciate the difficulties involved in trying to translate our ways of thinking into another speech and another place?
- Can we appreciate the difficulties other people face in trying to make sense of *our* culturally and linguistically determined ways of thinking and standards of relevance?

Questions like these challenge the very way we approach our ministry. They generate even more fundamental questions:

- What changes do we expect in people who accept Christianity?
- Are our expectations realistic or fulfilled?
- What response is necessary and sufficient (and indeed possible) from those who hear the gospel in an unfamiliar language or see it clothed in a foreign culture?

Neither Sapir nor Whorf formalized hypotheses or a systematic list of propositions on the relationship between language and thought. But drawing from their writings, we find some weighty principles:

1. All higher levels of thinking depend on language.
2. The structure of my native language influences the way I understand the environment. The picture of the universe shifts from one language to another.
3. Differences in the way people comprehend or find relevance in the wider world are *causally* related to the structure of their language.

These are serious propositions and not wild conjecture. Because of the enormous significance of language in mission, they merit serious consideration. They need not be *either* true *or* false, but might contain wisdom and helpful elements. We should be alert, however, to the word *language* and not confuse it with, or reduce it to, *literacy*.

ORDERING CHAOS

Even after years of living and learning, our control of the world is very limited and our ease is rather uneasy. The world can be very intimidating.

We may know how it feels to be where nobody speaks our language, where we sense our aloneness, ignorance, and lack of control. At best it is tedious, and at worse quite fearsome. Many previously familiar points of reference and points of view are no longer available or shared; much wisdom and experience now count for nothing; most frustrations cannot even be adequately conveyed to others.

Within our own social and linguistic group we can more or less tame our environment and make friends with other people. Only when separated from our comfortable world do we notice how dependent we were on the language that fitted us like a glove. Perhaps only then do we appreciate the creative or world-maintaining functions of our native tongue. Our language helps to create and maintain a predictable and controllable world, turning the threat of chaos into the potential for creativity. Not surprisingly, then, language tends to be conservative: we like to be able to say what we mean, mean what we say, and express our view of reality and our ideas of relevance with simple clarity.

Every group with a shared language[1] steadfastly builds and maintains its own world of meaning and, where necessary or advisable, resists or repudiates others' ideas of reality, truth, beauty, and relevance.

In Genesis we learn that Adam named everything in the world (Gen 2:20). Imagine you know the name, in Greek or Armenian, Gaelic or Cornish, for *tree* or *mother* or *sky* or *God*—then imagine being in a position of really wanting that knowledge but not having it. To be able to name is to have power. If I give you my name, I give you the power to name me; if I do not give you my name, you are ignorant of it—perhaps not *entitled* to it—and we remain strangers. Whoever legitimately says, "I name this ship *Titanic*," or, "I baptize you in the name of the Trinity," or, "I declare this bazaar open," is using words *performatively*, really bringing about what the words are saying, really using power. If you say, "I give you my word," "I call upon these persons to witness," "I swear . . . so help me God," you are engaged in a communicative act that binds you into a community and in a significant sense changes the world. You are reconstructing the order of things. You are acting with power.[2]

If language is power, those without it are powerless, whether they recognize it or not. I am quite powerless in Arabic and Russian. Sometimes I feel I can manage without them. But if ever I were in Omsk or Abu Dhabi, I would experience my powerlessness. A person who absolutely needs another language will want to become proficient in it. Anyone who wants some social or cultural (and thus linguistic) power must, in the modern world, become literate. Literacy is the ability to manipulate the formal system of a language through reading and writing as well as through speaking. Anyone who wishes to empower others to drink at the pool of knowledge encoded in a particular culture will usually concentrate on offering access to literacy.

Possession of language is widely seen as synonymous with literacy. Those who do not have literacy tend to be described—pejoratively or negatively—as *illiterate:* lacking something. But in our rush to offer literacy to others, we may have failed to notice and respect the genius of other people and their language. For the opposite of literacy is *not* illiteracy—except to those with an either/or mentality and according to a certain kind of logic. An alternative to, or companion of, literacy—that is, another way in which knowledge is encoded, stored, circulated, and transmitted—is *orality.*

Literacy is the capacity to negotiate the written form of language: the ability to read and/or write. *Orality* is the capacity to negotiate the spoken form of language: the ability to speak comprehensibly and fluently. Literacy is to letters, scripts, and texts as orality is to speech, discourse, and conversation. Literacy provides a good way to store formal knowledge, propositional truths, or fossilized facts; orality offers a good way to nurture informal knowledge and living truth. Literacy can be a fine museum; orality is a better laboratory.

If the purpose of mission is to transmit legal codes, eternal truths, absolute injunctions, and comprehensive catechisms, then literacy is arguably as necessary as Baptism. But if mission is more about communication between living people, about the uttering of a living word, about the incarnation of the word in culture, and about an urgent and vibrant call to action, then orality needs to be reexamined. Even if we are unconvinced that literacy should be relativized, we might consider the possibilities of ministry that employs *both* literacy *and* orality. If we are attempting to give a living and life-giving word of God while people are simply accepting the skills of literacy, there is a major miscommunication. But the tragedy would be just as great if we were to neglect the God present in people's own words and on their lips as we offer them the idol of literacy.[3]

Our question becomes simply this: *how* is the word to become flesh and dwell among other people? Must it be in an alien tongue and a complex written form? Or can we preach the gospel rather than the Bible, the Good News rather than the book, the word rather than the text? Can we be midwives to the Spirit rather than calligraphers of the letter or experts in the law? Can we focus on people's hearts rather than on tablets of stone? Or perhaps, in an inclusive spirit, can we learn to appreciate whatever resources are at our disposal, *both* orality *and* literacy?

LIBERATING LANGUAGE

One meaning of *universalism* is that there is a single truth, logic, and reason underlying all language. Classical Greek philosophy, on which much Western thinking is based, was universalist in this sense: truth is universal and universally accessible. The implication is that no matter what particular language one speaks, full communication is possible, since all languages tap into the same underlying reality.

This is a comforting and appealing theoretical argument. It upholds the unity of truth and logic even in the face of diversity of language. It has been espoused, at least implicitly, by many theologians and missionaries. And it is as dangerous as it is tempting. It strips individual languages of their world-creating-and-maintaining functions; it denies to languages their specificity (their unique and culturally determined properties); and it reduces language to its syntactical and grammatical components. This attractive argument overlooks the semantic component—the very meaning—of language. Phrases like "She flew off the handle" simply *cannot* be translated word for word into another language. This phrase has nothing to do with human aviation; and it remains meaningful whether or not it has a literal equivalent in another language.[4]

Whorf attempted to discredit and disprove the universalistic approach to language by invoking practical examples. He would not flatly deny the translatability of ideas, since experience demonstrates the possibility of translation. But focusing on language itself, he could assert that "a change in language can transform our appreciation of the cosmos" and that "each language performs [an] artificial chopping-up of the continuous spread and flow of existence in a different way." Whorf was an advocate of linguistic *particularism*.[5]

If people from different cultures and with different languages (as well as all-male or all-female groups) are presented with a chart showing the color spectrum from infrared to ultraviolet, they will "chop up" the spectrum and the various colors differently. *Gray* and *brown* turn out to be cultural and linguistic constructs: Dutch and French and English see them differently. Nor can one simply translate *chair* into *chaise* or *Stuhl* and claim an exact equivalence in French, German, and English. The French *fauteuil* denotes some things denoted by the English *chair,* while *chaise* denotes objects different from an English *chair*. There is much to be said for the claim that no two languages describe or itemize the world or relationships in quite the same way.[6]

LANGUAGE IN MISSION

Using a translator in Africa, I once referred to the third person of the Trinity as "the saving Spirit of God," thinking that this allowed him to create a more dynamic equivalent than if he translated the English *Ghost* or *Spirit*. But the translator thought he heard me say "the *seven spirits* of God," and proceeded to translate this theological novelty for the people! I picked this up, and since it contributed to the point I was making, I asked him who *the seven spirits of God* were. He said he had no idea but that I had said it, therefore it must mean *something,* so he translated it!

How many of our own well-intentioned lessons are lost in translation, yet how often are we quite unaware of what the people think we have said? We must *learn* to say what we mean, *learn* to pick up what people think we mean, *learn* to hear what people say, and *learn* to check if what we understand is the same as what the speaker meant to say. Language has great potential for the intercommunication of ideas, but it traps the unwary and causes untold confusion. Whorf's observations remain forceful and cautionary.

To move beyond a world of subjective meanings we need rules that are known and shared with others. Every language is a conventional system of shared rules and meanings. Unless two speakers hold in common a minimum number of rules and meanings, there will be mutual unintelligibility. This is even possible between two people who both *think* they are speaking the same language and communicating adequately. It is much more noticeable between people who speak quite different languages: but at least in that case, both parties *know* that they do not entirely understand each other.

Evangelization is communication. It cannot be undertaken at the whim of one party. True communication requires common ground. The simple goodwill of one party is inadequate. Nor can we forget that the gospel must be proclaimed in a *specific* language with its own structures, conventions, and meanings. It would be irresponsible to think that to transmit the gospel adequately we simply have to make people literate in our language and then proclaim it. Without some feedback mechanism enabling both parties to check that they understand and are understood, language is a very poor vehicle of communication.

Satisfactory communication between people with no common language (including those who communicate in a language that is foreign or secondary to one party) is impossible without concerted hard work on *both* sides. Teaching literacy skills in English to people who think and see and judge and pray in a completely different language and mentality does *not* magically enable them to think and see and judge and pray like their (British, American, Australian) teachers. If the gospel is to be translated *(carried over)* into another culture, then it must be translated *(transformed, converted, displaced)* from one linguistic world to another. This entails a fundamental upheaval of both the messenger and the message. But without it, the *meaning* of the gospel in all its richness and depth and subtlety and appropriateness—its *relevance*—will remain trapped between the covers of the Bible and remain a lifeless text.

Mutuality in mission is more than creating copies of ourselves by giving people our language and expecting them to adopt our ways. Reciprocity means that we will receive from others just as they will receive from us. It entails mutual enrichment. It requires mutual respect, and respect for God's presence in each other's lives. What are we prepared to receive from others? Do we still, deep down, believe without qualification that we have the "pearl of great price" while others are nothing but impoverished beggars?

LANGUAGE LEARNING

For years Elizabeth Brewster and her husband, Thomas, taught at Fuller Theological Seminary. After Tom's death, Elizabeth (Betty) continued their life's work by traveling all over the world to persuade missionaries to learn local languages.

Betty Brewster contests the notion that language learning is merely a necessary *means* or *instrument* of communication and mission, arguing persuasively that it actually *is communication, is mission.*[7] She quotes missiologist Charles Kraft. Asked how much time a short-term (two-month) missionary should spend in learning a language, Kraft replied, "Two months." Likewise, if the stay were six months, the missionary should spend six months learning the language. And if the service were two years or more, then two years or more should be spent learning the language. The issue is not to approach language as a formal task to be accomplished, much less a huge obstacle to be overcome, but to know the difference between *language learning* and *learning a language.*

Language learning is an integrated approach to daily living that builds on normal social activity. *Learning a language* is an isolated approach to mastery of grammar and syntax, and an intellectual or academic activity. Missionaries who believe they are not linguistically gifted balk at *learning a language* or become self-conscious and antisocial while doing so; or they stop trying; or they postpone most of their ministry until they feel proficient.

"Millions of people have studied a language without learning it, yet billions have learned languages without studying them," says Brewster. Of course: children learn language as an enjoyable social activity; *language learning is* communication. Missionaries are not children, and we cannot learn a subsequent language with the same facility as children learn their first. But we should not put our ministry, not to say our lives, on hold while we strain to learn a language. The Brewsters' method encourages people to become *belongers.*[8] Chapter Seven will examine this: becoming *outsider participants*, strangers, belongers. *Belongers* do not study *about* the language; they actually use the language, and they relate to the native speakers appropriately.

To be *language learners,* we must overcome individualism and self-sufficiency, learn to trust others, to be vulnerable, and to value other people and their resources. This is not impossibly difficult: to be vulnerable does not mean that we get beaten up but that we are open to possibilities. Language learners forge relationships of mutual indebtedness; they are involved in give-and-take: in gift-exchange.[9] They spend time with people, care about them, appreciate them, ask them questions, and value their assistance. This is communication, and it is already the beginning of ministry; it is not separate from, or preliminary to, ministry. Those who learn a language this way become drawn into, and part of, the normal processes of socialization; they begin to understand not only the formal meaning of words but the deeper cultural meanings of people's lives. To learn in this way is to appreciate not only cultural values but *gospel values:* aspects of people's lives that are *already* compatible with, or examples of, the core values of Christianity. This integrated *language learning* demonstrates God's presence before our arrival. It allows us to appreciate the grace we might overlook if we only think of cultures as flawed and sinful.

The Brewsters' teaching and dedication can be a Godsend to every missionary intimidated by the prospect of language school or afraid that learning a language will be disastrous. Academic study and language schools have their place, but the essentially social activity of language learning is irreplaceable. Once the Brewsters' insights are appreciated, we can discover for ourselves how language learning is communication and ministry.

When I was in Sierra Leone, I attempted language learning from a very special group of children. Some were learning their own language themselves, and we could happily make mistakes and discoveries together.

Several years later, I was finishing the last of a series of visits to the outlying villages, where I had been collecting small amounts of rice as the church members' dues. On returning to my house, I found that I had been robbed of almost everything, including all the rice I had collected, which was my livelihood.

I was utterly crushed. Evening found me sitting, head in hands, crying and wondering whether I could go on. Gradually I became aware that I was not alone. Finally, looking up, I found myself surrounded by that special group of children, standing silently in a circle. One by one they came to me, and each one put one penny in my hand. Then *Mahwah,* the youngest and my favorite, said quietly, "Don't leave, *kpele wa* [Big Beard]; we love you." Of course, I stayed. How could I not?

BEYOND LITERACY

Speakers must be able to determine whether they are making sense to others. But language may be used deliberately to conceal or confuse, to evade or prevaricate. Written language is particularly open to this possibility, since it is fixed, objective, and independent of both speaker/writer and hearer/reader. The written form of language is not responsive to readers, relying for its effect on purely linguistic conventions (grammatical, syntactic, semantic, and stylistic). Thus it is inherently less powerful a tool of communication than the spoken word. Spoken language has a feature that is edited out of written language: redundancy. Redundancy includes repetition, interrogation, tone, gesture, emphasis, and so on. It is highly efficient for refining, clarifying, and affirming.

Many people are surprised to hear that the spoken word can be more effective than written language. That is because they possess the tools and skills of literacy and they believe such proficiency is evidently a good thing. Other skills may be undeveloped, and they may not even know such skills exist. Those skills are particularly appropriate to societies that do not have and do not need literacy. These are *oral* societies, and *orality* is the medium of their language.

There is an unintended arrogance in the attitude of those who call themselves *Catholic* and refer to others as *non-Catholic*. If a Muslim were to refer to a Catholic as a *non-Muslim,* or the president were to refer to a woman as a *non-man*, it would not go unremarked. The assumption in each case is that there is one universal standard (Catholic, Muslim, man) and everyone who does not meet this standard is lacking something. So it is with the word *literate*. Many people imagine a world in which literacy is an objective, universal standard but where some people are *lacking*: they are called *illiterate* and perhaps regarded as in need of literacy. But there are other worlds than *literate* worlds and other people than those with *literacy*. *Oral* people are not *illiterate* any more than white people are *nonblack*. *Orality* is not the same as *illiteracy*, any more than poetry is *non-music*.

When we speak of nonbelievers, nonsmokers, noncombatants, or non-whites, we make belief, smoking, combat, or white the normal, the standard, the acceptable—and, implicitly at least, the good, the right, and the true.

Evangelization very frequently takes place in a context of minimal literacy. In today's world, literacy is widely desirable, but people without literacy are not without knowledge or wisdom, culture or religion. To think of people without literacy *only* as deprived is to overlook a cultural treasure trove. Missionaries need to appreciate *orality*, *oral* worlds, and the *oral mentality* of billions.[10] *Most of the people Jesus encountered did not use literacy, and Jesus never suggested that without it they would be incapable of receiving the Good News.* Orality was central to the preaching of Jesus. Yet much evangelism has assumed literacy as a prerequisite. Have we been missing something?

Missionaries often refer to the "dialect" of the people they serve. Why is this? It says a great deal about how people's speech forms are viewed (debased, inferior, nonstandard, ephemeral, insignificant), particularly when they do not have a written language. But even if they *were* dialects strictly so-called, they would not merit such condescension. They are languages—unwritten, local, without literate forms but systematic, sophisticated, and complex—and we should respect their integrity and uniqueness and learn that they can *only* be adequately approached on their own terms. *There are no inferior languages.*

That a language has a written form says nothing about its genius except that there was an overwhelming need for it to be written down. Only a fraction of 1 percent of the world's languages have ever had an indigenous written form[11] because it was simply not needed. Whole societies managed perfectly well with spoken language and human memory. A written form of language could be seen as an acknowledgment of the *failure* of a society to marshal and transmit its knowledge efficiently as much as of its success in coping with such knowledge.

Many literate people are dimly aware perhaps of the poverty of their memories; we can always "look it up" if we need some nonexperiential knowledge, or we can find a specialist. Our contemporary world is rooted in, and dependent upon, the Internet and specialists. Because we have access to literate forms of knowledge, our memories do not need to retain large amounts. Indeed, the mark of a good academic—an "absent-minded professor"—may be precisely the ability to know where to go for information rather than to hold it all in the head. Academics sometimes have very little firsthand experience and are rather limited in practical skills, whether hammering nails, fixing machines, raising families, telling stories, or doing good.

RELIGION AND RELEVANCE

Jesus preached—at times magnetically but always in a memorable, and therefore, a relevant way—to people who were predominantly oral. Both the structure of his preaching and the way in which his hearers assimilated knowledge facilitated active and interactive learning, retention, and transmission. Frequently Jesus draws people into the discourse and uses their responses to develop his teaching. He does not expect them to take notes, even when it is important to remember exactly what he says.[12] Yet he says some vitally important things that must neither be taken lightly nor misconstrued. But sometimes the evangelists seem to disagree about what Jesus said; and sometimes his words caused disagreement among his hearers. How do we interpret these things? One way would be to look at the broader context. In the very same century as Jesus (around 50 B.C.), Julius Caesar wrote his account of the Gallic Wars *(De Bello Gallico)*. Here he is talking about religion in Gaul:

> Many present themselves of their own accord to become students of Druidism, and others are sent by their parents or relatives. It is said that these pupils have to memorize a great number of verses—so many that some spend twenty years at their studies. The Druids believe that their religion forbids them to commit their teachings to writing, although for most other purposes, such as public and private accounts, the Gauls use the Greek alphabet. But I imagine that this rule was originally established for other reasons—because they did not want their doctrine to become public property, and in order to prevent their pupils from relying on the written word and neglecting to train their memories; for it is usually found that when people have the help of texts, they are less diligent in learning by heart, and let their memories rust.[13]

This famous passage has been used to argue that the pre-Christian Celts were illiterate. It demonstrates nothing of the kind but something often overlooked: the power of orality and memory. Jesus had this power, he appealed to it in his hearers, and he employed it in his preaching. Jesus was a master of an oral style of discourse, and his hearers were equally proficient listeners. He was particularly critical of those who had ears but failed to use them properly (Mk 8:18; cf. 4:9, 23).

The oral style[14] appeals directly to the imagination and the memory, to the listeners' capacity for storage and retrieval of information, and to certain conventions and rules. It does not depend on scribes or secretaries, tape recorders or books; the skills associated with these are irrelevant. The oral style appeals to human memories with a huge storage capacity (compared with literate, computer-and-book-using moderns), and actually helps enlarge the memory by testing and feeding it. The oral style of communicating and learning employs many forms of language. Some are also used by literate people; some have either atrophied or seem to have been lost forever.

What does it mean to say that literate people have lost the powers of memory enjoyed by other people (Greeks, Romans, or Celts who also employed literacy, and members of a thousand cultures without it)? Some of us realize our memory is not what it was, others claim to have a prodigious memory, and a few remain unmoved. But the fact that we are so deeply touched by literacy, individually and as members of a world that depends on it, explains why we cannot understand the capacity of a really powerful memory. Because we are literate, we might think that however powerful other people's memories might be, we can match them by other compensatory skills. This idea really needs to be erased from our minds and attitudes. I would love to persuade more missionaries of the largely untapped riches of orality and memory that can still be immensely helpful resources for relevant evangelizing. I would love to encourage missionaries to approach their task as Jesus did, from an oral rather than a literate starting point.

Jesus used parables, stories, proverbs, and other literary forms. We know this as a fact, but we may not understand its implications. First we have to understand the potential capacity of the human memory.[15] Then we might reflect on the people to whom we bring Good News: how do they pass their time, teach their children, instill values, and let people know about rewards and punishments? If we think about people who do not rely heavily on literacy, such reflection could produce great insight. If we could see Caribbean rap poetry, African praise-songs, medieval mystery plays, Indonesian proverbs, rural town criers, Appalachian storytellers, African-American "just-so" stories, and many other cultural forms as sources and resources for the transmission of the Good News, we would have taken a huge leap in the right direction.

GOSPEL AND GOSSIP

People everywhere must succeed in certain tasks or perish. Beyond the obvious provision of nourishment and shelter and the reproduction of the group, these tasks include the inculcation of a sense of group identity and the maintenance of certain standards. Without this minimum, groups break up and people fail to survive.

A sense of group identity can be forged in many ways, but particularly by the sharing of a common past and the production of a common effort. When people gather to share their commonness and transmit it to the younger generation, they are not simply passing the time or indulging in irrelevant and tedious duties. They are undertaking something critically important, and doing so within a relevant group. Everyone is there because they belong,[16] and *those who do not belong are not there in any significant or systematic way.* In essence, what the people are doing (though in a wonderful variety of forms) is telling stories. Storytelling is as old as people with language. Those who share stories share history and relevance and aspirations. So where is the missionary, the preacher-and-teller-of-the-story-of-the-Risen-One, when people's stories are being told?

Stories may include great heroic epics[17] or just-so stories, reminiscences or proverbs, folktales, and many other forms. They may be performed formally by famous people on special occasions or shared informally by the whole group at almost any time. The stories and narratives are often already known intimately by almost everyone, but sometimes they surprise by their novelty.[18] They may meet with quiet acceptance or raucous comment, and they may frighten or shame as often as they please and entertain. But all the time, cumulatively, and with great repetition and redundancy, by means of participation and pedagogy, they serve to bind the group together and to educate the members to the point where they simply cannot forget who they are and the values they uphold and respect. So where is the missionary, creative sharer, builder-of-the-community-of-faith-in-the-Lord, when these values are exposed and shared?

Stories are to oral cultures what laws and injunctions are to literate ones. But *story* must be expanded a little: there were both diversity and functional similarity between many oral forms. In Europe during the Middle Ages, troubadours, *jongleurs,*[19] and *goliards* (wandering singers, poets, gifted storytellers, and bawdy scandalmongers) used music and rhythm to enhance, recall, and transmit what they carried in their memory. They were tellers of tales and retailers of proverbs, purveyors of gossip and performers of pantomines. And they shared a social function: they highlighted the social group by marking its boundaries and mocking its deviants. They underscored the normal by appealing to the abnormal and licentious. They endorsed the righteous by criticizing the wayward. *By informing the community, they helped form the common memory.*

Gossip[20] derives from *God* and *sib* ("relation"). Originally it referred to a godparent. Gossip referred to rich and informative conversation about the extended family that was shared at christenings, weddings, and funerals. It probably contained prejudice and slander and innuendo, but these actually helped clarify what the group *disapproved* of. Only later did it become demeaned to tittle-tattle or talebearing and blamed on women.[21]

Gossip, folktales, and fairy tales—collected by the Grimms, created by Hans Andersen, or crafted by Disney or Doctor Suess—have a common significance in identifying virtue and disapproving of vice. Even today's popular music can be interpreted as a form of social control: it identifies cultural values, but it also has power to change them. However unlikely, these media could serve as soil in which the gospel might grow or as seeds that might bear good fruit at harvesttime.[22] By looking at people's actual modes of communication cross-culturally, we learn what they see as relevant and irrelevant. Only to carp and criticize and assault their worlds of meaning is counterproductive.

We could look for gospel values—those implicit, subtle, or informally held attitudes that echo the more explicit values declaimed by Jesus—within diverse forms of storytelling in predominantly oral societies. We would discover a surprising diversity across both time and culture. So where is the missionary, the proclaimer-of-the-Good-News-of-Jesus, when people gossip, when jokes evoke wry or raucous laughter, when communities gather to sing or hear the comedians and the jesters, the tellers of tales and the singers of songs?

There are many forms of orality in cultures with little or no literacy.

These help maintain the group's identity and teach certain social and moral standards directly and indirectly, positively and negatively. Literacy-dependent Christians may be blind and deaf to the richness of language that does not depend on literacy. Living in an oral culture, Jesus was instinctively sensitive to the oral uses of language. With so many oral people in the world today, we ourselves would do well to learn about the rich potential of orality.[23]

> In my time in West Africa I knew some proverbs, but I never understood how much they touched the people's hearts and minds. And yet I know now that my words reached out in a special way when clothed in terms or images that were familiar to them and evoked their own wisdom and memories. But more could have been learned, and I could have brought the oral gospel to an oral people,[24] or the community of storytellers to the riches of the stories of Jesus, in a much more effective way. A simple example: A proverb from the Mende of Sierra Leone says, "An empty sack cannot stand" *(beki wopu ee gu a lola)*. This means something very simple when translated literally; but what it really means is demonstrated by the context. It is said when a person is pressed to work harder or is justifying his or her exhaustion; a person with no *food* inside, cannot function. It really has nothing at all to do with bags; it is about bodies.

Evangelization must converge with people's actual lives. Unless the bringers of Good News really strive to come closer to people's experience, they will be in a wilderness of their own making. Jesus constantly met people on their own ground and spoke to them in familiar idioms and with memorable figures of speech. He allowed himself to be impressed, encouraged, touched, and comforted by their outreach and their gestures of hospitality or repentance. We, too, can discover many ways that people of oral cultures embody and manifest attitudes or virtues already highly compatible with his preaching. If we overlook or belittle such attitudes and virtues, we will have little to build on. If we really respect the people, we will respect their attitudes and virtues. If we are seen to respect the people and to be excited at the prospect of sharing the Good News we bring, we might continue to be relevant, and therefore interesting and worthy of attention.

Orality has many forms.[25] We have been using some: alliteration, repetition, triads (groups of three: phrases, questions, nouns, adjectives), and rounding (finishing successive sections with the same words). How do these affect evangelization? With an oral mentality and an oral approach we might project a living word more than a dead letter. There is a danger of literal-mindedness or formalism if we concentrate on *text* rather than *word*. The two are very different: Jesus *spoke,* and his words brought life. He had power over words and spoke performatively: "You are healed, your sins are forgiven," "This is my body," and so on. There is a whole theology about the word and the law, the spirit and the letter; but the theology of Jesus was in his living words. If we reduce the vibrant, direct message of the Scriptures to a recitation or a reading, we demean and destroy its efficacy.

If people ask for bread, will we give them a stone? If they hunger for a word of life, will we read them a book? If they need a word that heals, do we thrust a text in their hand? Bible and text are artifacts that make sense to a literate person but not to an oral person. But gospel (Good News), word *(logos),* and words (utterances, communication) can and should speak directly to persons and to hearts. Unless we speak to persons and listen to hearts that speak, there will be precious little communication, virtually nothing of relevance, and only a travesty of evangelization.

SPOKEN WORD AND GOSPEL

If every literate language handles reality in a slightly different way, what of oral languages? Most of us may never have reflected on the orality embedded in our own literate worlds, taking literacy for granted as synonymous with education. But millions of people are born and raised in an oral world, and they cannot possibly appreciate what a literate mentality might entail. So highly oral and highly literate people effectively live in different worlds with little idea of each other's experience of reality.

The move from orality to literacy represents a profound and fundamental shift in thought, in thinking, and in world construction.[26] Most of us have not consciously made this shift and are unable to appreciate its significance. But increasingly today, people born in strongly oral environments are becoming literate, while others, partially literate through schooling, find themselves in a rapidly changing environment that now reflects neither an oral nor a literate world at all adequately. They are confused and disoriented by the change. They may have acquired some practical skills, like signing their name or basic reading, but are bewildered by the trappings of a literate world and increasingly adrift from their familiar oral moorings. In a globalized and literate world where orality is interpreted only as illiteracy, very little is done to reap the fruits of orality or to use them for people in transition, worlds in transition, or the marginal ministries of Christian mission.[27]

We must not avoid the troubling question: how can someone socialized in a highly literate culture understand someone with no literacy but a wealth of oral skills? A person who speaks only English can—in principle—understand a Cantonese speaker, but not immediately and not without enormous toil and commitment. Language learning is required. This implies motivation, which leads us back to relevance. English speakers and Cantonese speakers know that mutual understanding is possible, but only when they actually try to communicate do they discover just how difficult that is. Likewise, literate and oral persons may imagine they can understand each other easily enough, but experience will show what a struggle that entails. Where evangelization is involved, hit-and-miss understanding is quite inadequate.

Whorf maintained that speakers of different languages are prejudiced—by virtue of their language itself—in relation to each other: "Every language and every well-knit technical sub-language incorporates certain points of view and certain *patterned resistance* to widely divergent points of view." Sapir is more radical: "It is almost as though at some period in the past, the unconscious mind of the race had made a hasty inventory of experience, committed itself to a premature *classification that allowed of no revision,* and saddled the inheritors of its language with a science that they no longer believed in nor had the strength to overthrow. [Therefore] the worlds in which different societies live are distinct worlds, not the same world with different labels attached" (my italics).

We must not overlook such arguments. Either we can translate the gospel into any and all cultures or we cannot. We believe we can, but the task is complex. We may *think* we are translating when we are simply dictating and failing to check on the message as received. And though translation *can* happen, some ideas will always be problematic, as we have seen. How will we translate "Lamb of God" into a culture without sheep? Sometimes we simply import foreign words or ideas and make them do duty in our own language: *nuance, naïve,* or *finesse,* for example. But now they are part of our language, they no longer mean precisely what they mean in French or to a French speaker; the *nuances* are slightly different. Translations of the liturgy into African languages are sometimes less than helpful if they import words like *prĭsti* ["priest"], *bredi* ["bread"], *or waini* ["wine"], or if the English word *priest* is rendered by the vernacular word for a diviner or "one who offers sacrifices." This kind of approach can be quite dangerous.[28] We must not be *naïve,* but we can use our language with both *finesse* and meaning if we are very careful.

Linguistic chasms can be bridged. We may never totally understand a speaker of another language, but we never succeed in understanding *anyone* completely: such is the inscrutability and uniqueness of every individual. But we must learn that when worlds are separated by literacy and orality, the first move depends on us. We literate people must acquire oral skills and a practical knowledge of orality. Oral people who become literate do not immediately forget an impressive range of skills that are also carriers of meaning and points of reference. Their world continues to rely on its oral underpinnings. But unless the literate Christian becomes schooled in oral skills, there will be no solid common ground on which to build new communities of belief, united in the living word of Jesus.

"HE SPOKE IN PARABLES"

Parables, especially the Kingdom parables, provide access to what a Christian mentality should be. They are particularly relevant in oral cultures.[29] They virtually embody the Good News: they tell it as it is. They are wonderfully illuminating for people who do not yet know Jesus. After all, this is part of the original purpose of the New Testament parables.

To teach not through catechism or law or abstract principle but through story and life experience: this is the way of Jesus. It is providential that we often encounter people so similar in oral mentality to the crowds in Jesus' day. We would be profligate to neglect his pedagogy in favor of texts and rules that bind and kill. The strength of parables is that they can be understood—in many ways and at many levels, partially and cumulatively, but understood nevertheless—by all who have ears.[30] But the Good News must pass through the ears of actual people and be heard by them according to their own genius and capacity.[31] We can tell the stories of Jesus and listen to the people's stories. We can introduce Jesus and communities to each other, simply and without pomposity, before stepping back in wonder at the outcome.

Language need not imprison thinking; it should not confuse but enlighten. It has power to do what we make it or let it do. It can be used to give and to take, to liberate and to enslave, to teach and to indoctrinate. It has enormous potential for stimulating and freeing thought, for illuminating reality, for transmitting deep insights and evoking profound emotions. Language gives wings to thought and challenges us to change and to action. How wonderful that we speak so explicitly of the *Word*, the communication within the Godhead, the utterance of the Creator who "said . . . and so it was." How stupendous that we hear and pass on the very message of God, spoken for all people and all times, *made flesh and dwel[ling] among us.* We were not given tablets of stone, formalized and immutable texts, or convoluted laws ridden with legalese. We were given a living, warm, active word, conceived of God and born uniquely in the hearts of all with ears to hear.

Here are strong words: they may be familiar; or you may be surprised at their source:[32]

> [The *Word*] is not to be equated with Scripture nor with the sacraments, yet it operates through them and not apart from them. The *Word* is not the Bible as a written book because "the gospel is really not that which is contained in books and composed in letters, but rather an oral preaching and a living word, a voice which resounds throughout the whole world and is publicly proclaimed." This Word must be heard. The Word must be pondered. "Not

through thought, wisdom, and will does the faith of Christ arise in us, but through an incomprehensible and hidden operation of the Spirit, which is given by faith in Christ only at the hearing of the Word and without any other work of ours." More, too, than mere reading is required. "No one is taught through much reading and thinking. There is a much higher school where one learns God's Word. One must go into the wilderness.[33] Then Christ comes and one becomes able to judge the world."

and as Bainton quotes further,

"Although [God] is everywhere and I may find him in stone, fire, water, or rope, . . . yet he does not wish me to seek him apart from the Word. . . . He does not desire that you should seek everywhere but only where the Word is."

The Reformers placed their emphasis squarely on "the word as the essential medium of the Divine operation in man. By *Word of God* was meant primarily not the language of the Bible, but the orally proclaimed biblical truth."[34] This is something for every minister of the word to ponder.

And a final thought. Some medieval paintings of the Annunciation depict Mary at prayer, an angel close by, and a dove—figure of the Holy Spirit—hovering above and radiating light. The center ray sometimes leads directly into Mary's (right) ear. The symbolism is clear: Mary conceived the Word of God *by hearing*. As Jesus said, more blessed even than his mother's womb and breasts are the ears who *hear* the Word of God—*and keep it* (Lk 11:27-28). We have the ability to speak living words; the people we encounter have ears to hear them.

Chapter 6

GIFT-EXCHANGE AND THE GOSPEL

Discovering Mutuality

ANTHROPOLOGIZING

On a good day, a cultural anthropologist might acknowledge that anthropology rarely discovers anything that is universal and truly enlightening: things are either universal (bipedalism, an opposable thumb) but fairly obvious, or truly enlightening but not universal. Self-deprecation does not, however, mitigate anthropologists' fascination with humanity, and actually there are some interesting universals.[1] One is exchange; it takes various forms (private, public, corporate, symbolic) and involves different actors (humans, spirits, gods, God).

Claude Lévi-Strauss (1908-) argued that human existence really begins when groups of people exchange their women in marriage. Marcel Mauss (1872-1950) saw exchange as the earliest solution to Hobbes's destructive human animosity, the "war of all against all." Exchange is central to social life, though more or less elaborated in different places.

Because of its universality, exchange should offer us some possibilities for translation, for communication with other people. If we can identify mechanisms or structures common to exchange cross-culturally, the process of translation should be even more effective.

GIFT, EXCHANGE, AND GIFT-EXCHANGE

The word *gift* is curious and interesting. Coming via Old Norse, through Old English and Middle English, it has common derivatives in Dutch and German, where *gifte* meant what English designates "gift," but in the neuter form it meant "poison." In Middle English one meaning of *gift* was "something given to corrupt: a bribe." Bribes evoke blackmail, a word derived from Gaelic, meaning "tribute formerly exacted from small owners by freebooting chiefs, in return for immunity from plunder." So a "forced gift" is offered or exacted for the privilege of freedom, peace, or being left alone. Browsing through the *Shorter Oxford Dictionary* rewards us with further associations: *gift* as "price," "marriage payment" (as Lévi-Strauss argued), "poison," "blackmail," and "agreement." Not all of these senses are current in English today, but the etymology demonstrates several useful things: it takes two (or more) to make a gift; and in particular cases the parties may have very different understandings of gift. If the notions are so variable within one culture, *across cultures* they might easily lead to major confusion. Gifts and poison may not be very far apart.

Considering the gift cross-culturally makes us broaden our customary categories to include not only material objects but offices, reproductive rights, filiation rights, entertainments, and various services. This is what Mauss discovered. Referring to lifelong or ongoing reciprocal moral relationships (gift-exchanges), he called them *total prestations*.

We must distinguish three institutions or activities: gift, exchange, and gift-exchange. They are different and carry different implications. The first two can be rational, contractual, and even commercial; gift-exchange is always a *moral* relationship.

Gifts can be given spontaneously, freely, and unilaterally—at least in theory. We think gifts are free, yet reflection convinces us that Mauss was correct: the gift is *never* free. This is because a gift cannot be absolutely separated from the giver, the intended recipient, and the underlying intention. A "free" gift that is not accepted is not a gift. If it is accepted but not appreciated, it has compromised the recipient or insulted the donor. If it is accepted and respected, some form of reciprocity is implied: not necessarily an immediate and equal repayment but a sign or token of acceptance, even if (only) a word of thanks. If we give gifts on birthdays or Christmas but have them returned or not reciprocated, we need to know why or we stop giving: clearly these are not really free gifts.

Exchange is a mutual transfer between two agents. Things of equal value are transferred: fish for bananas, dollar for dollar, so that when the exchange is complete both parties remain in the same status-relationship as they began. The Latin *do ut des* ("I give so that you give") expresses exchange quite well. Like gift giving, exchange does not necessarily imply a moral relationship, but the closer we come to true gift-exchange and the further we move from giving gifts or commercial exchange, the more we engage with the moral rather than the purely legal sphere. That is, the less we can appeal to law, the more we are governed by ethics.

Gift-exchange,[2] as Mauss pointed out, is part gift, part exchange, but different from both. It is an *institutionalized* social activity: not spontaneous but standardized. It is as rule-governed as chess and football.

To understand gift-exchange, we must understand its "grammar," be able to account for and explain its occurrences, and know what is appropriate or expected in different circumstances. Who gives exchanges (in a particular society)? When are they exchanged? Why? Who does not exchange gifts? What gifts are unacceptable, refused, or not exchanged? Perhaps most important: where is power in specific situations of gift-exchange? If we can answer these questions, our marginal ministry with others might be significantly enhanced.

We observed that behavior ought to be a manifestation of underlying belief, just as spoken language is a manifestation of an underlying set of grammatical rules. What might an act of gift-exchange reveal about underlying expectations and constraints? If we find some answers, we are close to accepting Mauss's dictum that "the gift[-exchange] is never free."

If gift-exchange is rule-governed, it can be interpreted, just like any other rule-governed behavior. But we can *misinterpret* what someone says or what a chess player or a football player intends. We can certainly misinterpret gift-exchange or apply the wrong set of rules. Severe miscommunication is always possible. What is the *meaning* of this or that bunch of red roses? How can we understand the *indebtedness* that results from a gift received? What is the meaning of marriage payments made by the bridegroom's family and accepted by the bride's? Once we get into areas of institutionalized and rule-governed behavior, we face the problem of understanding the rules and of seeing how they are used, perhaps abused.

SYSTEMATIZATION

Mauss gathered a dossier of case histories from many cultures. He contextualized and compared the characteristic patterns, slowly making sense of hitherto meaningless or bizarre behavior. The result became his classic: *The Gift*. Noticing that *obligation* appeared as a constant in gift-exchange behavior, he asked, "What is the principle whereby the gift received has to be repaid?" and, "What *force* or power is there in the thing given which compels the recipient to make a return?" Mauss was able to tease out a general pattern disclosing a surprisingly widespread *system* of behavior and values ("belief in action"). Far from a spontaneous or ad hoc mechanical transfer of goods and services, gift-exchange appears as *patterned behavior embodying clear moral values*; it creates and maintains personal relationships not only between private individuals but between groups and between *moral persons* or *statuses*.

Western capitalism and laissez-faire individualism belong to a system into which many of us were born. But there *was* life, gift-exchange, and economic behavior long before the eighteenth century and independent of the West. Before we look too closely at the logic and morality of gift-exchange cross-culturally, we should examine various notions associated with it.

The West glorifies individualism, private enterprise, and impersonal transactional systems. Laissez-faire—the doctrine of unrestricted freedom in commerce, especially for private interests—gives little consideration to persons or relationships; it is concerned with commerce. Prices are fixed, and the goal of business is sale or purchase. Everything has its price, and "money talks." But though the wheels of industry may run smoothly, human relationships may suffer. In order to transact business in our society, we need two or more major credit cards or other multiple forms of identification: an identification card is no longer sufficient to identify us. Our transactions are computerized and facilitated by plastic rectangles, not personalized and facilitated by human interaction. *Commerce* is a hungry deity that devours persons and grows fat on transactions. The world of Western commerce is a world of anonymity and isolation, individualism and technology. Fax machines and telephones, speculation and futures, interest rates and Dow Jones characterize our economic sphere of action.

Then there are gifts. The idea of gifts, with its emotional significance, is separated from our economic behavior and occupies an area of life marked by freedom and intimacy, human relationships and noncompetitiveness. We like to think of being surprised by gifts and surprising others or of allowing gifts to speak a thousand words. Gifts, we think, should be spontaneous. We may say of an unimpressive gift that it's not the gift that counts but the thought behind it. And so on.

But is gift giving so pure and noneconomic? We expect gifts for birthdays or other occasions. We feel cheated or insulted when our gift is not reciprocated. The gift we do receive sometimes seems insignificant or insulting. We feel obligated to give gifts in order to keep up appearances or because it is expected or good for business. What kind of spontaneity is there in the gift of roses from a compromised spouse or in the gift that cannot be refused or repaid but binds the recipient to the donor as a debtor? How easily and subtly can a gift become blackmail or hush money, payoff or payola? What language do we really speak with our gifts in a Western capitalist ethos? What is the *moral* value of a gift certificate that can be redeemed at the whim of the recipient for something the donor never thought of? And when gifts can be redeemed for cash, that all-purpose commodity which may so easily contain nothing of the giver, what have we come to? Is our own gift-exchange language the same as others'? Do our gifts say unequivocally what we want them to say, and do we receive donors' messages as unambiguously as we receive their gifts? We may have here some food for thought.

THE LOGIC OF GIFT-EXCHANGE

In *Argonauts of the Western Pacific* (1922), Bronislaw Malinowski, father of modern participant observation, identified a scale of gift-giving behavior among the Trobriand Islanders, ranging from real barter to pure gift. The first was understood to epitomize commerce and self-interest, while pure gift was held to manifest altruism and lack of self-interest in the form of spontaneity and simplicity. Others have interpreted so-called primitive gift-exchange (being too difficult to interpret otherwise) as an archaic economic system that forces people to circulate necessary goods so that ultimately everyone gets what they need. In this view, later and more sophisticated peoples would develop organized trading and a more rational approach to economics. Mauss accepted none of this. He emphasized repeatedly that gift-exchange in other cultures, as distinct from barter and gift giving, is *both* self-interested *and* disinterested. But it is also institutionalized, patterned into expected forms of behavior that persist over time and involve people in long-term relationships. It is not purely private, much less totally spontaneous; and it is certainly not simple. There may be exchange between specific individuals, but Mauss is talking primarily about *moral persons* and not private individuals. The notion of a private individual is very different from that of the socially responsible person in other societies. For Mauss, a moral person is an incumbent of a status position: a father, mother, wife, husband, chief, child, daughter, blacksmith, priest, and so on. We might say it is not just *any* father or mother but concretely *someone's* father or mother. There are no people in the abstract.

All societies, declared Mauss, are able to address and meet their economic needs. They do not need institutionalized gift behavior for that: there are marketplaces in which goods of equal value or worth are *bartered* and goods of unequal value or worth are *traded*. When one person gives another a bunch of bananas and receives a couple of fish, that is characteristically economic behavior. This is the essence of economic exchange and on no account to be confused with gift-exchange. When one person, after intense interaction with another, hands over several raffia cloths and receives a pig, this is also economic behavior. Bananas for fish is exchange of items of equal value, in this case classified as perishables. Raffia cloths and pigs are of unequal value, imperishable and dissimilar. But they are of roughly equal worth inasmuch as a person with pigs may gain prestige just as one with raffia cloths does. And depending upon market forces like availability, time spent in labor, or ease of replacement, a price will be negotiated in an economic way (arranging for the allocation and distribution of scarce resources) and unlike the straight barter or direct exchange of perishables.

Such negotiations may be direct, indirect, or delayed. They may seem to be similar or identical to the outsider's perceptions of gift-exchange. But they are very different from gift-exchange because they are differently motivated, differently patterned, and differently understood by those involved. They have a different meaning. In non-Western societies economic behavior is still characterized by human interaction—and this remains true in rural areas today. It is not impersonal, and it does contribute to the building up of relationships; but that does not make it gift-exchange. It makes it different from pure economics, though, because there is no such thing as pure economics divorced from human interaction.

Instead of seeing relaxed economic exchange in other societies as gift-exchange, we might note that in our own Western cultures economic transactions have often become dehumanized. They ought to be marked by cordiality, for they are undertaken by human agents. But cordiality has often been sacrificed on the altar of Profit, Efficiency, or Rationalization. What in other societies coexists in harmony—*both* economic exchange *and* gift-exchange—in the West is often separated and polarized, with the result that economics tends to pride itself on self-interest, contract, and profit, leaving gift-exchange to carry the responsibility for expressing relatedness, spontaneity, and altruism.

In the virtual absence of such a dichotomy, argued Mauss, traditional social systems show a *continuum* of behavior that *includes and merges* what people in the West try to keep separate: purely economic behavior and institutionalized gift-exchange.

THE MORALITY OF GIFT-EXCHANGE

We should not judge as simple economic behavior what is actually much more complex. What, then, might be our missionary approach to some behavior we encounter in other cultures? Mauss's insights about the structuring of gift-exchange gives us a way to understand what is rule-governed and systematic, if we address the code itself and try to solve the puzzle on its own terms.

People involved in the exchange of gifts are connected in *relationships* that may last a lifetime. One cannot lightly enter into reciprocal arrangements nor casually break them; honor, prestige, and self-respect are intimately tied up in ongoing gift-exchange. One party does not shower repeated and unsolicited gifts on the other nor relax into a comfortable position as a recipient. The rules—unwritten, even unstated, but certainly present and morally binding—indicate approximately when and in what fashion gifts shall be made. People in gift-exchange relationships are not *either* giver or receivers but *both*.

Mauss also pointed out how easily the mere bestowal of gift (simple gift giving) could become a manifestation of power and control if not regulated: "Charity wounds [the one] who receives, and our whole moral effort is directed towards suppressing the unconscious harmful patronage of a rich almoner."[3] This is a weighty statement and worth serious thought and discussion by anyone who is a giver. Givers who are reluctant to receive may uncritically accept the saying "Neither a borrower nor a lender be." They may even invoke the out-of-context biblical injunction that it is "better to give than to receive." St. Paul said that Jesus said this (Acts 20:35). We do not have Jesus' own word on the matter, but we do have Matthew's word that Jesus told his disciples to ask, seek, and knock, which would make them receivers in more ways than one: on another occasion he may have said it is better to receive.

Gift-exchange is *encoded,* and codes only yield to systematic and persevering investigators. We need to know the context and the parties involved. Not every gift offered or accepted represents approved behavior within a given society; manipulation and exploitation can tempt people. But much gift-exchange is as carefully orchestrated as the *Pastoral Symphony,* as minutely choreographed as *Swan Lake.*

Mauss discovered that the gift in gift-exchange is *an extension of the donor:* it embodies something of the personality or the spiritual essence of that person. One person entrusts another with his or her very essence by means of a gift. Respect for the gift, and at some point reciprocity, are necessary. The giver is, almost physically, in the possession of the receiver. This may sound fanciful, but it makes good sense if we imagine a world that is not crudely divided or dichotomized into persons and things. Such a world may be familiar to us, but it is of course a construct. In many societies things are attached to persons, and there is no absolute discontinuity between them. Person and object are already in relationship, so it follows that the exchange of gifts creates strong and lasting bonds between persons.

If the ideas we are discussing become fractured, an *opposition* is created between economic or contractual behavior and the gift. Then we have driven a wedge between persons and things. The gift as understood in Western cultures is our own recent invention: detached from the giver like the so-called "free gifts" we receive in the mail or gifts like checks or certificates that become whatever the recipient determines, not what the donor bestows. The gift studied by Mauss is very different: it is gift, loan, pledge, and self, all rolled into one.

THE MECHANICS OF GIFT-EXCHANGE

Some things appear to be simple, free gifts given by one person to another. But the true free gift is virtually impossible, not because we are incapable of altruism but because human beings are relational. As a knock seeks the opening of a door and a question hopes for an answer, a free gift demands a response. At its simplest, the response is the actual acceptance: a gift offered but not received is only a good intention. But if it is virtually impossible to identify a free gift, in the case of gift-exchange we do not even have to try. Gift-exchange is obligatory.

Social life consists of obligations and expectations, with accompanying sanctions: rewards and punishment. Human life in society depends on some responsibilities and promises. One social institution, critical for healthy and continuing social life, is gift-exchange. Mauss brilliantly reduced it to a set of three social obligations: the obligation to GIVE; the obligation to RECEIVE; the obligation to RETURN.

Looking at these obligations individually and together, we can make sense of otherwise odd behavior. Perhaps more important, we can understand some of our own interactions with people in other cultures and appreciate *why* they react in certain ways and how we, often inadvertently, trample on their expectations and their sensibilities.

The obligation to give

This applies not just to one party but to *everyone* who wants to be in relationship. Unless we give, we cannot be received. Unless we give, we remain centered on ourselves rather than open to the community. Unless we give, we will not receive and will thus remain isolated. People in individualistic societies may consider themselves independent and in no need of giving or receiving. But they also experience isolation, alienation, loneliness, and suicide. The obligation to give binds everyone who looks beyond individualism to community. The obligation to give, therefore, is as much a community obligation as an individual one.

Giving initiates chains of indebtedness and bonds of reciprocity. Gift-exchange reinforces self-giving and strengthens relationships. In close-knit communities, the refusal to give may be tantamount to an act of hostility. Whoever has but does not give will not only lose respect but might attract blame for unsolved mischief, even accusations of witchcraft.

The obligation to give does not imply that people must give indiscriminately to everyone. It is governed by rational concerns: strategic choices will include some people but not others. What is given to one person is not available for another—though it is possible to give *oneself* quite widely. But socially, those who want to live must choose to give.

The obligation to receive

If giving is intended to open up relationships, it is also necessary that gifts be accepted. Not to accept may be tantamount to a hostile act. Not to accept may at least be a statement of unwillingness to be in relationship. The situation is complex. The giver is initially in a superior position to the recipient because the giver opens up the situation and initiates the relationship and because the receiver becomes thereby indebted to the giver. Power is the underlying language of gift-exchange. But power *can* work both ways.

Indebtedness is no bad thing; it is the heart of gift-exchange. People *want* to be indebted to others, precisely because this indicates relationship. But no one wants to be indebted to *everyone* and to have no one in his or her debt. And to be indebted and unfree is totally demeaning. Whoever is not free to refuse is also likely to hate the donor. Debt can be crippling or potentially liberating. If a debtor is unable to repay, a dilemma is created: refusal to receive can be interpreted very negatively, yet being forced to receive may be the last straw. The whole issue is delicate, but mutuality is the key to appropriate indebtedness and gift-exchange.

The obligation to return

Return must be possible though it need not be immediate. Undue haste may indicate that a gift was not valued highly. To remain in debt for a long period may actually attest to the strength of a relationship. But if one is in long-term debt to another, one normally expects to have others indebted to oneself.

An immediate return would indicate participants of equal status and a weak gift-exchange relationship where mutual indebtedness has not developed. When the return is delayed, there may be a significant power differential. A Big Man may give lavishly, belittle his generosity, and tell the recipient that he is in absolutely no hurry for a return. His denial of any short-term need is a statement of power. Others are in his debt, and he is superior to them. They remain indebted until the gift is repaid. It may never be repaid. But a Big Man remains so by virtue of unclaimed debts.

If the recipient does not want or feel the need to repay immediately, there is freedom in indebtedness. But where the recipient *cannot repay* immediately, there is servitude. It makes no difference that the donor does not demand a return. This is a question of pride and reciprocity, and it certainly *does* matter both to the recipient and to the nature of the relationship. To the Westerner who feels that gifts should be free, these attitudes can seem incomprehensible or petty; to gift-exchange partners things are not so simple. To them, a nonreciprocal gift, an unreciprocated gift, or a simple once-only gift would be unfamiliar and even immoral notions.

To *return* is not to *repay;* these are quite different obligations. To confuse them is to compromise the very essence of gift-exchange. Without clarity here, any attempted communication will produce mutual incomprehension. A *return* keeps a *relationship* alive; a *repayment* concludes a *contract.*

The system may seem very neat, but there is potential for manipulation and rule breaking. Not everyone is a model of integrity, and life would be rather tedious if all the rules were kept all the time. A giver may exploit a recipient's reluctance to refuse, thus instigating an unwanted relationship. This would be blackmail or persuasion or seduction. Then gifts are indeed poison. But this is a travesty of gift-exchange and a means of *masking* the very thing it should disclose.

DEMAND SHARING IN AUSTRALIA

The oldest documented example of gift-exchange comes from Australia.[4] *Demand sharing* may go back more than forty thousand years, ever since aboriginal people gathered in small bands. The average band in an inhospitable land without agriculture is no more than forty souls. A band needs a minimum of about thirty lest it become too small and weak to survive; but the land cannot supply food or game for more than about forty. These subsistence bands are more or less egalitarian. But if someone comes dangerously close to death, the rules are clear: the needy person approaches another member and demands immediate help. Today the request might be formulated like this: "You'll be happy to lend me a couple of dollars, then." Since every person contributes to the band, it is in the general interest to attend to the particular need. It may require several people's contribution, but the money or its equivalent will be found. The request cannot be refused; the needy person is required to make the demand; and when recovered, he or she is only too aware of the duty to return something at the appropriate time. This is truly thought-provoking behavior.

THE *KULA* OF THE WESTERN PACIFIC

A well-known example of gift-exchange and ceremonial reciprocity involves many of the adult men[5] of several islands, some up to three hundred miles apart, between New Guinea to the west and the Solomon Islands to the east, in the Melanesian part of the Pacific. It is called the *kula* and it is still vigorous.

Preparations take months or years. Canoes are built and ritually prepared, and an expedition sets off to a specific island. This is no trading expedition, though trade objects are carried. But it *is* a community enterprise and not simply a group of individualists. Each seafarer *receives* either red-shell necklaces or white-shell armbands, depending upon his relationship to his partner on the other island and upon the affinity between particular islands. Shell for necklaces and armbands is neither scarce nor difficult to fashion. But these objects are *kula* valuables, *vaygu'a*, the most prized possessions of the recipients. They are not to be possessed or owned for long but must be given away relatively soon after they are received.

Several island communities constitute the *kula* ring. Necklaces are given by one partner to one of his other partners according to an established protocol and only in a clockwise direction from one island to the other.

Concurrently, in a counter-clockwise direction, go the armbands. There are many expeditions and an ongoing interchange in which valuables pass from one person to another in opposite directions. The rule is that those who receive the visitors give the gifts, and those who go on expedition receive the gifts.

> In 1996 I visited the Trobriands and was amazed that *kula* is so strong after perhaps half a millennium. Each armband and necklace is like a pedigree stallion, its history transmitted with each exchange. The more famous valuables are the more desirable, and even though one could actually make a *vaygu'a* oneself, it would have no history and thus no value: this is an antique exchange. The people were anxious and proud to show me their valuables and talk of their exchange partners. One purpose of the relatively speedy transmission of what has been received is to broadcast its pedigree (which is largely the litany of previous owners) far and wide. Anyone who is anyone is involved. Noticeably absent from the exchange were the expatriate missionaries, though, and I wondered why.

Everyone in the *kula* ring has one or several partners. *Kula* is a matter of relationships. Each partner gives one kind of object and receives the other (but not in direct exchange, for this is delayed and indirect exchange, in which large spans of time and many different partners are involved) according to formal ritual. But this is not formalism. Competition is fierce. Specially prized armbands and necklaces have long and well-remembered (oral) histories. A recipient of a famous piece is lionized even though he must give it away before long. But he will have several other similar objects, and he exercises choice in dispersing them among his other partners, bestowing the prized ones on special partners or clinging to a favored one for as long as possible.

The way of the *kula* is for the giver to *appear* to disparage his gift, to seem to be unattached to it and uncaring about giving it away. Then others will be impressed by his detachment, and his prestige will rise. The point of this *kula*-exchange is to keep the flow of goods in circulation and not to staunch the flow by holding them for too long. Partnership demands interaction through gift-exchange; someone who shows no largesse will soon be receiving only second- and third-rate *kula* goods, eventually forcing him out of this elaborate and ostentatious interaction.

The rules of *kula*-exchange and its context are very impressive. The general code of etiquette governing behavior is rigid. A presentation gift is obligatory, and as the expedition leaves, a countergift is made, at least equal in value to the opening gift. This is before the real *kula*-exchange gets under way. There is never any haggling or bargaining. This is far from barter and explicitly creates indebtedness.

We can see that gift-exchange can be ongoing, elaborate, and morally binding and is quite different from economic exchange. Reciprocity characterizes gift-exchange. Actual gifts are not as important as the symbolic exchange or total *prestations* that are communications of and between people. Strict rules and expectations are quite compatible with the development of interpersonal relationships. Reciprocal relationships can develop between peers, but asymmetrical relationships erode peer relationships. Gift-exchange relationships build on social relevance; if the relationship becomes irrelevant, it will atrophy. Unless relationships are nurtured, gifts may indeed become poison.

> I met three missionaries in the Trobriands. One, a fundamentalist from Australia, lived with the people and shared their lives; he was relevant and his congregation was growing. A second was a Melanesian who lived with his family and was well integrated into village life. The third, a Roman Catholic, lived alone, saw himself only as a giver, and refused to receive anything. He was isolated and perceived by the people as largely irrelevant.

THE *POTLATCH* OF NORTH AMERICA

Along the West Coast of North America, from Vancouver to Alaska, in societies that include the Haida, Tlingit, Kwakiutl, Nootka, and Bella Coola, the institution of *potlatch* was practiced in various forms. To understand it, we start with behavior.

The Hudson's Bay Company is sometimes said to have *really* made its fortune by selling blankets to coastal peoples who then threw many thousands of them into the Pacific and then returned to the company for more! There is some truth here; people did engage in orgies of destruction, beggaring themselves and their families. *Potlatching* became illegal but it is by no means dead. What does it mean?

Potlatch, from a Nootka word meaning "gift" or "the act of giving," connotes gift-exchange rather than unilateral gift. There are recorded cases of communities stacking up ten, twenty, thirty thousand Hudson's Bay blankets, throwing them in the ocean, and then watching them sink or sail away. Potlatches are (were)[6] institutionalized competitive exchange. They mark life crises or times of status change. They include the house-building potlatch, the vengeance potlatch, the face-saving potlatch, and the funeral potlatch.

Haida couples who want to be taken seriously will spend a decade or more preparing for a house-building potlatch. Then they invite friends and neighbors, and everyone works together throughout the winter months gathering wood and other materials for their new house and totem pole. The work is long and exhausting but broken by partying and feasting at the expense of the hosts. Costly though this may be, it is not yet a potlatch. Only at the conclusion of house building does the wife (in this matrilineal society, where descent is traced through the female line) throw a potlatch. All who have helped gather and are seated according to rank. The wife lavishes gifts of household goods, utensils, fur coats, and blankets on one and all. Closure is signaled when she gives her husband an old and torn blanket or token, indicating that nothing is left. All is finished, and in return for their new house and totem pole the couple have impoverished themselves before their friends; everyone is happy. The couple now have a house and friends who are disposed to help them; the exploited friends have some resources to help them in their own potlatch, and have extended their fellowship and interdependence.

A vengeance potlatch is different. An insulted man goes to whoever insulted him—and begins to destroy his own property.[7] He does not destroy what he does not really need but deliberately ruins, breaks up, or throws away what is most dear to him. The adversary is *morally obliged* to do likewise and to outdo the insulted person, or else he loses respect and status and ends up disgraced. Vengeance potlatches may have been involved when Hudson's Bay Company blankets were so profligately destroyed. But this is no wanton vandalism; it is a matter of honor and social standing.

Potlatches also take the form of lavish feasts given by a chief competing for support and social ascendancy. By deliberately beggaring himself, he gains status. But *everyone else is a short-term beneficiary* as well as in his debt in the long term. When a challenger to the highest status has finished his ostentatious display of wealth-in-use, the incumbent chief must try to outdo the splendor of his rival in order to maintain his position. Failure means loss of position; success ensures the flow of goods and services throughout the community, rather than their stanching and accumulation in the hands of the chief.

Where *kula* and potlatch exist, there are no misers[8] or hoarders: redistribution creates wealth in use. The more friends or clients one has, the greater one's prestige. These attitudes to wealth, relationships, gift-exchange, and prestige contrast starkly with behavior in societies where people seek to accumulate rather than redistribute, where interrelationship and indebtedness are considered *a bad thing,* and where the rich get richer and the poor get poorer. In capitalist societies, as riches accumulate and people become less related to others, they gain status and fame though they may have done nothing to benefit society as a whole.

Potlatching illustrates the obligation of giving, receiving, and returning. Unless one gives, one remains a nonentity.[9] The lesson is that people can and should be interdependent and not independent and that wealth is nothing if it is not being used.

THE *MUMI* OF THE SOLOMON ISLANDS

Bougainville Island in the Bismarck Archipelago was the point of departure for the southeastward colonization of the Pacific three thousand years ago.[10] Today it is part of Papua New Guinea. Here the Siuai people call their Big Man a *mumi*. Every young man's ambition is to become a *mumi*, and those who seriously pursue this goal work diligently and with great self-discipline. If a man can mobilize his wife, relatives, and friends, together they prepare a feast. As the number of his supporters increases, he builds a clubhouse or longhouse in which they can relax and eat. If he spends all his waking hours trying to please and his hospitality begins to impress, people start calling him a *mumi*. Those providing labor and resources expect acknowledgment or recompense, or they may be satisfied to bask in his reflected glory and be known as his intimates.

A *mumi* has no easy job maintaining his status.[11] Sooner or later someone will challenge for the preeminent position.[12] If the aspiring *mumi* remains ambitious, he must throw an enormous party, at which a record of all the food (pigs, coconuts, sago) and drink is kept. *Everyone is invited and everyone benefits*. The incumbent *mumi* must reciprocate with an even more lavish feast within the year. Failure to do so reduces him to the ranks, and the cycle begins again.

This is another example not only of rule-governed behavior but of redistribution. It is precisely in this communism or leveling out that human ambition flourishes. By contrast, where a capitalist mentality rules, ambition is often fed *at the expense* of the people in general. Here everyone benefits. Not that everything is perfect. It is not. But Bougainville may remind us that there are other viable ways of relating and living in society.

A *mumi*'s life is competitive and risky, and sometimes he fails. But his struggles and pretensions provide entertainment, diversion, and conversation for many. Arguably, many benefit marginally rather than few substantially; but few risk ruin if he fails, though many might be slightly inconvenienced. The more competing *mumi*s there are, the more goods and food are circulating. But even the most prestigious *mumi* is not immune to all strife. He cannot use force and often lives modestly in order to meet his obligations: "The giver of the feast takes the bones and the stale cake; the meat and the fat go to the others."

Before colonial policy outlawed it, controlled warfare was part of the life of many Big Men, and a way of obtaining resources. They would fight as allies or antagonists, and an incipient political system of opposition and alliance developed. But even here there was a significant element of interdependence and responsibility. The *mumi* was personally responsible for each of those he took to war: insurance had to be paid to the kin of any person killed, and the *mumi* was responsible for providing a fitting funeral. Such obligation would give pause to the more headstrong *mumi*.

MISSIONARIES AND GIFT-EXCHANGE

Reciprocity takes many forms and redistribution may be vital to society, but unless we take a long, hard look at other people's behavior, we will miss its real meaning. We may even overlook relevant points of entry for ourselves and the gospel. Using material on the *kula,* the potlatch, and the *mumi,* let us consider some important questions.

Do we grasp the force of a system of gift-exchange that is *both* rule-governed *and* spontaneous, that requires *both* personal initiative *and* mutuality? Do we understand people's respect for wealth *in use?* How might our own attitudes toward stewardship, savings, and personal unearned income be challenged and even reassessed? Are there parallels between our experience and some elements of potlatch? Can we identify any gospel values in potlatch or *kula* or the behavior of the *mumi?* Can we search for such values in other areas of people's lives?

If the world is a set of puzzles, those who venture to the margins can hardly avoid trying to solve some of them. But if gift-exchange is universal, we have a double challenge: to understand it in other cultures and to identify it in our own. If mutual indebtedness and reciprocity are expressions of our common humanness, gift-exchange is not only a universal phenomenon but a kind of universal language: it can promote communication, collaboration, and mutual comprehension. It might even highlight similarities underlying cultural features that seem so varied: ideas of the person, issues of ownership, mechanics of marriage, even principles of friendship or explanations of warfare. Beyond all these: what if gift-exchange can illuminate aspects of Baptism[13] or Confirmation, Eucharist,[14] and Matrimony? Then we would have a rich and relevant metaphor that could translate essentials of Christianity into every culture. We should reexamine the principles or rules of gift-exchange in a theological light.

The obligation to give

Missionaries do not doubt this: we are professional givers; we spend our lives refining our altruism and lavishing care on others. But do we realize that other people may feel the same obligation and the same need? We give on our terms, and if we do allow others to give, it may also be on our terms. Do we permit and endorse their giving *on their terms?*

Authentic gift-exchange is built on reciprocity. Where is the reciprocity in our giving? What do we know about other people's desires or obligations to give? If we inhibit people's customary patterns of giving, we demean them and appear aloof and insensitive to mutual indebtedness. If mutuality is a hallmark of gift-exchange and thus of humanness, do our hosts recognize this hallmark in us? In our concern to do good for others, are we insensitive to their desire to do good for us? Are we the "rich almoners" whom Mauss so criticized, who humiliate and antagonize by their charity?

The obligation to give is always matched by the right to give. No one is exempt.

The obligation to receive

Giving is not the prerogative or duty of one party. Both giving and receiving obligate those in gift-exchange relationships. Are we as attentive to our social obligation to receive as we are to our moral obligation to give? To receive is to hand the initiative to the donor, to empower or liberate the giver for a relationship. Not to receive is to refuse to place ourselves even temporarily in an inferior position. Yet someone must adopt that position, since without indebtedness there is no relationship of reciprocity and mutuality.

Even if we acknowledge our moral responsibility to be receivers, we may still receive *on our own terms*. Do we attempt to return almost as soon as we receive, so that we are not indebted? Do we emphasize other people's responsibility to give, so that we can receive upkeep or recompense for services rendered? Do we concentrate on money as a sign of reciprocity, rather than on other things? If money is our only currency or used as an all-purpose commodity, everything becomes reducible to money. Money does not fit easily within the context of gift-exchange; it belongs in the economic rather than the moral sphere. It may be more appropriate to use the currency of "fruits of the earth and work of human hands" than paper or coin. People are looking for *relationships* with us. So how do we show, and convince others of, our trust and acceptance—the bases of mutuality and essential components of authentic mission? We have to *learn* to be gracious receivers, to accept things we may not really want, need, or even appreciate. This might give us sympathy for others who have to accept the unsolicited gifts we press on them. It might teach us that there is more to life and to mutual relationships than our own perspectives and goodwill.

The obligation to receive is always matched by the right to receive. No one is exempt.[15]

The obligation to return

Mail-order catalogues are very popular. There is a legal obligation to pay within thirty days. A contract is involved *(do ut des):* the company sends the goods and you make the payment. You *repay.* After that, you owe nothing. The contract has been honored. There are no further obligations. Mail catalogues demand *repayment.*

But if you lend your lawnmower to a good neighbor for the last cut of the fall, you may forget it until the following spring, when your neighbor returns the machine in good order. And during the winter you borrow your neighbor's snowblower. Maybe the two of you hold on to each other's things. You have a relationship. You have mutual obligations. You will certainly *return,* but holding a neighbor's property symbolizes the relationship. You return it as your neighbor needs it. Neighborliness demands *return*.

To return does not mean that lawnmowers immediately return to where they started. Return is more of a quid pro quo, the exchange of one thing for another: lawnmower for snowblower. Return is explicitly *not repayment*. Unlike repayment, return *is delayed, sometimes indefinitely*. If you have your neighbor's snowblower after the last winter snow, you do not return it immediately. You hold on to it: you keep it in trust. You do not leave it to rust, but keep it in your garage.

The obligation to return is always matched by the right to return. No one is exempt.[16]

One blisteringly hot day in Africa, I was driving a Peugeot flatbed truck along the twenty-two miles of rocky, rutted, and rugged track between my mission station and the main road. After five or six miles, as I skidded around a bend, I almost ran over a body. Lying on her back in the blazing sun was a woman trying to give birth but already exhausted and nearly dead. The baby was in breech position, and the mother's friends had panicked and most had fled. We got her onto the exposed and oven-hot back of the truck, but there was no cover. The nearest good road was fifteen miles away, and it was sixty-seven miles to the hospital. At every bump I winced and the woman moaned or screamed. It took nearly six hours to reach the hospital.

The Catholic sisters immediately took her to Maternity, while I found a cool beer and began to shake with emotion. Less than an hour later the grateful mother called for me. She had delivered a baby of almost nine pounds, her fifteenth pregnancy and fifth surviving child. She was about thirty-four years old. She was very, very happy, and held the baby across her chest. As soon as I went in the room, she began to thank me and say that I had saved her life and given life to her baby. Without me her baby would not be alive. She owed the baby's life to me. The baby belonged to me. The baby was mine.

Before I could do anything, she held out her baby and I found myself holding it. "Its life belongs to you; it is yours," she said. I was deeply, deeply moved, and understood her words. I said a silent prayer that I would not do something stupid. I had no idea what to do.

Then I heard myself saying: "Thank you so much for this precious gift. I accept responsibility for the life of this child. I will always treasure this baby's life. But this child needs a mother. Will you be mother and look after this baby?" As if that were the most obvious thing in the world, she said: "Of course; I will be the mother!" And I handed the baby back to her.

In our missionary lives we have the opportunity to give, receive, and return. As we do, relationships are forged, indebtedness is accepted, lives are changed.

OUR OBLIGATION AND GOD'S

Missionaries are reasonable people and just stewards. They do not easily fall into debt, and they make speedy repayment. This attitude tends to minimize risk; it may indicate an avoidance of, or even an incapacity for, deeper relationships. But we missionaries are called to communicate cross-culturally and form Christian communities of interdependent people. How will we become less independent? How will we remain linked to people by obligations? How will we discover life-giving mutual indebtedness? Our cult of efficiency and legal contract can make us incomprehensible and unreachable. Unless we learn the language of gift-exchange, our message will not convince and our independence will compromise our relevance. Because of the vast resources at our disposal, we may give the impression we do not really need other people's gifts or services. This can make people feel helpless and insignificant. Sometimes we belittle their attempts at reciprocity. Sometimes, under the guise of good stewardship, we do not pay people justly or we pay them grudgingly. Sometimes our style is contractual rather than relational or interpersonal. To learn how to be in appropriate gift-exchange relationships could be immensely enriching for ourselves and for those we serve.

One of Christianity's major contributions is the idea that people can actually have a developing relationship with God: a truly amazing notion. Relationships need not be equal or symmetrical. Mother and child have an asymmetrical relationship. Man and dog have an unequal relationship. The Trinity is a God of relationship, in whom mutuality and self-giving are found; and this God respects each one of us. We are not equal to God, so we are not in a relationship of equality. But we are in a Covenant relationship, and God has pledged never to abandon us.[17] Our relationship with God is indeed mutual. What if we examine the obligations embedded in gift-exchange relationships and apply them to ourselves and to God? Could God have an obligation to give, to receive, and to return?

If we have a relationship with God, we have an obligation to give, to receive, and to return. If God has a relationship with us, God has a relationship to give and receive and return. Our faith lives, our God-related lives, could thrive if we took this seriously. God *must* give because God is self-giving. God *must* receive because God is gracious. God *must* return because God is in relationship. But we too *must* give because all we have belongs to God. We *must* receive in order to live. And we *must* return because we need relationship. It is not that we can *repay* God; that is impossible. But we can make a *return* to God. We can give God something. We can give God thanks; thanksgiving is the most basic sign of acceptance and of the desire to remain in relationship.[18]

God is pledged to accept our self-giving and to respond to our prayer.

This is not a contract *(do ut des)*: we cannot contract with God. It is a Covenant and it is relational *(quid pro quo)*. We are in an unbreakable Covenant with God.[19]

THE OBLIGATION TO LEARN AND TO CHANGE

We maintain that the gospel and the grace of God are free, unmerited gifts. Why are we so slow to follow up the implications? Free and unmerited these gifts may be, but they are *gift*: not gift as commodity but gift as exchange, as relationship. God is free and sovereign; still, a gift must not only be given but received. This applies also to God. We may need to reinterpret gospel and grace as gift, in the light of gift-exchange.[20]

How do we know whether a gift has been received? Some people have been committed for years to marginal ministry, yet their well-intentioned gifts appear to be untouched or unassimilated. What is the message here? Can missionaries not read, or are they simply unable to assimilate?[21] Why might such gifts not have been accepted if gift-exchange is a universal practice? Perhaps missionary gifts seemed meaningless, inappropriate, or embarrassing. Perhaps people have difficulty in understanding some of our best intentions and most valued gifts. *Good intentions are simply not enough.*

A donor is responsible for making a gift comprehensible if not acceptable, but a donor may need to acknowledge that a gift has not been accepted *in the form in which it is offered.* How flexible are we as donors? Do we allow people to refuse? How theologically and evangelically free are we to recognize other people's freedom to decline?

Our interaction is not always spontaneous and reciprocal because plans have been laid and policy set long before we arrive at our destination. We may have talked to people, but actually talked *down* to them. We may have listened to people, but perhaps *selectively.* Sometimes we craved relationships, but only as *givers.* Sometimes we set ourselves to learn from people, but only as their *teachers.* We brought a clear message, but maybe in the wrong *language.* Sometimes our language and our listening, our relationships and our teaching have been impregnated with power, righteousness, certainty, and the control of initiatives. We are not perfect, but mistakes can lead us to wisdom. Gift-exchange[22] may provide structure for our ministry and teach us the place of trust and risk taking, vulnerability and indebtedness, and mutuality in mission.

Gift-exchange is universal. It is a puzzle to be solved and a key to provide access. It offers a point of contact and embraces a world of meaning. It is a kind of language. It has the potential to become a way of ministry and a missionary method.

Here are some questions, some food for thought. If we can struggle with their challenge, we may be able to commit to a form of ministry that is more mutual and more responsive to relationships—with God and with our neighbors.

- How do we bring the message of the Good News as gift? How do we give it? How might we need to share (to exchange) it with others in new ways?
- How have we received the Good News? How do we show respect for the God who gives? What return do we give to God for what we have received? What exchange or return *can* we give? (See Mk 8:37.)
- In our marginal ministry, do we control patterns of giving and receiving? Do we favor contractual or economic relationships where reciprocal and moral relationships should flourish? Do we fail to respond to local themes and expectations?
- How can we possibly express Christian spirituality in a comprehensible way unless it is incarnated in people's lives, with their own rhythms and relationships, conventions and customs? How can we ever become belongers or participant outsiders in other cultures except through their own social institutions, of which gift-exchange is such a significant one?
- Are we now any closer to a culturally sensitive proclamation of the Good News? What have we learned about gift-exchange that could facilitate marginal ministry?

Chapter 7

STRANGERS IN THE PLACE

Learning to Be

SELF-HELP AND MUTUALITY

Inculturation[1] happens when faith and culture discover mutual relevance through life-enhancing dialogue. But *faith* cannot encounter *culture:* abstractions cannot communicate. Inculturation requires *people* of faith and *people* of culture for mutual encounter and transformation. Missionaries must encourage and support local communities to grow in response to grace. Believers cannot simply imitate other people or other churches: they must honor their own integrity. The universal church exists *in* and *from*[2] every local church. It is not a church of universal uniformity but of communion and diversity.

We are impelled away from familiar worlds and comfort zones, precisely in search of other people's worlds. Those worlds existed before and independently of us, yet we can also discover meaning there. We leave our own center but do not actually reach another's; we move only as far as our mutual margins. Margins are where encounters happen. The margin is the true center for God's mission and our discipleship. We cannot completely leave our own world of meanings and values, and we are never completely assimilated into another world; to think so would be presumptuous or aggressive. Individually, we are simply not that relevant. But neither do we fall into a void; we encounter others.

We want to be accessible and relevant even though we are only marginal to other people's cultures. We are not completely irrelevant: we may be strangers in the place, but there may be a place for strangers.

FOREIGN AND STRANGE

To feel foreign or strange is never comfortable: we wriggle or fidget as we resist the discomfort. Perhaps we keep still, look inconspicuous, and minimize whatever would mark us as outsiders. When all else fails, we look for a familiar face, a familiar anything.

Curiously, some of us (typically those from self-styled First World countries or English speakers) tend to regard *other people* as strangers even when we are in their country. So who *is* a stranger, what makes someone a stranger, and what attitudes are associated with strangers? To see others through our eyes is to adopt a perspective; to see ourselves through others' eyes is more difficult but a corrective to our myopia; to see ourselves as others see us may be a gift of God.

Some people enjoy the unfamiliar, others do not. Almost everyone tries to gain control by making sense or creating order. Some people in unfamiliar situations ask questions, look for assistance, and expect the best. Others strike a pose, act independently, and fear the worst. They tend to be pessimistic and to take a negative view of the people they meet. This can produce the poisoned fruit of xenophobia or racism.

The dictionary may be a refuge for tired minds, but it is also an Aladdin's cave of treasures. Under the entry for *foreign* we find words like *not pertinent, abnormal, alien, strange*. Under *strange*, we note *peculiar, odd, extraordinary*. Under *stranger* we discover "a person not easily explained, an unfamiliar person, and any person one does not know." Is it possible to consider ourselves *not pertinent, abnormal, not easily explained?* We may attach such labels to others; can we apply them to ourselves? This is important because, however we may appear to some others, there are times when, by definition, we are *strange* ourselves. Only when we acknowledge this will we begin to glimpse the impression our behavior creates. But we may never have been really vulnerable before others. We may always have found refuge in the security of a group of like-minded people. We may have been socialized to consider our values and attitudes as normative for everyone. We may never have sought the gift immortalized by Robert Burns.[3] If so, we may be unable to find an appropriate relationship to those we encounter.

DEFINITIONS AND BOUNDARIES

People position themselves and each other. They define their space and what it encloses. A definition is (by definition) a boundary. It marks the physical world or identifies the moral contours of virtues; thus truth, beauty, duty, and right become defined.

Those who disregard safety or who are impervious to pain might appear very courageous. People who do not distinguish friend from foe might seem very open-minded. But if such attitudes persist, those who hold them may soon cease to exist: societies cannot survive long unless they define or mark their own boundaries. People beyond our boundaries must be identified and labeled: they are *foreigners* or *strangers*. As such, they will be treated in culturally determined ways. Thus does the human species remake the world.

No two societies live in precisely the same relationship to the environment or to their neighbors. No two societies define their world in exactly the same way. Every society learns and takes for granted that its own definitions are valid and that its reality is really real. This is not problematic—until people step across the edge of their familiar world and find their definitions threatened and their reality judged idiosyncratic or false.

It is *normal* to find other cultures odd or unusual: compared with one's own, they often are. The opposite is just as true, but *others* may enter *our* world less frequently than we enter theirs. Unless we are careful, we may judge what is different or unusual to be inferior or bad, and what is familiar and our own to be good, even superior. Ethnocentrism is like a shadow: we cannot entirely shake it off. But those who leave their own world and enter the world of others must be careful that ethnocentrism does not become a stumbling block.

To abandon one's reference points completely is to throw away one's compass and walk on quicksand. It may seem trusting, but is so risky as to become imprudent and foolish. Yet if the compass swings widely and swimming is more appropriate than walking, to cling to compass and footwear would be both stupid and conceited.

It is *normal* to find other cultures confusing. That is because one who enters the world of another becomes the stranger. No society can afford to be unconditionally open to strangers. They do not belong. They are unfamiliar. They do not share the group's history; perhaps they do not share its values. People unwary of strangers have not always lived to tell the tale. There are no indigenous Uruguayans or Tasmanians today. For every forty Brazilian Indians before the arrival of the Europeans, thirty-nine were exterminated (from 1.2 million to 30,000). Native American Indians in the present United States were largely outflanked and crushed by strangers or poisoned by their dubious gifts. Relations between Hutu and Tutsi, Irish Catholic and Northern Irish Protestant, Serb and Croat, Palestinian and Israeli can deteriorate rapidly and shockingly. Trusting strangers can be very dangerous.

STRANGER AND HOST

No giver can thrive without a recipient. No stranger can live truly alone. Giver and receiver constitute a pair. A stranger, too, is half of a human pair: a dyad. But who is the other half? No stranger actually exists in total isolation, for that would be an asocial existence; the stranger is a social category. A stranger exists as such by virtue of the host: to be a stranger is, curiously perhaps, to be in relationship to another. Here is our first ambiguity: *host* can mean one who offers *hospitality* but also one who is *hostile*. The Latin root *host-* ("stranger, enemy") and the root *hosp-* ("receiver of strangers, host") are inextricable.

THE HOST

The rights of hosts

Strangers are *other people;* we do not normally define ourselves as strangers, much less as strange. This is because most of us stand within our own familiar world, comfortable with ourselves and our idiosyncrasies. Only when we wander into an unfamiliar world of meaning do we discover that *the other,* occupying a comfortable vantage point in a familiar world of meaning, labels *us* as stranger. Strangers are defined by others: the latter are at home, in place; the stranger is away, out of place. We know about "home team advantage": home team is *host team.*

The person who holds the initiative is the host. The stranger, out of place, needing food, hospitality, and safe passage, is immediately in debt to the host. It is appropriate and necessary that the stranger feel unsure, ill-at-ease, vulnerable: the stranger is not in control. Quick-witted strangers defer to their hosts, allowing them to take control. Such vulnerability attests to the power of boundaries: within a familiar world we are at ease; beyond, we are literally out of place, dislocated. As strangers should be sensitive to hosts' concern for their own safety, so hosts should take the fundamental human virtue of hospitality very seriously. But history records overtrusting hosts and unscrupulous strangers; so hosts must try to retain the initiative and dictate the rules of encounter.

Assuming the stranger accepts a position of deference and courtesy, thus allowing the host to be in control, stranger and host begin to communicate culturally, and interaction builds on their developing understandings. The stranger, intruder-in-need, is subordinate; the host, potential benefactor, is superordinate. Stated differently, the host is *one up*; the stranger, *one down*. Here is a potential relationship, but one built on unequal reciprocity.

The duties of hosts

Some people are just not used to being strangers and resist being dependent or vulnerable; the initial interaction will feel stifling and unacceptable. Some people bridle at the idea of putting themselves in the hands of another; perhaps they feel they might be exploited. This may be due to individualism and self-sufficiency. But sadly it misses an essential point about the host in relation to the stranger: the host must remain—both literally and figuratively—the host.

Even before any stranger arrives, hosts already have a sense of responsibility. Their responsibility *as hosts* may be among their most sacred duties.[4] Despite the risks, the human species wants to make friends. The very language of strangers is informative.

In English the dyadic term *host* can be paired with *stranger,* but equally well with *guest.* But in English *stranger* and *guest* are not equivalent. They sometimes denote two very separate categories with very different sets of expectations. We may think of a stranger as someone with no real identity, and certainly not as a friend. A guest may be much more familiar, someone we know and entertain freely. The fact that we categorize strangers differently from guests indicates that we also treat them differently. Language categorizes our world, and our categories assume an almost objective status.

In many languages the word for stranger *is* the word for guest: the lexicon does not have two different words. A "stranger" therefore should be treated as a "guest" is to be treated. A guest is not simply someone one knows but may be someone one does not (yet) know—but who nevertheless warrants preferential treatment. The dyad or relational pair in such societies as these is *host: guest/stranger.*

Treating a stranger as a guest confers social status on the stranger. It gives the stranger an identity, transforming anonymous outsider into named participant. The stranger *does not become an insider* but is brought across the boundary that previously separated stranger and host: the rules may be unwritten and even unformulated, but people do not treat others in a random or ad hoc fashion. If strangers are well treated, the society has developed this behavior pattern and maintained it over time through socialization patterns. Where hospitality is taken seriously, every host bears the weight of responsibility. It takes a host to make a guest, but it takes a stranger to make a host.

The expectations of hosts

As people move in and out of each other's worlds, several questions arise. Do strangers show adequate and genuine deference to their hosts? Do they willingly acknowledge their hosts' authority? Do strangers allow themselves to be appropriately positioned as strangers according to the legitimate rights of hosts? Or do they try to seize initiatives, to make their own expectations clear, even to make demands? If so, they are refusing the role of stranger. They are impeding their hosts from claiming their own rights, undertaking their duties, and offering hospitality. Strangers may rationalize their own behavior, claiming virtuous independence or respectful self-sufficiency. They may show ostentatious humility or naïvely protest that they do not want to impose. But if they fail to allow the other to be host, they give offense and show great disrespect; worse, they sow seeds of confusion wherever they pass.

Being a stranger is not easy; but it is *necessary* if people are to succeed in crossing boundaries and discovering new relationships. To be strangers willingly is to respect the cultural rules, to defer to our hosts, and to allow them the common courtesy of moving us between categories. It is impossible for us to move *ourselves* across the threshold of another culture, except by aggression. That is the responsibility and the right of those into whose worlds we hope to enter.

A stranger must be sensitive to the context, discovering what is appropriate. In principle, that is whatever meets local conventions, whatever makes sense within this particular world of meaning. Strangers have no right to dictate what is appropriate: they are outsiders, perhaps guests, certainly *strangers*. They must learn how to behave rather than jump to unwarranted conclusions and behave as barbarians. Conventions in the host culture may be as different from one's own as the local language is different. But cross-cultural communication is possible if both parties respect and commit to the process.

Hosts have obligations and legitimate expectations. One reason strangers may feel ambivalent about their hosts' responses is that the hosts are testing their responses. There is an element of cat-and-mouse behavior as a host seeks to control the situation and determine whether the stranger acquiesces. Unless the host's expectations are met, the stranger may never move beyond the most preliminary stage of encounter.

The ambivalence of hosts

Hosts will always be somewhat apprehensive of strangers, even when treating them like guests. Treating them as guests may mitigate any possible aggression, but the issue goes beyond potential aggression. From the perspective of those who define them, strangers are *not like us*. In the short term at least, because their behavior is not fully understood, they are not always seen as consistent or totally comprehensible.

It makes good sense for hosts to treat strangers rather formally as they try to get their measure. Initially, hosts may be ambivalent about strangers, the more so if there are several. Strangers are unknown. They may bring gifts and have access to resources, yet their motives are hidden. They may be dangerously powerful. Interaction is likely to demonstrate some of this ambivalence,[5] which is entirely understandable. In due course, ambivalence will resolve itself into acceptance unless it hardens into rejection.

Every missionary is a stranger. Some of us are familiar with being "homecomers" —returning to familiar loved ones who welcome us warmly and treat us with unconditional acceptance. But strangers are not homecomers and cannot expect to be treated as such.[6] We must be prepared to be strangers; we go into *unfamiliar* places to be among *unfamiliar* people. Strangers are welcomed with formality rather than unbounded warmth. That is the price of hospitality, which is itself the basis of relationship. Without relationship there will be no new communities. Without trust there will be no relationship. Without hospitality there will be no trust. But unless we approach as strangers, there will be no hospitality, for hospitality is the welcome appropriate for a host to extend to a stranger.

THE STRANGER

To become a stranger effectively and with dignity entails two unfamiliar processes. First, the learning process that transforms us as we encounter a new reality. This involves both *understanding* and *standing under*: the former, the familiar absorption of external information; the latter, the willingness to be absorbed into another world, even if one does not fully understand it. The second process required of us as strangers is the suffering process that allows us to grow as we negotiate the necessary discomfort and distress. This involves both risk and trust.

Failure to learn and to be open to new experiences will mark us as stubborn, ill-mannered, and therefore untrustworthy. Yet overeagerness may mark us as gullible and imprudent. True respect for the host culture—and willingness to risk and to trust—is always likely to make us comfortable and may require compromise. We face the paradox and the pain of cross-cultural encounter. We want to help people, yet we are infants in many ways. We want to be vulnerable and trusting, yet we must not compromise our integrity. As we guard ours, we must respect theirs; to do any less is to fail at a basic level.

The stranger as receiver

If strangers can prepare to be unprepared (unsure, unfamiliar), they will have less reason to worry about hiding their ignorance. They must gradually learn to accept hospitality: it may not come easy, and it takes place as life goes on. Hospitality is culturally determined and shaped; strangers cannot anticipate it. They *will* be caught unawares by the expectations and habits of hosts. Unless they are willing to change some attitudes (to personal hygiene, privacy, eating and drinking, and so on), their hosts will be unable to classify them; they will remain anomalous.

Strangers need a strong sense of personal identity; they must be rooted yet resilient. Otherwise they will do one of two things. They may compromise totally, which their hosts certainly do not expect, since part of strangers' attraction is precisely their quaintness and otherness: their *strangeness*. Or they will remain slaves to their own Western habits—of dress and demeanor, food and friendship, housing and hospitality.[7]

A stranger cannot *demand* legitimation (community approval). It is the hosts' right to *accord* this when appropriate. It depends on the stranger's credibility, which likewise cannot be foisted on the community.

Yet without legitimation and credibility the stranger remains peripheral, distant, and not socially significant.

Neither legitimation nor credibility is automatically conferred. Time must pass; privacy may be invaded; vulnerability may be probed; some confusion and isolation will be felt. In the end it still does not depend on the stranger alone but on the progress of relationships. Somehow the stranger must be grafted onto the native stock. But before this can happen, the surrender of control, the experience of cognitive dissonance,[8] and the exposure to the scrutiny of the community ("culture shock")[9] must take place.

The stranger as resource

Highly individualistic people believe that independence, resourcefulness, and self-sufficiency are cardinal virtues. To avoid owing anything to anyone, they acquire every imaginable machine and gadget. Some may trumpet their willingness to lend. But other people, no less individualistic, are just as determined *not* to borrow or to become indebted; thus, generosity is not actually tested. Such attitudes actually create barriers, cognitive or ideological if not actual, because they are nurtured by an *ethos* of competition rather than collaboration. Individualism and competitiveness are not benign and can easily turn into xenophobia. Strictly, xenophobia indicates *fear* of strangers (or the *other*), but may express itself in *distrust* or *disregard*. Our capacity to distinguish and define, to stereotype and to stratify may be understandable; but however we rationalize negative attitudes to outsiders or to the *other*, they run contrary to cultural, not to mention evangelical, imperatives.

Societies need outsiders,[10] and the gospel needs to embrace everyone. Otherwise cultures stagnate or collapse under the weight of their own hubris (or are destroyed by outsiders), and Christians become complacent and selfish, betraying the very gospel they preach. At the very least, every group needs to find mates beyond its own members. Apart from so-called marriage by capture, this produces some self-interested alliances with strangers. Strangers may always be ambiguous but are never totally irrelevant. Potentially, they are a vital resource. Strangers may need to be turned into allies, but if a group's interests warrant it, the necessary process can and will be undertaken.

The stranger as alien

Given the human capacity for setting boundaries and limitations, a total stranger may be perceived *initially* and *primarily* as an alien. If a group lives within a strong, bounded microcosm, what is outside is also unknown, unfamiliar, and therefore alien; and the stranger comes from the outside. The less known about strangers or their origin, the more likely will bizarre properties and habits be projected onto them. This convention underscores the divide between *us* and *them*.

Whatever a group may do to accommodate and transform unfamiliar strangers, they first perceive them as alien: strange and unfamiliar. Historically, some strangers have never been transformed because the potential hosts have not really engaged in relationships with them: hosts have thus *not* transformed strangers. At other times strangers may be kept at the edges of society and hounded—or perhaps tolerated or used in some contractual ways; yet they are treated as objects *because* perceived as alien and by definition *not-one-of-us*. Unless people acknowledge others to be like themselves, they will be unable to treat them as such. Low-caste, and particularly no-caste or *outcast*, people of India are a case in point. The lower their status, the more powerless they are to become acceptable to higher castes. Like nonindentured slaves, they are used and abused by others. They are not treated as human beings *(us)* but as aliens *(them)*.

> In Pakistan I was taken by a group of missionaries to meet some of the local people called the Marwari Bhil. They are of Hindu stock, living in a Muslim state. They are not even part of an official caste: socially the lowest of the low. There are some Punjabis, also originally from India but members of the lowest caste, the sweepers. A few of these have become Christian. Yet they look down on their Bhil neighbors and cannot yet see how un-Christian this is. When we visited the Marwaris, they were delighted and very hospitable. They put us at our ease and fed us with their simple food. They said that we (the missionaries) treated them as human beings, unlike everyone else in Pakistan. For me this was a profound encounter that left an indelible impression of how *us* and *them* can become *we* and how *we* can become fractured into *us* and *them*.

If we who consider ourselves benign, compassionate, and nonthreatening have suffered as strangers, we should understand victims of xenophobia, people categorized as alien and stripped of their identity and human dignity. But we might also feel for those who are xenophobic: it is not always realistic for strangers to expect to be welcomed unequivocally and magnanimously. Those who treat others as alien and strange often do so because they cannot relate to them or feel threatened by them. Until such a situation is changed, their alien status will continue to work against them. Missionaries are sometimes in unenviable positions, but they may also have great potential.

Some missionaries, treated as alien, might be able to withdraw and return home. Those determined to stay may be reduced to frustration, anger, or depression. Better, in many ways, for the host to take the initiative (to assimilate or expel) than to leave a stranger in a *liminal*[11] state, indefinitely marginal. This would lead to stagnation and social and spiritual death. Fortunately, because *stranger* is a social category and part of a dyad, the passage of a stranger can be charted, and strangers can take heart. But a word of warning: when considering the stranger as an alien, some might respond, "Not me!" Some strangers resist the categorization and refuse to be seen as problematical. If they are also missionaries, they have some serious work to do. They need to learn to live in the transitional status of alien, and they certainly need to become alerted to the plight of others who live permanently in that condition.

The stranger as guest

Finally we are on more comfortable ground: most of us respond well enough to being treated as guests. But there are serious implications here: when a stranger is being treated as a guest, someone in the local community is probably being deprived. The guest's convenience is the community's inconvenience. This is no bad thing: it is the cost of openhanded hospitality. But hospitality is not limitless; the smiles on the faces of hosts will be strained after a relatively short time. Guests need to be able to read the signs.

Because the guest *is* a stranger, it is not up to the guest/stranger to refuse hospitality; that betrays a desire to control. The guest must be gracious but sensitive to the possibility of overstaying the welcome. To approach the role of guest with a self-important attitude is to insult the host and to demean the process. This is no basis upon which to announce a gospel of service, ministry, and respect for persons.

> An exception to prove the rule: I had been living in West Africa for several months. The paramount chief had welcomed me warmly, though I knew him to have no intrinsic interest in Christianity. A paramount chief has a house or hut in each village of the chieftaincy, or else a room will be prepared when he arrives. Each village traditionally gave a woman as wife to the chief. But if the chiefdom was large or the chief past his prime, the designated woman might remain in her own village.
>
> Once, when I was in a remote village, the hut designated as the paramount chief's was provided for my accommodation. But so, too, I discovered, was the chief's wife in that place. The chief's hospitality was evidently quite extensive. When I came back to my room after a service, a smiling, toothless, and somewhat self-conscious woman offered her personal hospitality. It seemed appropriate for me to decline, so I thanked her for the thought and bade her good night in a rather loud stage whisper for everyone's benefit.

Strangers, even guests, have no absolute rights; the initiative belongs to the host. To be a guest can be delightful, affirming, and the preamble to developing relationships and mutuality; but it is also delicate. Every authentic stranger *must* learn to be a guest, and not simply as a means to an end. An acceptable guest can be converted or transformed by hosts into an appropriate long-term stranger. But whoever does not learn to be a guest will never become relevant and worthy of trust.

ASSIMILATION OF STRANGERS

To be a host is demanding. A host must modify certain attitudes and expectations in order to treat the stranger graciously while retaining control. To be a stranger is no less demanding: a stranger must modify certain attitudes and expectations in order to treat the host deferentially while not becoming servile. Every stranger must construct a world of meaning from a world of puzzlement.

Anthropologists caution us: a vulnerable stranger[12] may adopt a rigid attitude to the hosts and become too serious and withdrawn. However understandable this may be, it marks the stranger as inflexible, formal, and difficult to assimilate. Stranger and host both aspire to some measure of assimilation, but this is delicate because each is wary of the other's expectations and likely to transmit ambiguous signals.

We previously noted[13] that three obligations are key to unlocking cultural meanings. Now we discover three stages of assimilation.[14] These stages are not totally separable and may not clearly follow in sequence. It may not be as easy to specify them in advance as to interpret them in retrospect. But they can be named: a *preliminary* stage, a *transitional* stage, and a stage of *incorporation*.

Preliminary

Initial contact is characterized by formality, hesitation, and tentativeness. The intruder wants to be accepted and the host does not want to be outflanked. Certain markers indicate to everyone the *preliminary* nature of the interaction. Conventionally there is an introduction, preceded by the announcement of the stranger. The ritual scrutiny of the stranger follows, probably with pointing, touching, stroking, poking, searching, observing, and commenting. There may be laughter and some embarrassing moments as the stranger is assessed and compared with more familiar points of reference. But the clearest indication of the preliminary nature of the interaction relates to time: the stranger is kept waiting or hanging around, and there seems to be a great deal of time-wasting: this helps establish that the host is in charge. The more the stranger tolerates and even encourages this, the more likely he or she is to be gradually assimilated. But it is not always easy, and often very tedious for efficient, time-based people.

Anyone new to a cross-cultural situation knows that time can hang very heavily and it is not easy to keep frustration at bay. One must learn to relax and not become agitated. Agitation is contagious, and we should not make our hosts ill at ease. Fortunately, relaxation can be just as contagious: if we take our cue from our relaxed hosts, we contribute greatly to the well-being of all. If we cultivate a relaxed air, we help our hosts relax, too. But this can be a real test of our resilience.

Transitional

Time passes; this is as necessary as it is inevitable. Gradually, and assuming the stranger is not despised or ejected, attitudes will change. Formal acts of hospitality and kindness begin to diminish. The stranger may sense some cooling off on the part of the hosts. What was relatively structured behavior now becomes frustratingly unpredictable, changeable, even random.

As the *transitional* or *liminal* (*limen*, "threshold") stage is reached, the stranger may be treated very casually or even left to manage alone. But the casualness or randomness is only apparent; the transitional period is by definition inconsistent and necessarily confusing. The stranger is being brought across a threshold and is no longer completely outside (stranger) nor completely within (host). The threshold is neither in nor out and therefore a powerful symbol of betwixt-and-betweenness. Crossing the threshold marks a new beginning; waiting at the threshold allows for mature decision making or reminds people that a boundary is about to be crossed, a new encounter about to take place.

It is important that the stranger have the flexibility, trust, and perseverance to remain committed to the process, instead of allowing frustration or anger to have full expression. This may be very confusing.

Characteristics of the transitional phase include some proffering and acceptance of gifts, some reciprocity but no firm commitment, some mutual modification of attitude and status between the parties. Neither stranger nor host is entirely happy or comfortable, but neither wishes to abort the process and each is questioning some basic assumptions about self and about the other.

In a sense, the whole of any meeting between two persons or two groups, from the same or different cultures, is transitional, since there is always call for personal and mutual reappraisal. Circumstances may warrant the indefinite delaying of commitments. But human associations may also mature and pass beyond the liminal, as people settle into a committed relationship. Insofar as they do so, we can identify the third phase of a social interaction: *incorporation*.

It had been months. Months of not knowing whether I was really welcome or merely tolerated. Months of oscillating between receiving wonderful hospitality and effective abandonment. I did not know where I was with the local people. Sometimes I felt certain that I had made the initial transition, only to fall back to a feeling of alienation from the people I had come so far to serve.

One day an old lady walked to my modest house at the edge of the village. She knocked on the door and I answered. I beckoned her to come inside, and she crossed the threshold. Opening a cloth she held in her hand, she revealed three fresh eggs. I thought she wanted to sell them, and I remember thinking that I really did not want them. I also knew she could not afford to give them to me. But that was what she had come for: to make me a gift.

I was deeply touched by her simple yet profound kindness. Something told me that this was more than a token gift; it was a sign that I was acceptable to the community. Months of uncertainty seemed to melt away as I received her gift.

Incorporation

If some level of incorporation is achieved, the relationship will be modified. Now there is spontaneity and trust, very different from the previous ambivalence and inconsistency. But the transition is not inevitable.

Sometimes the incipient relationship simply crumbles. Incorporation always depends on mutuality, but even an incorporated person is not structurally equal to the host. The host is always superordinate. Unless the stranger/guest acknowledges this by appropriate attitudes, incorporation cannot occur. The incorporated stranger *remains a stranger,* at least for a long time. In Europe a person who moves into a rural village continues to be referred to as a stranger after thirty years or more. Sometimes even their grandchildren—who, like their parents, have been born and raised there—have been known to be called strangers. What expectations might a stranger reasonably entertain? Acceptance by the host is not carte blanche: the stranger is still subject to the rules of hospitality as mediated by the host. The stranger/guest is not strictly free and must remember the rules of precedence and the respect due the host. Another paradox: if the stranger wants to remain free and not become beholden, incorporation is actually not desirable. If the stranger wants to remain indebted and perhaps move to a gift-exchange relationship, mutual indebtedness must actually be sought.

Some incorporation without total absorption or assimilation is the most any outsider can hope for. But unless long-term strangers are working through the transitional phase and toward deeper incorporation, they will not receive credibility and will fail to become relevant to the group. Any long-term plans strangers may have, based on the assumption that they are relevant, will come to nothing.

AMBIVALENCE OF STRANGERS

The role and status of stranger are inherently ambiguous, and every stranger will feel somewhat confused and unclear. Since some people seem congenitally indisposed to confusion and unclarity, some strangers instinctively try to manipulate situations and restore some order and control. The more they struggle, the less gracious they appear. The less gracious they appear, the more difficult life becomes for everyone. A stranger's ideas of courtesy, etiquette, and graciousness may have to be revised.

What should strangers/guests do when offered excessive hospitality? What should they do when cast in the role of receivers? What should they do when cast in the role of honored person?

> Trekking from village to village, I found it necessary to travel in a group: there were books, bedding, a camp bed, and toiletries to be carried, and sometimes food. I rarely knew the way. Schoolboys or youths were usually happy to accompany me even though it meant a long walk with a load on their head. But they were wise: they knew that when I arrived at a village, I would receive hospitality. They knew I could not eat nearly as much as I would receive. They knew there would be plenty for them.
>
> Sometimes the trek meant a day off from school. Sometimes they would have relatives in the village. Some of them were just good-hearted companions. But all of them knew there would be food. One thing a receiver or guest can do is to be a medium for redistribution. Redistribution can go a long way to making friends and building community.

Hosts may be imprisoned by their own hospitality. A host's behavior is not spontaneous but governed by convention. The host expects the guest's response to be constrained by the same conventional rules. Initially, the guest will be indulged; this is a mark of hospitality. But generosity is also a language: it says that the host can afford to be lavish, wishes to be excessive, and will impoverish the host community as a visible sign of respect. The first obligation of the guest is to learn to relax and let this happen. The guest's discomfort is no reason for a protest or attempt to turn the tables. The host is in charge; the guest is not.

But the conventional rules of hospitality do not operate indefinitely. This will bring some relief for the guest, and certainly for the host. If an insensitive guest continues to drain the community's resources, early welcome will quickly turn sour. The guest must be learning to read the signs: the formal and indulgent phase is coming to an end, and the guest is now being moved from the initial phase into the liminal or transitional phase.

We emphasize that the host needs to be in control. The host has a great deal to lose if a guest seizes the initiative. A stranger may be treated with generosity and preferential treatment, but such openhanded hospitality may leave hosts vulnerable to exploitation. On the other hand, it may be the host who has an eye for the main chance: if a guest is treated well, the host community may benefit from the host's gratitude. The relationship between the two may be unclear as each seeks to show respect yet exploit the situation. Thus, a diligent stranger may find an opportunity for advancement. There are many examples of hosts treating strangers with conscious indulgence, and strangers in turn moving rapidly from the periphery toward the center of power and influence.

> Thousands of Chinese were brought into Hawaii as indentured slaves and laborers in the early nineteenth century. By dint of industry, quiet ambition, support from the extended family, and opportunity, some achieved the status of entrepreneurs and politically powerful figures in a couple of generations.
>
> Many Pakistani people who moved to England in the past couple of generations became shopkeepers and worked long hours and every day; and some became millionaires. Such upward mobility, while admirable in many ways, may give pause to hosts when faced in the future by apparently helpless strangers. They may fear that if they are too welcoming, they may live to regret it.

POSSIBILITIES OF STRANGERS

Reflecting on the social identity of the stranger, we notice that it is not always negative. What advantages might there be? Here are seven possibilities to conclude these reflections.

Sharing histories

What do strangers and hosts know of each other? They may desire to bond and to commit themselves to each other, but they are ignorant of each other's pasts. True strangers have no common experiences. They do not understand each other's socialization processes. They do not know about the social function of *significant others, legitimators,* or *peers.* Nor do they understand the distribution of power and authority. Initially they do not even know experientially whether they share a common humanity. But they must determine this if cooperation is to be built up.

The history of human contact between indigenous groups and strangers is uneven. Travelers' tales (especially after the Middle Ages and into the era of European discovery in the sixteenth century) sometimes narrated encounters with fantastical beings who walked upside down or appeared grotesque. Sometimes the visitors attributed subhuman features to the local people. One recalls stories of cannibals: the word comes from

Arawak in the West Indies, and cannibalism was alleged by the Spanish to characterize the local people.[15] But there are stories from an earlier age, when people were more prone to assume that strangers were human like themselves. If people think of others as fundamentally different, they tend to demean or even demonize them. One party's air of social superiority may metastasize into an air of moral superiority, spreading the cancer of xenophobia.

From the stranger's perspective, it is important to know something about the hosts and their lives: the stranger is dependent, vulnerable, outnumbered. Yet if the host knows virtually nothing about the stranger, significant problems also arise. It becomes almost impossible to interpret all of the stranger's reactions. It also becomes difficult to locate the stranger appropriately within the world of the host. But unless the host community succeeds in fitting the stranger into the existing social framework, the latter will be unable to establish a credible identity.

Despite such dangers, hosts and strangers can, given the opportunity, *share* their respective history and experience. Each can illustrate and explain their behavior and perhaps belief. Such sharing presents an opportunity for forging a common agenda. At least it allows a host community to place the stranger on its agenda, however peripherally.

The history and experience of host and stranger are different: each must resist the temptation to claim superiority. People with different histories approach problems from different perspectives, and this can prove mutually beneficial. The possibility of sharing histories and perspectives is the possibility of reaching new levels of cooperation.

Pooling resources

Every local world yields local resources that can be harnessed to deal with local problems. A stranger comes from another world. The stranger's resources may not exist in the host's world. The stranger's resources, including explanations or approaches, may not always make sense to the host. But every local world subsists within the global world, and every local world has problems in common with every other local world. Resources from different worlds can be carried to new worlds, and new solutions to old problems can be found. The stranger's resources are not necessarily better than those in a local world, but they are different. Different approaches, solutions, and wisdom can be shared to mutual advantage.

Driving along a rock-strewn road in West Africa, I blew a tire for the second time in a few miles. There was no other spare. I was fifteen miles from my destination; fifteen miles in the opposite direction was the nearest garage. The car came to a stop, miles from anywhere. Yet within minutes a handful of men had congregated round the car. The problem was obvious to all, but I could see absolutely no solution.

I was already mentally planning to stay in a nearby village for the night when two of the men, unbidden and without consulting, jacked up the car and started removing the flat tire. As I watched and wondered, they carried it into the bush. Since I could not travel anyway, this did not inconvenience me. In a very short time they came back, rolling the tire. They fixed it in place, tightened the nuts, and released the jack. Smiling, they told me to drive on. I was completely mystified and could not even believe their solution would work: they had packed the tire with grass.

I did drive on. I drove the fifteen miles to the mission, slowly yet in comfort and safety. A few days' later I drove all the way back down the road, thirty miles, to the gas station. The mechanic fixed the tire the way I would have if I had had his tools.

But I did not have his tools, so even with theoretical knowledge and practical experience I would still have been unable to take the tire off the rim and patch it adequately. I could not even have imagined the solution proposed by the local community. Even when I saw it, I hardly believed it. But it worked.

The sharing of local resources, approaches, and solutions can be a real blessing.

Opening microcosms

People living within small, bounded worlds develop a strong or closed microcosm. Their world is focused largely on itself, often becoming highly self-sufficient. Other people live within microcosms that are open to the wider world. They, too, have boundaries, but these do not exclude outsiders. People who live within an open or weak microcosm are hunters, travelers, mariners, nomads, or conquerors. Those within strong microcosms tend to be farmers and settlers.

Because every local world exists within the wider world, we can correlate microcosm and macrocosm. Where the microcosm is strong and meaning is largely found within, the macrocosm will be correspondingly weak and largely irrelevant to people's lives. Those living within a strong microcosm may need to patrol its borders and maintain its integrity by carefully controlling the passage of strangers. Those living within a weak microcosm are correspondingly open to the macrocosm and less concerned to patrol boundaries and monitor the passage of strangers. Not that they dispense with boundaries or fail to discriminate among strangers: those without boundaries soon lose a sense of their own identity; those who are completely open may find others taking advantage. There is always need for balance, flexibility, and willingness to change.

Strangers may be a catalyst for opening up societies. But strangers are ambiguous. Where they are welcomed spontaneously and easily, the microcosm is probably already weakened and the community already open to the wider world. But where a community is closed, strangers may not be as warmly welcomed and the microcosm thus remains strong. So whether strangers are an advantage or not depends on many variables, not simply on the strangers' goodwill. Yet however self-sufficient they may be, strongly bounded societies will always be limited by their own experience and imagination. Not only does the stranger come from another world; in other worlds people do things differently. By opening up a local microcosm, the stranger offers alternatives: alternative ways of thinking and of doing. This is potentially beneficial, since it helps extend the range of possible solutions to local problems. Yet it depends on the acceptability of the stranger in the first place, and strongly bounded societies tend to resist alternative ways of doing things unless and until they perceive new reasons and develop new needs.

> A rural African community was decimated by a high infant mortality rate. The medical missionary sisters discovered that the local midwives were cutting the umbilical cord with a piece of sharpened bamboo, which they then wrapped in a cloth until the next baby was born. Babies contracted septicemia from the infected bamboo, and many died.
>
> The sisters assembled the midwives, instructed them in sterile technique, and issued to each of them a packet of five razor blades to replace the bamboo. They were told to use and then to discard the blade. They would receive more blades as necessary. After a year the infant mortality rate was as high as ever. The sisters were perplexed, the midwives angry, the mothers increasingly afraid.
>
> After some research and much prevarication from the midwives, the sisters discovered that the midwives were indeed using the razor blades instead of the bamboo. But in these poor rural communities, razor blades were hard to come by and nothing was wasted. So the midwives would wrap the used razor blade in a cloth, use it until it was dull—and sell the other razor blades in the community. Not only were the babies dying from the very same cause as initially; the community was now disenchanted with the sisters for promising a dramatic reduction, only to find that the new solution was a complete failure.

Alternative solutions can be helpful if translated into the local cultural idiom. But opening up closed microcosms is no unmitigated blessing. People must be helped to live with alternatives and to prosper within an expanding world, otherwise strangers' gifts will turn to poison and local hospitality will turn to hostility.

Offering solidarity

Initial reactions to a stranger may be ambivalent as insiders ask questions. Why has this person come here? Is the stranger seeking something or bringing something? Is the stranger a spy or bent on destruction? This possibility is sometimes enough to turn host communities very quickly against a stranger. Sometimes the conventions of hospitality break down in face of the perceived threat; even if they are observed, the stranger may be treated with coolness or suspicion.

Perhaps the stranger is worthy and well disposed. A host community must determine strangers' intentions, but it is not always easy. If a self-sufficient and ostentatious, strong, articulate stranger approaches a poor and needy community, the community may be ashamed of its own impoverishment. Subsequent relations will be affected by that shame. If local people cannot act as hosts but feel worthless, "one down," and indebted, the consequences will be grave. Beggars can't be choosers; but those forced to beg and expected to be grateful can be deeply hostile to the benefactors they cannot refuse.

A priceless gift a stranger can bring to a needy community is the moral gift of solidarity. Today many communities feel abandoned by the wider world or victims of terrible violence within their own country. They suffer physical, moral, and spiritual deprivation. A stranger may be an agent of incalculable good. To convince such people that the stranger would not want to be anywhere else, or with anyone else, is to begin to rehabilitate those with crushed self-esteem or verging on despair. When the stranger becomes recognizable as a friend and the host is able to embrace and be embraced, stranger and host have been transformed into a community of friends.

Enriching lives

Every culture can benefit from strangers. But strangers are beneficiaries as well as benefactors, and the development of authentic relationships depends partly on the stranger's gracious willingness to learn and to receive. There will be some tension between the insider and the outsider, superordinate host and subordinate stranger. This is because, while each needs to acknowledge their respective structural positions, each is also capable of putting the other at ease and thus developing increasing mutuality. The tension, then, is between assertiveness and deference. But the encounter between two people or two communities with different backgrounds and capacities carries the potential for one of the most profound of human experiences. It is the experience of moving beyond differences to similarities, beyond strangerhood to friendship. It may be a long, hard road, but to reach its end is to celebrate unity at a profound level.

Every encounter with a stranger is a risk. A blood transfusion is potentially life-giving to a patient, and a stranger is a potential life bringer to a depleted community. But blood transfusions can kill: contaminated blood may not be detected until too late. A stranger's goodwill cannot halt the spread of the measles he carries; a blood donor's generosity cannot make her rhesus-positive blood acceptable to a rhesus-negative person.

Encounters can be enriching. The assimilation of strangers into host communities can enrich the lives of both. The contribution of a stranger who freely engages with others out of a genuine desire for mutual exchange may be beyond price. This is the summit of human encounter.

Mediating hostilities

Local communities carry the seeds of their own destruction. Villages, corporations, families, or even spouses may experience a souring of relationships. This can produce hostility and antisocial behavior. Sociologically, a faction is a fragment or group within a wider group; it is opposed to another faction on a particular issue. When institutionalized, factionalism can become utterly destructive and virtually unresolvable if communities become polarized. Then there is no arbitrator, and no possibility of reasoned discussion. Maybe not until one party is utterly exhausted will some semblance of normality return: the embers of factionalism may burn for generations.

The stranger may be an unlikely arbitrator or mediator. But the stranger may be the only person trusted by both sides. This assumes the stranger has been assimilated over a relatively long period and is not still in the *preliminary* or *early transitional* stage. It also assumes that *because* the stranger is well into the *transitional* stage, the stranger has met the host group's expectations and acquiesced in being scrutinized, tested, and taught. This stranger is not authoritarian or disrespectful but vulnerable and supportive; this stranger is deemed to have the community's interests at heart.

If members of factions do not trust each other, they may then turn to the trusted stranger who may help resolve the impasse. Then the faction will dissolve, and enemies can begin to talk to each other without losing face. Without the stranger's contribution, these things would have been unimaginable or taken forever. The stranger who helps mediate lives offers a precious gift to the community. Perhaps even more important for those who wish to learn cross-cultural lessons, a stranger may acquire the moral authority of a *significant other* and even find a place on the local agenda.

Sharing worlds

The third stage of assimilation is *incorporation;* but the *fully incorporated* stranger is a contradiction in terms. Practically, incorporation is limited, and for good reason. The stranger has been socialized in a particular world, has acquired values and practical principles, and has developed an aesthetic and moral sense. Those things cannot be abandoned any more than human beings can slough their skin. We take our socialized selves with us wherever we go. Resocialization can and should take place, but we remain largely who we have become as our cultural formation has stamped us. Likewise for those we encounter. The challenge is to communicate, to share, to experience mutual modifications *consistent with our respective integrity.*

A stranger cannot become an insider. But a stranger does not need to try. It is the quality of relationship between insider and outsider that matters. A fully assimilated stranger would cease to be a stranger[16] and lose the voice and perspective of the stranger, so critical to mutually enriching dialogue.

The stranger *may* hope to become a participating rather than a nonparticipating member of the community. The *participating outsider* has great potential for contributing to, and benefiting from, a community. A *nonparticipating outsider* would have little relevance (a tourist, traveler, parasite) or be resented (an occupying army or colonial government). A stranger cannot be a *participating insider* because a stranger is an *outsider.* But a stranger should not be reduced to the status of *nonparticipating insider.* Those are the pariahs, the criminal or deviant classes, or the insignificant.

The stranger can aspire to being a participating outsider, so long as the stranger remains an outsider and yet participates. To remain an outsider means not to assume too much, not to make inappropriate demands, to remain socially marginal (servant), to be disinterested (not clinging to status). To participate means to discover one's place on the agenda, to contribute to the felt needs of the community, to be a servant, yet to be able to challenge and support, to be spiritually and culturally life-transmitting and life-propagating. These are challenges for every missionary stranger. To them we turn next.

MISSIONARY AS STRANGER

Doing Marginal Ministry

BIBLICAL ATTITUDES TO STRANGERS

The Bible is full of meetings between strangers and hosts, and it would take a biblical scholar to explore the theme adequately. We will raise a few points, offer a brief set of references, and encourage readers to pursue the topic. The Bible is a rich and relevant source of reflection for any missionary trying to understand service in other cultures.

Biblically,[1] a stranger is not a member of the tribe or in-group. As such, the stranger is a potential if not an actual enemy. Gradually the Israelites began to develop their own self-consciousness as the Chosen People, becoming concerned about maintaining their identity and not allowing it to be compromised by the beliefs and behavior of strangers. Hospitality nevertheless remained an important virtue and a sign of graciousness and generosity, sophistication and refinement. Whoever was allowed into the community became *entitled* to hospitality, just as we find today in many cultures. It would have been unthinkable to invite people in and then to neglect them.

Where there were strangers, there was tension. Rules of hospitality notwithstanding, strangers might be unbelievers, barbarians, heathens, pagans, or members of other categories of ambiguous or problematic outsiders. If an outsider was categorized in this way, the duties of hospitality might conflict with the demands of purity (exclusiveness) or proselytization (assimilation or conversion).

There was another tension: even assuming strangers were not perceived as threatening, they had to be contextualized or located within the insiders' social world. Social groups must balance two imperatives: alliance and descent. *Alliances* are social relationships created by marriage. *Descent* is relatedness based on common ancestry. But alliance and descent are like two sides of a coin: in order to perpetuate a group by descent, alliances are necessary for providing spouses (the incest taboo drives a group to create pair-bonds between its own members and members of other groups). Also, a major reason for undertaking alliances is to ensure the perpetuation of one's group (by befriending potential enemies and thus assuring one's own survival). Formal or informal alliances make every group dependent on other people, just as the creation of a descent line or lineage is only possible with outside assistance. In other words, human beings are bound to other human beings with unavoidable yet problematic social links and responsibilities.

Strangers in the Bible are not an undifferentiated category. We distinguish strangers as *nokri* and strangers as *gêr*. The strongest negative connotations are associated with *nokri*. Anyone designated *nokri* would attract suspicion and hostility. Still, some movement of status was possible even for a *nokri*. A stranger could also be a temporary guest and actually rise to the status of *permanent resident alien,* or *gêr*. In fact, if we want to understand the situation of strangers in biblical times, we should make a study of *gêr*. To appreciate the nature of the call of the Chosen People and of the Covenant itself, this kind of study is required. Moreover, if we missionaries are to contextualize ourselves within other cultures, we certainly need to understand the possibilities of strangers and to learn how to be strangers in a strange land. The biblical record can help us.

The history of the patriarchs is the history of boundaries and transitions, exile and incorporation. Abraham was a stranger *(gêr)* in Egypt (Gen 12:10; 17:8; 20:1). Likewise, Moses in Midian (Ex 2:22) and Lot in Sodom (Gen 19:9) were *gêr*.

The *gêr* occupied an ambiguous place in society and enjoyed an uncertain position. Lack of sharp focus or of clarity of role and status was emblematic of a *gêr*. Though a *gêr* could expect not to be oppressed, and indeed to receive charity and even asylum, the latter could never be *demanded*. The *gêr* therefore might sometimes be exploited or refused respect, and so it was advisable to have a protector or a patron. It was possible, as a stranger *(gêr),* to rise to some social prominence, to become wealthy, even to possess land. *But such a stranger was never assimilated to the very center of society.*

We saw the importance of *legitimation* for strangers;[2] the same social mechanism applies to biblical strangers. We also noted the virtual impossibility of missionaries becoming completely incorporated. They may be accommodated and given protection. They may find an appropriate level of relevance and become part of local agendas. But they cannot expect to become pivotal or essential except in unusual or extreme circumstances.

The story of *gêr*, however, goes beyond the cases of individual aliens or outsiders. It becomes a theme running right through the history of the Chosen People and on into the mainstream of our own (Christian) history. Israel itself was *gêr* in a theological sense. Israel existed—settled, dwelt, lived, flourished—in the land that was Yahweh's land and not simply a commodity belonging to the people.[3] Individual members of the Chosen People would have been taught to think of themselves as a *gêr* of Yahweh, with all the implications of that relationship (Ps 38:13; 118:19). This is critically important for our understanding and for our missionary lives. Israel had to go through a gradual and painful *process* as the people learned to respect Yahweh. Similarly we have to learn to be strangers in strange lands, to discover appropriate behavior, and to show respect to our hosts. Lessons from biblical history offer enlightenment for our own journey.

Some might argue that with Jesus things have changed and that old lessons and old relationships do not apply. They might deny that the Christian is *gêr*. After all, St. Paul does say, "So you are no longer aliens or foreign visitors; you are citizens like all the saints, and part of God's household" (Eph 2:19). But in reference to "the world" we are indeed *gêr*: we have here no abiding city (Heb 13:14). So we might profitably ask ourselves some questions. What do we need to learn from biblical scholarship in order to understand the notion of "stranger" better? Have we—wrongly—resisted becoming strangers in other cultures? Have we tried to manipulate other people and define ourselves rather than allow ourselves to be defined by others? How might we learn to know and to take our place as strangers in other cultures? Perhaps the most fundamental question: is it possible to be truly missionary in the spirit of Jesus *without* undertaking to be strangers ourselves?

JESUS AS STRANGER

In the climactic twenty-fifth chapter of Matthew's gospel, Jesus—the *Son of Man (huios tou anthropou)*—presides over the Last Judgment. We recall the majestic cadences: "I was hungry, and you gave me food; I was thirsty and you gave me drink; I was a stranger and you welcomed me. . . ." We understand the implications and we take them seriously. We are sensitized to giving food, giving drink, welcoming people, and so on. This is excellent as far as it goes. It just does not go far enough; it does not carry us where it should.

Each of these Corporal Works of Mercy presents us with a pair, a dyad: hungry one/food provider; thirsty one/drink provider; stranger/host, and so on, through the last three dyads: naked person/clothes provider; sick person/visitor; and prisoner/visitor. We may take these works of mercy seriously but *tend to respond as the provider, not as the needy person*. We may be extremely sensitive to hungry or thirsty people, to strangers or people who need clothes, to the sick or imprisoned. But though the Corporal Works of Mercy engage us with needy persons, in almost every case we act from a position of superiority and initiative, even of control.

Jesus did not say, "I want you to be kind to the stranger (the *other*)," but, "I was a stranger (myself)." If we are to be as Jesus was, we cannot be content to help strangers: *we must become strangers ourselves*. Being kind to strangers is worthy and necessary; but it is not sufficient. Jesus humbled himself (Phil 2:6), but this point is prefaced with a very pointed statement: "In your minds you must be the same as Christ Jesus" (2:5). This leaves us with some significant challenges.

STRANGER RELATIONS

The stranger/host dyad is unequal. The host is always *one up* in relation to the stranger, who is always *one down* relative to the host. A person who is kind to strangers acts from a position of structural and moral superiority; the stranger who receives kindness is always in a position of structural and moral inferiority. This is simply the way things are. It is not that strangers are intrinsically inferior, simply that they are structurally or socially inferior. Likewise for the superiority of the host. When Jesus says, "I was a stranger" (Mt 25:35), he is acknowledging his social position as inferior. But when we say we will be kind to strangers, we are *not* doing what Jesus did: we are locating ourselves as social superiors. It is rather easier to be kind to a stranger than actually to become one. This is what we must ponder.

In order to understand the dynamics of the relationship between strangers and hosts—and between hosts and strangers—we distinguish two scenarios: first, when you are the stranger and I am the host; and second, when you are the host and I am the stranger.

When you are stranger and I am host

In this situation *I am in control.* I have the initiative. Events unfold at my home, in my village, on my turf. I am superordinate or one up; you are subordinate or one down. I have more authority than you. I may be very kind and indulgent, but I hold an initiative that you do not and cannot. You not only depend on me to an extent; you are indebted to me.

If the situation lasts indefinitely, it can create *internalized oppression:* a frequently unresolved or only partially expressed anger, rage, or hatred due to the burden of indebtedness spiced with feelings of impotence. Historically, the oppression of a perceived subordinate has produced such internalized oppression in African Americans or Native Americans in the United States, Irish people in Ireland, Hutus in Rwanda, and any systematically oppressed or subordinated people. Feelings of internalized oppression can be generated by insensitive missionaries in the people they encounter. Internalized oppression itself is due to outsiders usurping the role of superordinate and failing to act as appropriate strangers in other people's native land.

When you are host and I am stranger

In this situation *you are in control*. You have the initiative. Events unfold at your home, in your village, on your turf. You are superordinate or one up; I am subordinate or one down. You have more authority than I. You may be very kind and indulgent, but you hold an initiative that I do not and cannot. I not only depend on you to an extent; I am indebted to you.

If the situation lasts indefinitely, it can create *dominance* by you and unwholesome dependence—even resentment—by me. It can cause me to lose my own self-esteem, and even to see my own capacities wither. It can lead to serious dysfunction and produce violence or passive aggressiveness in me.

From either/or to both/and

In Jesus we see the leader, the master, the teacher. As such, he was appropriately in charge, in control, using initiative and inspiring others. But he did not remain in this position for very long: he often yielded the initiative, affirmed others, humbled himself. Not only did he do this; he demanded it of others. First he reminded them that he was legitimately one up: "You call me Master and Lord, and rightly; so I am" (Jn 13:14). Then he called their attention to what he had just done, to the surprise and consternation of the twelve: he has just washed their feet. This was the epitome of servanthood, requiring Jesus literally to go one down.

Jesus made subordination, going one down, a requirement of his followers: "If anyone wants to be a follower of mine, let him [her] renounce himself [herself]" (Lk 9:23). Yet in the very same chapter of Luke's gospel, we encounter the disciples wrangling about hierarchy and competing to be the greatest. Again Jesus subverted the established order and called his followers to do likewise. We read, "Whoever exalts himself will be humbled, and whoever humbles himself will be exalted" (Lk 14:11). Calling James and John, he said, "You know that among the pagans the rulers lord it over them, and their great men make their authority felt. This is not to happen among you. No; anyone who wants to be great among you must be your servant, and anyone who wants to be first among you must be your slave, just as the Son of Man came not to be served but to serve, and to give his life as a ransom for many" (Mt 20:25-28).

Not that Jesus was never served by others: clearly he was. John's gospel records Jesus as a wedding guest (2:1-12) and a guest at supper hosted by Martha and Mary (12:1-8). A theme of the synoptic gospels is table fellowship, and Jesus is often the recipient, whether dining again with Martha and Mary (Lk 10:38-42), as guest of Simon the leper (Mk 14:3-9), or inviting himself to Zacchaeus's house (Lk 19:1-10). We know these stories well.

But Jesus also acted as host, entertaining motley groups of tax collectors and sinners (Mk 2:15-17) and on one occasion challenging his host with these words:

> When you give a lunch or dinner, do not ask your friends, brothers, relations or rich neighbors, for fear they repay your courtesy by inviting you in return. No; when you have a party, invite the poor, the crippled, the lame and the blind; that they cannot pay you back means that you are fortunate, because repayment will be made to you when the virtuous rise again. (Lk 14:12-14)

For Jesus, the solution to the problem of hierarchy and dominance was to be both master and servant, both one up and one down, both host and guest, both stranger and host. He challenged his disciples to adopt the same behavior patterns, thus undermining the tendency either to self-aggrandizement or to competitive display. Jesus required the open handedness of the host and the graciousness of the guest or stranger. Repayment was not to be demanded, especially of the poor. Rather, generosity to the poor was intended to generate real (though asymmetrical) relationships, even friendship. The poor may not be able to *repay*, but they can make a *return* by their free acceptance and gracious thanks.

HOST, GUEST, AND STRANGER

Being the host has its own rewards; the weight of responsibility is balanced or exceeded by the glow of satisfaction hospitality brings. Being the guest can be equally rewarding; to be acclaimed and feted may be very congenial. But when the "guest" is really a stranger, things are not always so pleasant or predictable; a stranger is in an ambiguous position, dependent and vulnerable, though in principle quite responsible and socially important. It is easy to see why the roles of host or guest are more congenial than that of stranger.

Yet Jesus said unequivocally, "*I* was a stranger." Looking at his life, we see that he actually cultivated the role and status of stranger. But it is equally true that other people treated him as such. As a self-declared stranger, he had nowhere to lay his head (Mt 8:20); he consorted with undesirables (Mt 9:10-13), making himself a pariah. He called his disciples to emulate him and warned them of the radical estrangement it would provoke (Mt 10:24-39). And he constantly crossed boundaries, whether territorial, religious, or ethnic (Mt 15:21-31), or boundaries of gender (Lk 8:1-3) or kinship (Lk 8:19-21).

But his life is also marked by other people's treatment of him as a stranger or outcast. He came to his own and his own did not receive him (Jn 1:11). He went home and his relatives tried to restrain him, convinced that he was out of his mind (Mk 3:21). Returning from the wilderness, he came to Nazareth, where he initially found favor; but in no time at all, people became enraged and threw him out of town (Lk 4:16-30). Clearly this man was regarded as strange, and became estranged from many people. "I was a stranger" is a measure of his vocation and his response.

The disciple is not greater than the master. What they did to the one they will do to the other (Mt 10:17-42). Discipleship is a costly business; its price is estrangement, being regarded as strange. Those who follow Jesus must choose to be strangers.

To choose to be stranger is to undertake an inferior role, but it is also to take the risk that others might practice genuine hospitality and exercise their full humanness. In other words, it is to undertake encounters, to promote relationships, and to facilitate mutuality. As people who cross boundaries and enter other worlds, we have no business to claim the role of host or one up, and every reason to acquiesce in our role as guest/ stranger or one down. Such is the interplay of human relationships, even a stranger may assume the role of host. But this requires both time's passage and the host's satisfaction.

To be able to embrace both the role and status of stranger and that of host is not a matter of manipulating relationships or "getting even." It is much more subtle. It can prevent *oppressive* asymmetrical relationships. An outsider (stranger) may remain an outsider and a stranger, but appropriate role switching helps create a measure of true mutuality, even though structurally the relationship remains asymmetrical. A parent remains a parent but can learn from time to time to receive, to give, to be guest as well as servant. This is one of the symbolic functions of Mother's Day, Father's Day, or birthdays. Even the internalized oppression can be neutralized if the one down can sometimes be one up. Many institutions like the armed services have long traditions of role reversal, with officers serving the ranks at least once a year. Unwholesome dependency can be mitigated if host and guest or host and stranger occasionally change places.

Finally, careful attention to the obligation to control and concede, to serve and to be served, to give and to receive will help to build up a community that is not rigidly stratified by rank or privilege but truly striving for mutual indebtedness and the celebration of a common humanity. But unless those who wish to treat strangers well are also willing to become strangers themselves and take the risk that others will treat them well, such a community can never be achieved.

As host, Jesus took appropriate initiatives, gathered people, served them, and used his one up position for the benefit of others. He helped to restore dignity to outcasts and marginalized people, those demeaned as *other*, and strangers. As host, he was necessarily one up, and they were one down.

As stranger, Jesus revealed himself as the *kenotic*, or self-emptying, one and showed that it is entirely possible to relinquish control and to lay aside privilege. He allowed other people to be the host, to take initiatives, to make choices, and to be of service. As stranger, Jesus was necessarily one down, and another was one up.

THE STRANGER ON THE ROAD

The account in Luke's gospel (24:13-35) is a superb illustration of the possibilities a stranger can open up. We have already considered a handful of advantages. The Emmaus story offers us the chance to see exactly how the example of Jesus can help those who would be missionaries and strangers.

The context is important. It is the first day of a new week, and two disciples of Jesus are leaving town, dejected and even disillusioned (v. 17) by the execution of Jesus. They might have been encouraged by reports of the empty tomb, but women (v. 22) were unreliable witnesses, and they chose not to believe their own—presumably male—friends (v. 24). These almost-fugitives are essential to Luke's purposes, which are to teach lessons of universal significance: missionary lessons, we might say.

The disciples are too preoccupied to notice Jesus, who initiates the conversation with a question. The immediate response is to identify Jesus as a stranger.[4] To them he appears as *unknown, strange, not familiar, not belonging to the group*. It is precisely as such that Jesus allows the encounter to develop.

Jesus *questioned* the "insiders," and their initial depression gave way to some animated and self-committing talk (v. 21). The stranger simply *listened* attentively as they told their story. Whereupon he *responded* in a rather surprising way: "You foolish men!" he said. But presumably before they could respond, he took their own story and *reinterpreted* it with conviction, authority, and evidently plausibility. Still not disclosing his identity, Jesus *accompanied* the travelers to their destination and *did not impose;* but in a *courteous* manner, he prepared to continue. He *was invited*—with some enthusiasm (v. 28)—*to be their guest*. The stranger has now been transformed by the hosts into a bona fide guest, invited and not self-imposed, deferential and not self-important.

The stranger grows increasingly significant from this point on. First it is Jesus, the stranger, who takes the bread and offers a blessing. Why? Perhaps it would otherwise have been omitted; perhaps Jesus was offering a clue to his identity by showing his hands; perhaps it was a gesture of authentic service and relationship: *giving* thanks (to God) and *giving* bread (to his hosts). Whatever the reason, this action was a "releasing mechanism": their eyes were opened (v. 31), just as their eyes had been held closed or bound (v. 16). They recognized him then, just as he disappeared, leaving them with their own heightened emotions and reactions: mouths babbling, hearts burning (v. 32).

Thanks to the stranger the disciples now understood the meaning of their own experiences. He had interpreted what they could not. Their lives were revolutionized, and they literally turned and retraced their steps, from despondency to hope and from disbelief to faith. They could now augment the evidence of the Resurrection with the witness of their own senses.

We cannot fail to notice the attitude of Jesus the stranger, who *questioned, listened, responded, reinterpreted, accompanied, did not impose, was courteous, was invited,* and *became a guest.* It is a recipe for us. Jesus accepted the disciples on their own terms, in their own context, with their own preoccupations. His attention to them also provided him with a means of access to the deepest levels of their lives. He waited for an opportunity to engage with their agenda and to become relevant. In the encounter between hosts and stranger, enlightenment was offered and received, conversion became possible. Meeting at the table offered a moment of fellowship and sharing, not only of food but of meaning. It was a missionary moment.

Following the example of Jesus, we might aspire to breaking through in other people's lives, to finding how to become part of their agenda, to discovering how mission can become an intrinsic part of life. Following Jesus, we can learn how to share stories and how enriching that can be. Following Jesus, we can appreciate how alternative interpretations or responses can clarify and resolve.

MISSIONARY POTENTIAL

We do not leave the security of home in order to become loners. If we did, our approach would be seriously flawed. We are committed to sharing the Good News of Jesus Christ and to announcing the present and approaching Realm of God. These are essentially social activities. The Realm of God, the Body of Christ, bespeaks relationship, interrelatedness. It is fortunate that those who come as strangers are actually making the first tentative steps toward encounter and relationship. How can we go wrong? We are strangers, and strangers are half of a pair; if we build on the initial encounter, we will be communicating appropriately. If only it were that easy!

We know several things: that the host's agenda must be respected; that strangers may be manipulated; that we may have a low tolerance for friction in our lives;[5] and that we are so well socialized, it may be difficult for us to question our own belief or behavior. The danger is that we might remain unreconstructed or unconverted strangers. If so (and because we are already seen as strange or abnormal), we might remain indefinitely irrelevant or not pertinent though we live in another world for years.

We are living through a period of serious reappraisal of the missionary task and of our relationship with local people and local churches. Many missionaries are much less certain of the best way forward and much more aware of some past mistakes. This need not undermine the missionary commitment, but it ought to moderate intemperate missionary zeal or arrogance. Perhaps in our uncertainty or self-consciousness we will give greater credence to the Holy Spirit and the local people. This would surely facilitate more respectful and collaborative missionary methods.

Strangers can show respect for hosts, admit their uncertainty and powerlessness, ask for assistance, and thus demonstrate their openness, integrity, and desire for relationships. But we missionaries are sometimes our own worst enemies. The very qualities that facilitate our cross-cultural encounters (adaptability, initiative, risk taking, creativity, independence, and so on) may create problems for our hosts. The host *needs* to see indications of dependence, deference, conformity, and predictability. So we must live in creative tension. We must trust the skills and virtues that facilitate our survival in other cultures; but we must listen to the voices and read the expectations and reactions of our hosts in order to adapt and be comprehensible—able to be understood and able, literally, to be grasped or embraced.

To realize our potential as cross-cultural communicators and allies, we need to work constantly to *accept our marginal and ambiguous status*. We are not the primary agents of mission but collaborators and assistants: servants. The primary agent is God's Spirit, and we must not muzzle the Spirit or try to wrest initiatives from God. The primary respondents to God's call are the people themselves. We may need to learn how that modifies our own position. If we try to intercept God's message in the hopes of relaying it to the people, we may badly distort it. If we try to model the only possible and authentic response to the gospel, we will certainly reflect only a shadow of God's glory. If we presume too quickly to be God's mouthpiece, we may overlook the still, small voice with which God likes to animate the silence. If we patronize and dominate the interaction with other people, they may never gain access to the light so necessary for their own growth. It is good for us to be on the edges, at the margins of our own worlds. That locates us where we really have to work with others. It also calls us to learn the meaning of their language and their world.

All this demands of us a role shift and a status change. The measure of our missionary commitment is that we do not cling to privilege and comfortable certainties but choose to become servants and learners. That is difficult for anyone but especially one sent by an institutional church with a proud history. We are called to repent and be converted as much as we are called to call others to repentance and conversion.

Not far from our familiar world as well as further afield, there are many marginal people and marginal groups or castes. Serious Christians should be among them because that is our calling. But our "being with" must be compassionate and encouraging and neither threatening nor self-important. It is not enough for us to know that our world is populated with refugees, outcasts, prostitutes, prisoners, or homeless people. It is not enough for us to know about, or even to know in passing, a few abandoned, abused, exploited, or condemned people. As disciples of Jesus, we are called to do as he did: to make friends among the poor, to love concretely and not in the abstract, to spend and be spent for others. As we try to do so, we will become more aware of how shallow we are and how far from the people. True encounter with the other will expose us to the glare of God's justice. Then we will see increasingly that we contribute to oppression through sexism, consumerism, ageism, clericalism, racism, classism, and the rest. We will admit that these offenses are not just against abstract categories but against real persons loved by God if not yet by us. As disciples, we cannot legitimately escape from the marginalized and the needy. As we encounter them, we discover that there is less and less escape from ourselves.

Christians must be in the business of constantly trying to read the signs of the times. The twentieth century saw human misery on an unprecedented scale. The twenty-first must not catch us closing our eyes to injustice or turning deaf ears to the cries of the poor even as we speak words that promise new life. How well are we supporting people incarcerated as political prisoners or women trapped in the morass of prostitution? How effectively are we reaching out to those caught in addictive behavior or exploited as members of minorities, whether ethnic, sexual, religious, or economic? How close are we to the powerless, the weak, the exploited, the homeless, the poverty-stricken, or those without status? As people who cross boundaries and labor at the margins, we should be very close because these evils proliferate at the margins, where real people are ground down and where hope grows ever dimmer. Unless we are close to people, our work is vain and our words are hollow.

To accept to be marginal and a stranger is to place oneself at the disposition of the God who calls. To embrace the status of a servant or stranger is to approach and empower other people and to dare to infuse some trust into a world where self-interest and suspicion so often walk unimpeded. To choose to be a stranger is to be a true disciple of Jesus.

JESUS: STRANGER AND MISSIONARY

Jesus "did not cling to his equality with God, but emptied himself, to assume the condition of a slave, and became as [we] are" (Phil 2:6-7). We simply cannot internalize this passage without being profoundly affected by its implications. The condition of a slave is not radically different from that of a stranger waiting on a host or negotiating the one down status. The stranger depends on other people's initiative and indulgence. The stranger waits to be given a social identity. The stranger is not self-made or independent. If Jesus had come as a powerful, high-status, self-important, demanding figure, insisting on privileges and the dignity of his office, what respect would that have shown for others, and what freedom would it have extended to them? He was not like that; he came as a servant-slave *(doulos)*. He came as a stranger.

Jesus was sent on an urgent mission to the victimized and those on the margins (both near ["the lost sheep of the House of Israel": Mt 15:24] and far ["all who labor"; gentiles; Samaritans; "everyone": Lk 16:16]). Nevertheless he had no permanent base or home of his own. A carpenter's son and a carpenter himself, he was not from the right family to make much of a mark. He had little personal status. In due course, Jesus deliberately chose his disciples from people at the religious and social margins, including, of course, women. His marginal ministry took him to the boundaries where he encountered people living at the edge: lepers and other sick or contaminated people, those living in caves or in the hills, tax collectors and "sinners," even little children.

Jesus had nothing to gain in terms of status or reputation from the people he frequented; they had nothing to give. Yet he walked with the crippled and talked with the mute, he ate with the starving and drank with the dry. His faith was strengthened by the infidel Syrophoenician woman and the Roman soldier, and he was edified by sinners and purified by an impure woman's ointment. In the heart of paradox and reversal he found and brought clarity and restoration. For all *our* preparation, rationalization, education, and orientation, unless we get to the heart of Jesus and his approach to other people, we will never get to the heart of the gospel or transplant it into any body.[6]

Not only did Jesus seek out and move among such people. He took the powerless and empowered them, took the withered and regenerated them, took the wounded and healed them. He showed them that they mattered and that God loved them. He needed them as they needed him, because he needed relationship. But he also sent them to teach others, to be the media for his message. As J.D. Crossan put it, Jesus was a "nobody" who gathered "a community of nobodies." And together they changed the world, from the margins to the centers. Jesus the marginal missionary calls, co-missions, and sends us too.

These forgotten people abound today. They are addicts (alcohol-, food-, drug-, tobacco-, power-, sex-addicts). They are victims of the *-isms* of others. They are throwaways of the modern world (refugees, migrants, survivors of war). They are handicapped or challenged (physically, mentally, emotionally, morally). And yet, no less than us, they are counted among the people for whom Jesus came. They are not far from where we live: just out of sight and maybe out of mind, but not beyond reach.

We are called to become and to be missionary *in the Spirit of Jesus:*

nothing less and nothing else. If Jesus came as a servant, slave, and stranger, and if he operated as such people do, we must become his followers in the same spirit. Jesus deliberately used the potential of his socially inferior identity and attracted the attention of the curious: "Who is this man? Can anything good come out of his place? Where does he come from?" The answer, then and now, is the same: "Come and see." So what *do* we see if we look?

- Jesus moved, listened, responded, shared, and adapted. He did not lord it over others. He was gracious. Jesus rejoiced and he wept, he knew when to ask for advice and he was able very simply to give advice.
- Jesus identified and worked with the local community. He was collaborative, picking unlikely people to be close to him and to carry the responsibility after him. He was compassionate, taking pity on the crowds around him and the people in general but also encountering the man in the tree and the woman at the well: individuals in their particularity.
- Jesus shared himself, his time and energy, his presence and power, his prayer and his passion. He effectively incarnated and contextualized himself. He discovered the significance of gift-exchange: of giving and receiving and returning, of making moral relationships of mutual indebtedness.
- Jesus was able to name his needs. He was psychologically and spiritually grounded and rooted. He could state his need for privacy and prayer, for companionship and consolation. He did not burn out through misplaced zeal: he was able to withdraw, to be alone, to go to the hills.
- Jesus experienced linguistic and cultural adaptation, transition, assimilation. He used forms of language that engaged and entertained and informed people, telling stories, preaching, spinning webs of words, holding people spellbound. He made sense. He connected with his audience, using question and answer, dialogue, gesture, participation.

So what *do* we see if we look at Jesus? And how *do* we apply the lessons to ourselves? Jesus was always set for the falling and rising of many; his magnetism saw to that. In whatever he did or said, Jesus never became less than challenging and relevant[7] to quite disparate groups of people: insiders and outsiders, important people and nobodies, self-righteous and sinners, women and men—and children. Can Jesus, servant-stranger, teacher-learner, host-guest, first-last, one up–one down, teach us and inspire us to be more credible preachers-of-the-living-word, more passionate lovers-of-the-unlovely-and-unloved, more Christlike missionaries?

STRANGERS, FOR GOD'S SAKE

The idea that Christians welcome strangers (Mt 25:35-45) is challenging and attractive. Certainly we are called to reach out to the needy, the stranger, the *other*. But the other is not always or inevitably a stranger; and sometimes it is *I* who am the needy one, the stranger. Christians committed to mission should be sensitive to the role switching that is part of every encounter. Nor should we think we will always be treated as we might like, when we venture beyond our comfortable world. To do as Jesus did, we need to be willing—and must consciously undertake—to become strangers in strange lands and even in our own. We are called to be countercultural: not to worship Caesar but to be followers of The Way. We have here no abiding city (Heb 13:14).

If we cross boundaries, we enter other people's lives. If we are not strangers (appropriately one down and hoping to receive hospitality on our hosts' terms), we are intruders. People who are quite well disposed to strangers will be confused or threatened by intruders. People who are more than willing to be hospitable are not willing to be taken advantage of. Some Christians are gracious and trusting of their hosts: they allow themselves to be contextualized as *strangers*. They do not try to control, dictate, seize initiatives, or proselytize. It is more likely, other things being equal, that relationships can then develop in a mutually satisfying way. Such mutuality is the only basis for authentic evangelization.

For many years I had worked among poor and homeless people in Chicago, preparing and serving meals, trying to be unostentatious, thinking I was serving as Jesus might have served. Week after week I would spend an overnight at the shelter, sleeping under the piano, comparing mission in Chicago and mission in Africa, and wondering why it did not feel quite right.

One night, while serving the meal, I noticed Rosalee. I could see her out of the corner of my eye and knew she was heading in my direction. Rosalee was mentally ill and not able to live alone, but she was a live wire with a loud mouth. She could be devastatingly perceptive. Without preamble, she challenged me: "You know the trouble with you, Tony?"—and I knew she intended to tell it to me straight. "The trouble with you," she said, "is that you don't ask *us* what *we* want to eat."

I was flustered, defensive, and upset, and I said, "You mean you don't like the food?" "The food is fine, " said Rosalee. "So, do you want something different?" I asked her. "No," she said quietly.

But I still didn't understand, and I said, "So, if the food's all right, and if you don't want anything else, what's the problem?"

"The problem," said Rosalee, "is that you don't ask *us*. If you ask us, we'll tell you that we like the food and we want it. But then it will be our choice, and not just yours."

That was perhaps the most important pastoral lesson I ever learned at first hand. It came from a "crazy woman." Sometimes such people tell the truth in a way our friends never would and maybe never could.

Every week after that, the women at the shelter would say "thank you" after the meal. Before that, they never had. And I had always wondered why.

There is nothing automatic about the process of forging relationships. We may not realize that we intrude even though we try to be unobtrusive. We may not realize how staunchly we strive to be in control or how we presume to know what's best for others. We may not realize that others have a right to be consulted about our best intentions on their behalf. But we *are* intruders, we *are* disruptive, and we may not even have asked permission to invade another world. We may not be sensitive to the feelings, needs, and even the rights of others. We may fail to share our own feelings of isolation and ambivalence, either with our peers or with those we come to serve. Even worse, we may experience all the normal features of culture shock and of being strangers—the transition, the frustration and restlessness, the ambivalence, marginality, and *liminality*—without really understanding what is happening. If so, we miss a golden opportunity to share some of this with those we encounter or to use it as a way to become authentic missionaries. We should thank God, then, if someone like Rosalee shares her insight.

If we do recognize that we are experiencing a stranger/intruder syndrome, there is lots we can do. We can remind ourselves that we are marginal, transitional, ambiguous in other people's lives, and we can try to accept what that entails. We can actually choose to venture further and further from our comfort zone and to trust ourselves to those who live at the edges of our comfortable little world. We can reflect that Jesus, sent to the outcasts and those on the margins, also had to choose, to seek, and to find the needy. If we gather all this knowledge and experience into prayer, we can allow ourselves to be graced as strangers.

And yet . . . so strong are our socialization processes and expectations, we may balk at the challenge. We may simply not identify ourselves as poor with the poor, weak with the weak, or marginal with the marginal. We may, implicitly at least, see ourselves as strong, resourceful, independent, pioneering, personal saviors. We may even stop short and refuse to go to seek out and find the needy, expecting them to come to us and maybe even thinking we are giving them the initiative in this. A stranger's identity is not easy to wear, and missionaries are prone to misunderstand it, misapply it, or rebel against it.[8]

Historically (due to cultural, colonial, or evangelical perspectives), missionaries sometimes reacted quite strongly in an attempt to reverse their stranger status as quickly as possible. They demanded to be treated with respect, as guests, celebrities, even civilizers or God-bringers. This was, of course, not always so then, nor is it today; but such attitudes sowed seeds of confusion that have survived for many, many years. One consequence is that some of the people we go to today already expect us to be difficult to deal with. The sins of previous generations may leave their mark today and tomorrow. Those of us who take mission seriously must also examine our own self-image. If it is crudely that of giver, initiator, superior, or teacher, then its sad effects will continue to be felt by another generation of missionaries and those who receive them.

A final note of warning needs to be heard, even by people who truly seek the well-being of others and who truly believe that *goodwill is not enough*. These sensitive and mature Christians use neither gospel nor Christianity to intimidate or proselytize. The warning is this: in recent years we have become increasingly aware of some of the more unintended and dangerous consequences of missionary activity. We know our potential for opening up local worlds or microcosms to be a positive and even necessary component of evangelization. But there are side effects that we must address.

This delicate and complex issue warrants much greater sympathy from missionaries than it has so far received. The place for an extended consideration is not here, but an image may spur reflection. Think of the manicured green of a golf course. Perhaps the drainage is not effective or the layout could be improved. But if someone cuts a deep furrow up the fairway with a heavy tractor and plow, things will never be the same again. If the resident club members have not been consulted, they will be understandably put out. If, as the plow rolls in, they are informed that a presidential committee made the decision, they might be quite outraged. But perhaps they signed a member's contract, and the small print already allows for this "improvement." Then they might feel powerless, and it could be years before their resentment surfaces. If the members had been consulted in a timely fashion, they might have been given some freedom of choice or some alternative provisions. At least a majority would have been part of the decision to modify the golf course. They might even have felt sufficiently involved in the process to commit themselves to a long-term vision for golf course, benefactors, and beneficiaries.

Missionaries are not imperialists but agents of a God of freedom and of love. We may take initiatives in good faith, only to find a generation later that we have contributed to a situation worse than the one we encountered. It is not enough to wring our hands and blame the local people. We have an initial responsibility to determine whether we are perceived as relevant to local agendas: to apprise, to listen, and to interpret. We also have a responsibility not to abandon the people we claim to serve.

Because of their different pasts, insiders and outsiders will always have some difficulty in positioning or relating to each other. If a stranger clings to privacy, a host will not be able to retain the initiative or to "position" the stranger. If a host seems too curious or demanding, the stranger may feel overwhelmed. But if a stranger is kept at arm's length and treated very formally, it can become uncomfortable and oppressive.

On the other hand, if a host remains indulgent and in control, everyone might become resentful. Where resources are stretched, a host will begin to resent the stranger. If a stranger feels powerless to reciprocate and to relax, the stranger will begin to resent the host. And if the local community suffers, its members will begin to resent both host and stranger.

Relationships between insiders and outsiders, strangers and hosts, tend to preclude true reciprocity, frankness, and collaboration. If each party wishes to move forward, it will only be as each begins to sense that formal relationships are inadequate and something else must be built on their foundation. But who takes the initiative? The insider is unlikely to know what the outsider has in mind; the stranger-outsider may sense resistance from insider-hosts who want to hold on to their legitimate position of strength. So the next stages of the journey may never be reached to everyone's satisfaction. Mutual respect may not blossom into true friendship unless there is a real basis of equality and shared knowledge. Gift-exchange is more than the exchange of commodities: it is an enduring moral relationship. It can stand as a model for those who go in Christ's name, though some missionaries and some local people never achieve enduring moral relationships. But better by far to have tried and failed than never to have tried at all.

A STRANGER CONCLUSION

After trekking for many miles under a tropical sun, I arrived, hot and needy, in a remote West African village.

After greeting the chief, I submitted to some stroking and poking by the more adventurous, giggling children. Many of the people had never seen a foreign stranger before, and some of the smaller children ran away in tears.

I then asked the chief for access to the toilet facilities. His response was a broad smile and an even broader gesture: he gestured by opening wide his arms and turning his hips, embracing the whole horizon over which I had just come.

So I retraced my steps and found a spot in the primeval forest. Huge fallen trees lay silent and decomposing; an awesome sight. Thick, impenetrable vegetation was all around. A perfect and very private place.

But at a critical moment, I noticed a pair of eyes looking straight at me. Then another, and another; I was not alone!

Clothing myself in my dignity and the rest of my attire and

pretending not to have noticed or to be in any way self-conscious, I returned to the village.

But the eyes were there before me. Everyone in the village was waiting, laughing, and gesticulating in my direction. Among the giggles, the gossip and the revelation were passed with great relish and a loud voice: "He is white *all over!*"

It can be very important for us to submit to some mild indignity as we allow ourselves to be tamed, contextualized, and appreciated. The communication breakthrough that day was critically significant: now I was "unmasked." Even though I was still rather odd and definitely a strange stranger, I was at least identifiably human.

Around the middle of the second century, when the followers of Jesus of Nazareth were a curiosity, they began to attract the attention of the one ups, the socially significant people. One of these, Diognetus by name, attempted to discover more about these "Christians." The anonymous *Epistle to Diognetus*[9] is an attempt by one of them to explain who they were and what they stood for. It is rather long and a little dualistic; it is understandably partial and biased; but it offers wisdom that we could profitably travel with. Here, in conclusion (and with inclusive language), are some extracts:

> Christians are not distinguished from the rest of people either by country, speech, or customs; the fact is, they nowhere settle in cities of their own; they use no peculiar language; they cultivate no eccentric mode of life. Certainly, this creed of theirs is no discovery due to some fancy of inquisitive people; nor do they, as some do, champion a doctrine of human origin. Yet while they dwell in both Greek and non-Greek cities as each one's lot was cast, and conform to the customs of the country in dress, food, and mode of life in general, the whole tenor of their way of living stamps it as worthy of admiration and admittedly extraordinary.
>
> They reside in their respective countries, but only as aliens. They take part in everything as citizens and put up with everything as foreigners. Every foreign land is their home, and every home a foreign land.
>
> They spend their days on earth, but hold citizenship in heaven. They obey the established laws, but in their private lives they rise above the laws. They love everyone and are persecuted by everyone. They are poor and enrich many; destitute of everything, they abound in everything. They are dishonored and in their dishonor they find their glory. They are calumniated and are vindicated. They are reviled and they bless; they are insulted and they render honor.
>
> Doing good they are penalized as evildoers; when penalized, they

rejoice because they are quickened into life. The Jews make war on them as foreigners; the Greeks persecute them; and those who hate them are at a loss to explain their hatred.

In a word, what the soul is in the body, that Christians are in the world. The soul is spread through all the members of the body, and the Christians throughout the cities of the world. The soul dwells in the body, but is not part and parcel of the body; so Christians dwell in the world, but are not part and parcel of the world.

Christians are known as such in the world, but their religion remains invisible. The world, though suffering no wrong from Christians, hates them because they oppose its pleasures. Christians love those that hate them.

Christians are shut up in the world as in a prison, yet it is precisely they that hold the world together.

Christians, when penalized, show a daily increase in number on that account. Such is the important post to which God has assigned them, and they are not at liberty to desert it.

. . . COMING BACK

GOOD MANNERS ARE NOT OPTIONAL

Returning one last time to Africa, here is a story about "coming back."

Augustine Baio was large and genial. I liked him but did not really trust him. I always thought he would take advantage if I turned my back. He was a self-styled "builder" and he was to build a simple mission house. My knowledge of building was scant, but between us we drew up a plan of sorts, and he assured me he could turn it into a building. I left him mixing cement as I set off for a week's trek to a number of villages.

On my return, I had to wade through a mile of swamp before climbing the gradual rise to my mission. But as I approached—in slow motion because of the swamp—I could see what looked like a new shape against the skyline: my new mission house! But the closer I approached, the more I knew something was very wrong. At last I could see that a new wall stood there, maybe *fifty feet long, perhaps ten feet high, but without a single break for doors or windows!* It was like the Great Wall of China.

I lost my patience then, and I started to rant. As I approached, my voice got louder and my insults more barbed. The "builder," meanwhile, was just sitting on top of the wall looking down. I continued unabated but gradually realizing that he was actually smiling at me! Even more intemperately I shouted, "What are you *doing?"*

But Augustine was not in the least put out. His smile grew even bigger as he sat, literally looking down on me. And in a rather relaxed and understanding voice, he said, "Fadda, you did not say good morning!"

I was dumbfounded. Yet instinctively I knew how rude I had been. So, churlishly but obediently I said, "Good morning." And then I realized that Augustine had not been listening to a word I had said and that all my huffing and puffing had been completely wasted. Not

161

to have said good morning meant that the day had not begun. What had been said counted for nothing.

But I discovered something very important that morning: in being required to say "good morning" I had to look at, and greet, my temporary adversary. Even as I did so, my heart and temper cooled, and it was possible to be almost reasonable. Augustine Baio escaped my wrath. My disgraceful behavior was overlooked—not for the first time. Augustine lived to build another wall. And I had something to put down to "experience" and to resolve never to repeat.

Good manners are not optional. We must treat each other as human beings. Only when and as we do will we become human beings ourselves.

FROM MISSION IN REVERSE TO REVERSE MISSION

Perhaps God is a little like Augustine Baio. God builds while we are away doing other things. God would like us to say "good morning" when we return. God helps us to see with new eyes what has been happening in our absence. We may not understand it all. God helps us to begin again, but our eyes may need to adjust, our vision may need to clear, and our judgment may need to be modified. We may seem to be home, but we are not returning to the Homeland. This is a Newfoundland.[1] What new lessons remain to be learned? What new treasures may still be discovered?

Mission in reverse has come to describe[2] the impact made on a person by other people and other cultures:

The mission-in-reverse approach teaches that the minister can and should learn from the people ministered to—including, and perhaps especially, from the poor and marginalized people. By taking these people seriously, by listening to them . . . personal relationships are developed, and the dignity of the people is enhanced. Such presence to people is seen as necessarily allowing them to be the leaders in the relationship.[3]

The mission-in-reverse approach has been implicit throughout these pages; without it, how will we be converted? Here is another challenging characterization:

[Mission in reverse] is incarnational because it attempts to imitate Christ's own entrance into our world and his total identification with a particular culture—an identification so complete that he was not recognized as God. It is dialogic because dialogue seems to be the best way in our day to describe how we can enter the world of others, at least when dialogue is seen primarily as an attitude and not simply as a technique.[4]

By contrast, *reverse mission* is sometimes confused with mission in reverse, and sometimes considered synonymous with it. But *reverse mission* can describe the riches brought back by those who have worked in the vineyard of another culture. There may be some risk of "occasional brashness"[5] on the part of enthusiastic returnees, but they can bring a revival of hope and mission to the church they left behind. The same should be true of us. If and when we find ourselves back in the familiar territory we used to call home, we only have to look for the margins and the marginalized, to move there and invite others to do the same. Then reverse mission will be a fan to the embers, kindling flames and producing encouraging warmth where the need is greatest, while mission in reverse will allow us to experience our own continuing conversion. If we return seeking our conversion and bringing gifts, we should discover numerous opportunities for authentic gift-exchange.

In the previous pages we have used the word *missionary* and referred continuously to mission. Now we have described mission in reverse and reverse mission. Yet these pages have not explicitly or exclusively referred to mission *ad gentes*. This warrants a word of explanation. I do not seek to minimize the importance of mission to "the nations" (*gentes*). Nor would I deny its continuing validity among the peoples who have not yet even heard the Good News of Jesus Christ. But in this book it has been my intention to speak of mission as it applies to, and is required of, *every Christian*. Therefore I have not privileged either the far distant reaches of the globe or those lifetime missionaries who belong to institutionalized communities like the Mennonite Mission Board, the Division for Global Mission of the ELCA, or the numerous Roman Catholic religious orders.

All Christians share a common baptismal identity. This ought to forge a global missionary community that crosses denominational, gender, and ministerial boundaries. Such boundaries may serve a useful purpose, yet the mission confided to every baptized person should be something that can be undertaken wherever particular Christians happen to be, and together.

Unless we realize—that is, make *real*, not just intellectually but *incarnationally*—the missionary significance of our common Baptism, we perpetuate the divisions in the community that Jesus so wanted to heal. On the last night of his life he prayed,

> May they all be one. Father, may they be one in us, as you are in me and I am in you, so that the world may believe it was you who sent me. I have given them the glory you gave to me, that they may be one as we are one. With me in them and you in me, may they be so completely one that the world will realize that it was you who sent me, and that I have loved them as much as you love me. (Jn 17:21-23)

PARTICIPANT OBSERVATION
AND OBSERVANT PARTICIPATION

Participant observation is the standard methodological approach of anthropologists. It requires a serious, intensive, and rather prolonged encounter with people one does not know and to whom one appears as a stranger. But participant observation is only professional language for what every missionary must espouse. In more theological language, it is what Pope John Paul II refers to in his mission encyclical:

> Missionaries must immerse themselves in the cultural milieu of those to whom they are sent, moving beyond their own cultural limitations. Hence they must learn the language of the place in which they work, become familiar with the most important expressions of the local culture, and discover its values through direct experience. Only if they have this kind of awareness will they be able to bring to people the knowledge of the hidden mystery in a credible and fruitful way. It is not of course a matter of missionaries renouncing their own cultural identity, but of understanding, appreciating, fostering and evangelizing the culture of the environment in which they are working, and therefore of equipping themselves to communicate effectively with it, adopting a manner of living which is a sign of Gospel witness and of solidarity with the people. (RM 53)[6]

This is an expression of participant observation, which itself represents an invitation—and a challenge—for us to engage with other people's lives as we attempt to understand them. It is an invitation to *participation*. This does not imply that we unilaterally decide when and in what fashion to participate and when not to: that would be far too controlling. Participation may sometimes be required when we least feel up to it, just as it may not be warranted even though we might love to participate.

But participant observation also requires *observation*. This can be just as demanding as appropriate participation in other people's lives. Sometimes we fail to observe what we are actually doing: we have the experience but miss the meaning. We must cultivate *observant* participation, and not mere passive participation. Psychologists tell us that highly literate people forget about 98 percent of what they read, 80 percent of what they hear, and 70 percent of what they see. But when we are actively engaged, we learn much better and recall much more efficiently. When we participate by seeing *and* hearing, we retain 50 percent of the information we gather. When we are actually speaking, we retain 70 percent of the information we impart. And when we are as fully and actively engaged as possible, we retain a full 90 percent of what we were saying and doing simultaneously. Participant observation and observant participation can go a long way to enabling us to assimilate the meaning of other people's worlds and to endear ourselves to the people themselves.

EXPERIENCE AND MEANING

"We had the experience but missed the meaning." Sometimes, in revisiting former attitudes and old haunts, we are touched by enlightenment and we see as if for the first time. Perhaps we needed the past in order to make the mistakes without which we could not learn for the future nor be forgiven for the past. Perhaps in God's Providence what we thought of as the *passing over* that would carry us to our life's work was only an introduction to our *coming back,* more chastened and wiser but ready for the work that lies ahead. We had the experience; maybe only now can we understand the meaning.

But if the Christian missionary journey is really never-ending, did we accomplish anything by passing over in the first place? Again T.S. Eliot offers a wonderful insight: "To make an end is to make a beginning. The end is where we start from."[7] A growing realization of this writer is that the question itself—whether we accomplish anything—is both unanswerable and inappropriate. We indeed may have accomplished very little of any consequence. God, meanwhile, may have been quite challenged to write straight with our lives' crooked lines. God's grace may have been supporting our hosts and those who had to put up with our posturing and petulance. God's amazing grace must have been very active in minimizing the effects of our own sinfulness and arrogance as we lived in the Wonderland of other people's lives. It is one thing in hindsight to claim that mistakes are integral to life and learning; quite another to understand our own need of repentance for the mistakes that hurt other people. Sometimes I think that those who listen to and tolerate some of the excesses of missionary zeal are more virtuous and long-suffering than any missionary.

Nevertheless it does seem appropriate to suggest that one advantage of our passing over and coming back is that we can return renewed, reinvigorated, and actually relevant to the communities we may have left behind long before. Donal Dorr concludes a recent book[8] with a chapter entitled "Bringing It Back Home." He reiterates the point that Christian mission cannot be a part-time pursuit and *missionary* is not an optional adjective for Christians. *Missionary* describes every authentic Christian who cultivates a "frontier mentality" and seeks out "frontier situations." He identifies three applications of the word. *Missionary* denotes those who leave home intending never to return; those who spend significant though limited amounts of time in foreign parts; and those who remain in their own locality but seek out and work at the margins or edges, the social or geographical boundaries.

Explicitly at least, this book has addressed missionaries in the first and second of these categories. But the third kind of missionary is just as important. Implicitly at least, it has been our focus, too. The litmus test of authentic missionary Christians is a faith that impels them from the centers to the edges, from their familiar zone of comfort and control to an unfamiliar zone where comfort is compromised and ministry is undertaken. In an era of secularization and the postmodern rejection of moral responsibility, the number of practicing Christians appears in steep decline. But relatively speaking, the number of true Christian missionaries today is by no means insignificant. Many labor unsung in inner cities or institutions, supporting terminally ill brothers or sisters, working in homeless shelters, looking after the elderly who are also mentally ill, waiting for desperate people to telephone for help. In a postmodern world, many of our contemporaries are admirably capable of dealing with unpredictable individuals and open-ended situations or with personal powerlessness and institutional obtuseness. Marginal ministry challenges us all to live with paradox rather than in complete clarity. So those in the process of *coming back* may bring with them some priceless skills for continuing their missionary commitment in the Newfoundland.

Mistakes from which we learn can generate learning. Experience on which we reflect can disclose meaning. Learning and meaning can distill wisdom. But wisdom cannot mature without challenge and change, risk and resolve. Wisdom is not given to the fainthearted or overcautious. At least we can say that those who attempt to live up to their baptismal call are walking in the paths of wisdom. As Paul Clasper once said, if we want to remain the same, it is best not to venture out.[9] But we *must* venture out; we *cannot* remain within our comfort zone, for we are Christians and we are called. Therefore we must not aspire to remaining the same, but can be reassured by the prophet:

> Young men [women] may grow tired and weary,
> youths may stumble,
> but those who hope in Yahweh renew their strength,
> they put out wings like eagles.
> They run and do not grow weary,
> walk and never tire. (Isa 40:30-31)

Mission truly is an adventure. Simmel might have been correct in saying that adventure is for the young,[10] but Isaiah was right in saying that God can renew God's people's strength. We do not get any younger, but we do not need to. The renewal we experience is generated deep within us and does not depend on youthful energy. The renewal comes from the peace that Jesus promised. The world cannot give it, nor can the world take it away; but those who know this abiding peace are sustained—in a changing world and in the midst of sadness and sin—by the God whose mission they serve.

NOTES

Preface

[1]Rodney Stark, *The Rise of Christianity: How the Obscure, Marginal Jesus Movement Became the Dominant Religious Force in the Western World in a Few Centuries* (Princeton: Princeton University Press, 1996): 212, notes that the classical philosophers "regarded mercy and pity as pathological emotions" because they involve the provision of *unearned* assistance. He adds that Plato removed the problem of the needy from his ideal state by dumping them over its borders. "This was the moral climate in which Christianity taught that mercy is one of the primary virtues—that a merciful God requires humans to be merciful. Perhaps even more revolutionary was the principle that Christian love must extend beyond the boundaries of family and tribe [; ...] even beyond the Christian community."

[2]These presentations became a book called *Gifts and Strangers: Meeting the Challenge of Inculturation* (Mahwah, NJ: Paulist Press, 1989). The present work represents a complete revision and elaboration of themes in that book.

Introduction

[1]Johannes Quasten and Joseph Plumpe (eds.), *Ancient Christian Writers: The Works of the Fathers in Translation* (Washington, DC: Catholic University of America, 1948).

[2]John Dunne, *The Way of All the Earth: Experiments in Truth and Religion* (Notre Dame, IN: University of Notre Dame Press, 1972): ix-x; 180. Cited in David W. Augsberger, *Pastoral Counseling Across Cultures* (Philadelphia, PA: Westminster Press, 1986): 36-40.

[3]The first operational helicopter, invented by Igor Sikorsky, dates from 1939; the first true marine submersible, *Bathyscaphe,* invented by Auguste Piccard, dates from 1947.

[4]Donal Levine (ed.), *Georg Simmel: Selected Writings on Individuality and Social Forms* (Chicago: University of Chicago Press, 1971): 187-98.

[5]Levine, 1971: 188, 190.

[6]Levine, 1971: 191-2.

[7]Levine, 1971: 194.

[8]Dunne, 1972: x.

[9]See Chapter Four.

[10]This is explored in Chapters Seven and Eight.

[11]Peter S. Adler, "The Transitional Experience: An Alternative View of Culture

167

Shock. *Journal of Humanistic Psychology* 15, 4 (1975): 13.

[12]Paul Clasper, *Eastern Paths and the Christian Way* (Maryknoll, NY: Orbis, 1980): 126-7.

1. Movement and Mission

[1]Donal Levine, *Georg Simmel: Selected Writings on Individuality and Social Forms* (Chicago: University of Chicago Press, 1971): 187-98.

[2]Levine, 1971: 198.

[3]AG, 1, 5; also *Redemptoris Missio,* 1991, 71.

[4]David Bosch, *Transforming Mission* (Maryknoll, NY: Orbis, 1991): 389.

[5]Bosch, 1991: 390.

[6]T.S. Eliot (1888-1965), *Four Quartets* (1941): "The Dry Salvages" (New York, NY: Harcourt, Brace, Janovich).

[7]George Santayana's (1863-1952) *bon mot* is actually "those who cannot remember the past are condemned to repeat it."

[8]Some people prefer *missioners*. And increasingly the word *missional* is being used, to describe both Christians and the church itself. These words will be used from time to time in the narrative.

[9]Clifford Geertz, *Available Light: Anthropological Reflections on Philosophical Topics* (Princeton: Princeton University Press, 2000): 42-67. This reference, 42.

[10]Geertz, 2000: 46.

[11]St. Paul says "all beings in the heavens, on earth and in the underworld, should bend the knee at the name of Jesus" (Phil 2:10). The prophet says that Yahweh speaks and says "By my own self I swear it; what comes from my mouth is truth, a word irrevocable: before me every knee shall bend" (Is 45:23).

[12]Anthony J. Gittins, "Ethics, 'Hard Words,' and Liturgical Inculturation," in Kathleen Hughes, (ed.), *Finding Voice to Give God Praise* (Collegeville, MN: Liturgical Press, 1998). Also Bernard, 1998; LeCompte and Schensul, 1999.

[13]Dunne, 1972.

[14]Clasper, 1980: 126-7.

2. Meaning and Communication

[1]David Barrett, George Kurian, Todd Johnson (eds.), *World Christian Encyclopedia: A Comparative Survey of Churches and Religions in the Modern World* (New York, NY: Oxford University Press, 2001): 2: 243; figures taken from Dalby, 2000.

[2]"There are any number of different languages in the world, and not one of them is meaningless" (1Cor 14:10).

[3]For other definitions of, and approaches to culture, see Alan Barnard and Jonathan Spencer (eds.), *Encyclopedia of Social and Cultural Anthropology* (London and New York: Routledge, 1996): 136-7; Clifford Geertz , *The Interpretation of Cultures* (New York: Basic Books, 1973): 88; Chupungco (1996); Hiebert 1976; Ingold, 1994: 327-733; Luzbetak, 1988; and for a nuanced and comprehensive view, Schreiter, 1997: 29, 46-61.

[4]Geertz, 1973: 89.

[5]"Man cannot stand a meaningless life," said Carl Jung, in Anthony Storr, *Feet of Clay: Saints, Sinners, and Madmen: A Study of Gurus* (New York, NY: Free Press, 1996): 202. Also 152, 198-9, 200, 203.

⁶Peter Berger and Thomas Luckmann, *The Social Construction of Reality* (Garden City, NY: Anchor Books, 1967) is the most accessible exposition of the process whereby culture helps shape and fill our understanding of reality. Reality is "socially constructed" inasmuch as perceptions of what is really real vary cross-culturally. Through socialization the external world is selectively brought to our consciousness, and we are taught how our community understands, interprets, and relates to it. Once socialized, people cannot easily think their thought is wrong. It is tedious or frankly difficult to be resocialized to a different way of thinking or to an appreciation of worlds with which we are not familiar. Language is one of the major lenses through which we encounter worlds. Anthropologists and missionaries, among others, attempt to negotiate multiple socially constructed worlds.

⁷In Chapter Seven we consider different kinds of outsider and distinguish the *participant outsider* from the *non-participant outsider*. It is this latter that we refer to here.

⁸In some cultures, people who are perceived to be *different*, whether mentally or physically, are chosen to be shamans or ritual agents. They would say that the mental or physical characteristic is the sign God uses to identify such a person to the community.

⁹For a highly critical view of orthodox psychiatry and a trenchant argument, Thomas Szasz, *The Myth of Mental Illness* (New York, NY: Harper and Row, 1974 [revised edition]), is compelling. For an alternative view but an equally interesting read, Michel Foucault, *Madness and Civilization* (New York, NY: Random House, 1965), remains evergreen.

¹⁰Again Clifford Geertz, *Local Knowledge: Further Essays in Interpretive Anthropology* (New York, NY: Basic Books, 1983): 73-93 ("Common Sense as a Cultural System"), says it all, or most of it.

¹¹Ziauddin Sardar, *Thomas Kuhn and the Science Wars* (New York, NY: Totem Books, 2000): 53.

¹²Michael Jackson, "The Man Who Could Turn into an Elephant." *Paths toward a Clearing: Radical Empiricism and Ethnographic Enquiry* (Bloomington, IN: Indiana University Press, 1989): 102-18.

¹³For the "couvade" or lying-in of men, in Brazil, see Patrick Menget, "Time of Birth, Time of Being: The Couvade," in Michel Izard and Pierre Smith (eds.), *Between Belief and Transgression* (Chicago, IL: Chicago University Press, 1982): 193-209. For men who wound themselves, see Ian Hogbin, *The Island of Menstruating Men* (San Francisco, CA: Chandler, 1970).

¹⁴Steven Lukes, in a justly famous article (Wilson 1970: 194-213), talks about different forms of rationality (R) and distinguishes R1, R2 and so on. R1 would represent whatever is *universally* accepted (objects fall *downwards*), while R2 represents what a whole community accepts as really real (spirits, witchcraft), even though other communities may disagree. This would be local or contextual rationalities. Though different from R1, these cannot be said to be *a priori* irrational, says Lukes. Missionaries might find this rather enlightening.

¹⁵Thomas Kuhn argued forty years ago that anything outside the conceptual and practical scope of an operative paradigm must be seen as irrelevant. (Sardar, 2000: 30).

¹⁶A very sensitive treatment of this issue is Vincent Donovan, *Christianity Rediscovered: An Epistle from the Maasai* (Maryknoll, NY: Orbis, 1979).

¹⁷We also know stories of local people who were at a loss to understand why

missionaries would bathe fully clothed, or indeed disrobe only to replace day-clothes with night clothes when going to bed. Normal behavior can often seem bizarre when circumstances change.

[18]E.A. Judge, *The Social Patterns of Christian Groups in the First Century* (London: Tyndale, 1960): 107.

[19]Geertz, 1983: 120, 119, maintains that we (he's talking of anthropologists) need to be more than simply puzzle solvers; we need to be diagnosticians. He talks of "a science that can determine the meaning of things for the life that surrounds them." And we cannot assume that the meaning *for others* is the same as the meaning *for us*: "most people, I am convinced, see African sculpture as bush Picasso, and hear Javanese music as noisy Debussy."

[20]Lamin Sanneh, *Translating the Message* (Maryknoll, NY: Orbis, 1989).

[21]The notions of *lost* and *found* in translation are explored in another essay of Clifford Geertz, "Found in Translation: On the Social History of the Moral Imagination" (1983: 36-54).

[22]Developed in Gittins, "Belief and Faith, Assent and Dissent," *New Theology Review* (1989b): 65-85.

[23]Gittins, 1989b.

[24]Vatican II, "The Church in the Modern World" *(Gaudium et Spes)*, 43, in Flannery, 1996.

[25]*Lausanne Covenant 10*, 1974, in James Scherer and Stephen Bevans, *New Directions in Mission and Evangelization, 1* (Maryknoll, NY: Orbis, 1992): 257.

[26]See the Nonsense Exercise in the next chapter. We cannot always infer meaning simply by observation, nor *in abstracto*. What is the meaning of a kiss? Think of Rodin, think of Judas, think of your mother.

[27]Igor Kopytoff, "Knowledge and Belief in Suku Thought," *Africa* 51, 1981: 709-23.

[28]Frank Manning, "The Prophecy and the Law: Symbolism and Social Action in Seventh Day Adventism," in Carol Hill (ed.), *Symbols and Society* (Athens, GA: University of Georgia Press, 1975: 30-43), shows how religious symbols serve to synthesize a people's *ethos* and *worldview* (see Ch. 4, below).

[29]Hill, 1975: 1-10, provides a useful survey and introduction to this general area.

[30]A very important, classic, and somewhat modified article is Robin Horton's "African Traditional Thought and Western Science." It can be found slightly abridged, in Wilson 1970: 131-71; and in full with some discussion in Robin Horton, *Patterns of Thought in Africa and the West* (Cambridge: Cambridge University Press, 1993): 197-258.

[31]See Chapter Four.

[32]An excellent and evergreen reflection on this subject can be found in John Beattie, *Other Cultures* (London: Cohen and West, 1964): Ch. 5.

[33]Andrew Walls has a superb article on the contrast between *proseltyes* and *converts* in the early church. "Old Athens and New Jerusalem: Some Signposts for Christian Scholarship in the Early History of Mission Studies." *International Bulletin of Missionary Research* (October), 1997: 146-53.

[34]Jan de Vries, *Perspectives in the History of Religions* (Los Angeles, CA: University of California Press, 1977): xv. The introduction to a book that looks at a variety of approaches to religion.

[35]Geertz, 1983: 16.

3. Sense and Nonsense

[1]Noam Chomsky, *Syntactic Structures* (The Hague: Mouton, 1957).

[2]The most recent statistics indicate that there are 300 *ecclesiastical traditions* and a staggering 33, 820 *denominations* in the world today. But this is rather confusing. An ecclesiastical tradition is defined as "a church's or denomination's main tradition, family, rite, churchmanship, etc., with which it is most closely connected historically. Global total of all major traditions: 300, including 27 Roman Catholic rites and sub-rites" (David Barrett et al., *World Christian Encyclopedia: A Comparative Survey of Churches and Religions in the Modern World* [New York, NY: Oxford University Press, 2001]: 2: 659). A denomination is defined as "an organized Christian church or tradition or religious group or community of believers or aggregate of worship centers or congregations, *usually within a specific country*, whose component congregations and members are called by the same name in different areas, regarding themselves as an autonomous Christian church distinct from other denominations, churches and traditions" (Barrett, 2001, 2: 658) [my emphasis].

[3]There are many excellent and accessible surveys of applications of the linguistic analogy. Terence Hawkes, *Structuralism and Semiotics* (Berkeley, CA: University of California Press, 1977); M.L. Foster and L.J. Botscharow, *The Life of Symbols* (Boulder, CO: Westview Press, 1990); Steven Pinker, *The Language Instinct: How the Mind Creates Language* (New York, NY: HarperPerennial, 1995).

[4]Even worse: a standard assumption was that "culture" was synonymous with "high civilization" and that people beyond Europe simply did not have culture: they were barbarians or heathens, and whatever social organization they may have had was fatally corrupted and sinful.

[5]A *generative grammar* is a linguistic theory that attempts to describe the tacit knowledge that a native speaker has of a language, by establishing a set of explicit, formalized rules that specify or generate all the possible sentences of a language, while excluding all unacceptable sentences.

[6]The heavy work of clearing the ground in preparation for planting rice had been going on. The young man had been felling a tree. His foot caught in the root and he was struck as it fell. Perhaps his neck was broken then: certainly the trauma contributed to his death. The following night, in a fever, he dreamed about witches (what Lucy Mair called "the standardized nightmare of the group") and wickedness. During the night he went outside to relieve himself, but collapsed between his hut and his neighbor's. To be discovered outside during the night is a bad thing. He would have been questioned and encouraged (morally forced) to "confess." The reality of his dream experience was more important to him than the fact of his accident the previous day. *Secondary elaboration of belief* (the way explanations are sought and found in terms of a prevailing belief-system) would have helped cluster the circumstantial evidence into a watertight and circular case: perfectly logical and quite undisprovable. This kind of event can provide a wonderful pastoral moment for many of us, but only when the local reality was treated with the seriousness it deserved.

[7]Compelling and controversial is José Comblin, *The Meaning of Mission* (Maryknoll, NY: Orbis, 1977). This extract from pp. 33-4.

4. Merging Agendas

[1]These words are not always used consistently in the literature.

[2]Clifford Geertz, *The Interpretation of Cultures* (New York, NY: Basic Books, 1973) treats *ethos* and *worldview* (written as two words) in "Religion as a Cultural System" (esp 89-90); and in "Ethos, World View, and the Analysis of Sacred Symbols," (*passim*, esp 141). Though indebted to him, I use *worldview* as *the way things could be and should be*, which is slightly different.

[3]Barry Barnes (*T.S. Kuhn and Social Science*, London, UK: Macmillian, 1982): 9.

[4]Peter Matthiesson, *At Play in the Fields of the Lord* (New York, NY: Vintage Books 1965/1987); Barbara Kingsolver, *The Poisonwood Bible* (San Francisco, CA: HarperCollins, 1999). These are two of the more recent—and chillingly effective—reminders of the danger of well-meaning missionaries who are insensitive to people and their cultures.

[5]Jack Dominian, *Cycles of Affirmation* (London, UK: Darton, Longman & Todd, 1975), has spent a lifetime looking at human capacity for and resistance to change.

[6]As I drafted this, the saga of the American "spy" plane and the Chinese authorities was unfolding. The Chinese demanded a formal apology, consistent with their sense of outrage. Meanwhile the Americans said they had nothing to apologize for. A formal apology in diplomatic language was offered and accepted, though both parties knew it was more conventional than real.

[7]Extremely helpful material can be found in Michael Cole, John Glick et al., *The Cultural Context of Learning and Thinking* (New York, NY: Basic Books, 1971); also Michael Cole and Silvia Scribner, *The Psychology of Literacy* (Cambridge, MA: Harvard University Press, 1981).

[8]The classical text is still Peter Berger and Thomas Luckmann, *The Social Construction of Reality* (Garden City, NY: Anchor Books, 1967). The authors show how people are socialized to become members of their respective groups; they show how freedom and constraint operate socially; and they show how the operation of sanctions maintains social worlds.

[9]The notion of *moral* authority is expanded to cover what is deemed *situationally* or *contextually demanded*, whether or not it is objectively honorable or ethical.

[10]The Jesuit *Ratio Studiorum* of 1599 is the classic educational text here (Vincent Duminuco, *The Jesuit Ratio Studiorum of 1599: 400th Anniversary Perspectives* [Bronx, NY: Fordham University Press, 1999]).

[11]A recent and helpful study of missionaries and socialization is Birgit Meyer, *Translating the Devil: Religion and Modernity among the Ewe in Ghana* (Edinburgh, UK: Edinburgh University Press, 1999).

[12]In *dual systems* "a people follows the religious practices of two distinct systems. The two systems are kept discrete; they can operate side by side." Robert Schreiter, *Constructing Local Theologies* (Maryknoll, NY: Orbis, 1985): 145. Syncretism is "the mixing of elements of two religious systems to the point where at least one, if not both, of the systems loses basic structure and identity" (Schreiter 1985: 144). Since the mind accumulates information sequentially, it has to mix or combine the new and the old. Some *syncretic* assimilation is quite normal. Thus the tenets of Christianity can be woven into the fabric of actual lives to produce many varieties of Christian understanding and behavior. The degree of acceptable

syncretism is debated, but "good" and "bad" syncretism are sometimes distinguished. Robert Schreiter, "Defining Syncretism: An Interim Report," *International Bulletin of Missionary Research* 2, 1993: 50-3.

[13]This observation will strike Christians of different denominations in different ways (another illustration of the maxim that each one receives according to his or her capacity or predisposition to do so). (Roman) Catholics generally have a more optimistic view of culture than do Protestants: their respective evaluations of the sin and the grace in human life differ. If human nature is essentially corrupt, and all is grace, culture will be perceived as fatally flawed. If human culture is the basis for the human response, then despite the human propensity to sin, culture will be perceived as foundational to transformed humanity.

[14]Harlan Lane, *The Wild Boy of Aveyron* (London, UK: Paladin, 1979). This is a classic account of studies done on a boy found in the forest and apparently not raised in human society. It places us in the context of early nineteenth-century thinking, and describes the struggle toward a definition of *human*, which fascinated both humanists and theologians for years.

5. Proclaiming Good News

[1]We mentioned a figure of 13,500 languages in the world today.

[2]In his classic work, J.L. Austin, *How to Do Things with Words* (Harvard, MA: Harvard University Press, 1962), demonstrates various aspects of language: the *locutionary* (bearing semantic content); *illocutionary* (warning, asking, promising, etc); *perlocutionary* (affecting the listener by frightening, amusing, etc.) and *performative* (performing the very act that is spoken).

[3]Wilfred Cantwell Smith has a fine essay, "Idolatry in Comparative Perspective." He shows how easily we can come to worship our own ideas of God rather than God, in John Hick and Paul Knitter, *The Myth of Christian Uniqueness* (Maryknoll, NY: Orbis, 1987): 53-68.

[4]*Dynamic equivalence* is a translation which, while not literal, is nevertheless true to the deeper meaning. It translates terms or phrases with an eye to total context. We have to find *meaningful* translations as we take the Bible from one culture to another. How might we translate "lamb of God" to people who live in Arctic wastes? Could we ever think of something like "pig of God" for people who live in Pacific pig-cultures, or does this offend our own sensibilities too much? Some languages may not start a sentence with a demonstrative ("this"), but state the substantive first ("bottle"); thus the English "this is a bottle" is rendered "the bottle it is this one." For those who accept the real presence of Jesus in the eucharist, there is a significant theological problem if the *bread* ("this") is raised but identified *first* as "*body*"; we think of the power of consecration as effecting the change *from* "this (bread)" *to* "my body." Languages that say "my body it is this one" leave us with a problem of identification (is "this" *bread,* or *body*?). Translation can be a theological and semantic minefield. But even minefields can be negotiated in various ways.

[5]Margaret Miles, *Image as Insight: Visual Understanding in Western Christianity and Secular Culture* (Boston, MA: Beacon Press, 1985) demonstrates this wonderfully, as she discusses oral language and religious imagery.

[6]Linguistic relativity in this sense is an illustration of the incommensurability of worldviews. See Ziauddin Sardar, *Thomas Kuhn and the Science Wars* (Cambridge, UK: Icon Books, 2000).

[7]E. Thomas Brewster and Elizabeth Brewster, "Language Learning *Is* Communication—*Is* Mission," *International Bulletin of Missionary Research*, 1982: 160-4.

[8]The booklet referred to above, also contains "Bonding and the Missionary Task," another essay that explains becoming a *belonger*.

[9]This is the topic of the next chapter.

[10]The *World Christian Encyclopedia* gives the global literacy rate at 76.7% of adults (over 15 years). This seems impossibly high, but even if it were strictly true, it means there are well above a billion adult "illiterates" in the world. Whatever else they are, these people are *oral*, and as such they receive and transmit their culture effectively without recourse to literacy.

[11]Walter Ong, *Orality and Literacy: The Technologizing of the Word* (New York, NY: Methuen, 1981) says that only about 108 languages have ever had indigenous writing (and we quoted 13,500 languages in the world today, and countless that are no longer spoken).

[12]Martin Luther: "Christ did not command the apostles to write, but only to preach; the Gospel should not be written but screamed." Cited in Miles, 1985: 104.

[13]Caesar, *De Bello Gallico*, Book VI, Ch. 13 and 14. See Ellis, 1994: 55, 162-7, for a discussion of Celtic and Druidic literacy and orality.

[14]Ong, 1981; Miles, 1985.

[15]Possibly the best history of the art of memory in English is Frances S. Yates, *The Art of Memory* (London, UK: ARK Edition, Routledge and Kegan Paul, 1984).

[16]This is the same language Betty Brewster uses. Brewster and Brewster, 1982.

[17]Three references here to the "greats": Parry, Propp, and Lord. Albert Lord (1960) showed how Balkan epic-singers learned their prodigious feats of memory, and how they produced "creative-memory" renditions for hours on end. His work was inspired by the classicist Milman Parry who worked on the Homeric epics and their transmission (Parry, 1971). Vladimir Propp (1968) argued that all folk-tales of a certain type share a common structure that can be discovered beneath the variations. This insight is used by Kelber (see n. 23), discussing the Markan parables; it helps explain how they might be memorized and retold in their integrity.

Helen Waddell, *The Wandering Scholars* (London, UK: Constable Co., 1927/1987), studied the "Vagantes" whose repertoire of songs and poetry was prodigious: another indication of how much a memory trained to deal with oral rather than written information can retain and transmit.

Isidore Okpewho (1979, 1992) has been studying the epic, and myth, in Africa.

[18]A good storyteller, especially of "creative" stories, will presumably refine the stories and then tell them in several locations; it would be less than sensible to give one's best stories only a single telling! And I imagine that Jesus would have told the same parable on several occasions. Each telling is special; there is no such thing as "the original" for a storyteller, since each rendition is original and slightly different. Perhaps our search for the "original" occasion of Jesus' stories or parables is misdirected; if each has something special to tell, and none need have absolute priority, we can approach them with a certain freshness.

[19]"The *jongleur* sings an oral text," says Brian Stock (*Listening to the Text: On the Uses of the Past* [Baltimore, MD: Johns Hopkins University Press, 1990]: 25).

[20]Gossip: in Old English and Middle English, equivalent to godparent (God+sibb),

or sponsor at baptism. Later, "idle-talker." The word refers both to "god-talk" and to "family/familiar talk." Patricia Spacks, *Gossip* (Chicago, IL: University of Chicago Press, 1985). Also Alan Barnard and Jonathan Spencer, *Encyclopedia of Social and Cultural Anthropology* (London and New York: Routledge, 1996): 266-7.

[21]This is another story; this shift has a political and anti-woman history, as Marina Warner has shown. *The Beast and the Blonde: On Fairy Tales and Their Tellers* (New York, NY: Farrar, Straus and Giroux, 1994): 20-2, 33ff.

[22]One has only to reflect on the multi-million dollar industry of "Christian music" or Hollywood biblical epics to know the appeal of the oral, aural, and visual media today.

[23]Many literate people today have not lost all their oral skills. Missionaries might profitably explore the oral culture of those they serve. Werner Kelber, *The Oral and the Written Gospel* (Philadelphia, PA: Fortress Press, 1983), deals with the spoken word of Jesus and of Paul, and the transition from their speech to the written gospels and epistles. Also Herbert Klem, *Oral Communication of the Scriptures* (Pasadena, CA: Wm Carey Library, 1982).

[24]Kevin Maxwell, *Bemba Myth and Ritual: The Impact of Literacy on an Oral Culture* (New York, Frankfurt, Berne: Peter Lang, 1983), shows how literacy brings a new way of thinking (one that leads away from the mentality of Jesus or Paul as much as it leads to the text). More recently, Joseph Healey and Donald Sybertz, *Toward an African Narrative Theology* (Mayknoll, NY: Orbis, 1996) and Kofi Ron Lange, "Inculturation and Proverbs from Dagbani, Ghana," in Gittins (ed.), 2000: 135-44, have done fine work in this area.

[25]See David Rhoads and Ian Michie, *Mark As Story* (Philadelphia, PA: Fortress Press, 1982).

[26]Jack Goody (1968, 1986, and 1987) has produced some of the most interesting work in the field of orality and literacy. Also Ong, 1981: 3; Miles, 1985.

[27]Ernesto Cardenal, *The Gospel in Solentiname* (Maryknoll, NY: Orbis, 1982, 4 vols), showed how a small Christian community shared the word of God and discovered immense practical wisdom. The good news comes alive among people gathered to reflect and pray the gospel. What can happen in Nicaragua can happen anywhere.

[28]Currently, within the Roman Catholic community, there is a crisis centering on the issue of translation. *Dynamic equivalence* (note 4, above), a very standard approach, is regarded as unacceptable, and the Latin *editio typica* is required to be the basis for all translations. This threatens to produce the most literal or bland liturgical texts, if not chaos.

[29]Again, I am suggesting that virtually any community will respond to oral modes of learning, because they survive even in highly literate cultures.

[30]Barbara Reid (1999, 2000, 2001) shows the transformative potential of parables.

[31]William Bausch (1984) writes about storytelling and gives examples and practical advice for those who would like to explore this potential of the minister's trade. Also Rosemary Haughton (1973).

[32]From Roland Bainton, *Here I Stand: A Biography of Martin Luther* (New York, NY: Abingdon Press, 1950): 224. All the direct quotes are from Martin Luther himself.

[33]This assertion may take us back to the earlier treatment of *passing over*

(Introduction), or of the demands of *participant observation* (Ch. 1).

³⁴Walter R. Wietzke, *The Primacy of the Spoken Word* (Minneapolis, MN: Augsburg, 1988): 32.

6. Gift-Exchange and the Gospel

¹Donald Brown, *Cultural Universals* (Philadelphia, PA: Temple University Press, 1991); Kwasi Wiredu, *Cultural Universals and Particulars* (Bloomington, IN: Indiana University Press, 1996).

²I write gift-exchange with a hyphen to distinguish it from gift or gift giving, and mark it as mutual, reciprocal, and governed by moral rather than legal norms.

³Marcel Mauss, *The Gift: Forms and Functions of Exchange in Archaic Societies* (London: Cohen and West 1950/1970): 63.

⁴Nicholas Peterson, "Demand Sharing: Reciprocity and the Pressure for Generosity among Foragers," *American Anthropologist* December (1993: 860-74), has a wonderful ethnographic account of *demand sharing*.

⁵The *kula* is only one example of gift-exchange. But it is competitive exchange. Some men only dream about *kula* partners, as some Western capitalists dream about getting rich.

⁶Potlatches were made illegal in the 1930s but continue, in a modified way, as part of local life. A derivative is the "give-away" practiced by many Native American societies from the Plains. On occasions such as christenings and weddings, everyone who comes is given a gift; people come and receive rather than come and bring gifts. The hosts really impoverish themselves, but the guests build up their social capital.

⁷A thought-provoking example is the following, from another part of Papua New Guinea: "Wakasilele's friend presented him with a large pig. Wakasilele is a *Big Man,* a tough, stony-faced leader with a ferocious temper and a haughty pride. His friend was not a *Big Man*, but left Wakasilele speechless with emotion when he gave him the pig. 'Why is he being given the pig?' I asked. 'Because his friend is angry with him,' I was told. The friend had earlier brought Wakasilele some shellfish from the coast, but the latter had churlishly spurned the gift. The giver was ashamed, insulted and indignant. To point out to Wakasilele in the most humiliating way possible that he [Wakasilele] had committed a breach of good manners, his friend presented him with the most valuable asset he possessed—a pig. The emotion Wakasilele was struggling with was shame, and presumably contrition" (Michael Young, *Fighting with Food* [Cambridge, UK: Cambridge University Press, 1971]): xix.

⁸The English word *miser* is a direct loan from Latin: it means an unhappy man (sic). A miser is one who has everything but no friends. *Kula* exemplifies a social mechanism that distributes things as widely as possible, thereby gathering friends. A truly rich person may have no money and no things but many friends. A person who gives a dollar to each of twenty friends may have no money but many resources; a person who hoards the money is a miser *because he has no friends*.

⁹Not everyone engages in *potlatch*. Strategy determines how and when one engages in various kinds of exchange behavior.

¹⁰Patrick Vinton Kirch, *On the Road of the Winds: An Archaeological History of the Pacific Islands* (Berkeley, CA: University of California Press, 2001).

¹¹Douglas Oliver, *A Solomon Islands Society: Kinship and Leadership among*

the Siuai of Bougainville (Cambridge, MA: Harvard University Press, 1955). Maurice Godelier and Marilyn Strathern (eds.), *Big Men and Great Men: Personifications of Power in Melanesia* (Cambridge, UK: Cambridge University Press, 1991). Marvin Harris, *Cannibals and Kings* (Glasgow, UK: Fontana, 1977).

[12]A potential challenger will be lobbying for support, rather like a politician planning to run for office. If the challenger realizes he cannot win, he withdraws by hosting a feast and inviting the ranking *mumi.* This is quite a contrast with democratic politics: candidates who withdraw from the race are not noted for graciousness to the opposition.

[13]Piet Korse, "Baby Rituals, Ritual Baths, and Baptism—A Case from Congo," in Gittins, 2000: 119-34.

[14]André Fossion, "The Eucharist as an Act of Exchange," *Lumen Vitae* (1980): 409-16.

[15]A fundamental human right is the right to survival. Everyone has the right to food; a starving person who exercises this right is not stealing.

[16]If a neighbor insists that you keep his lawnmower, you are entitled to decline this offer. Neighborly generosity should not make others feel uncomfortable. But if you have your neighbor's snowblower but need to rearrange your garage, you surely have the right to return it.

[17]There are numerous biblical references to God's promise not to forget or abandon us. (Deut 4:31; Ps 9:12; 2Kg 17:38; but especially Is 49:15).

[18]Thanks-giving and for-giving are two fundamentally human capacities. We cannot pursue forgiving or forgiveness here, but it too has a place in the theory of gift-exchange.

[19]Walter Burkert, *Creation of the Sacred: Tracks of Biology in Early Religions* (Cambridge, MA: Harvard University Press, 1996: Ch. 4, "Hierarchy," and Ch. 6, "The Reciprocity of Giving"), contain real insight.

[20]There are many significant statements about *gift* in the New Testament. Read in the context of the present discussion, they may yield further insights. For example, Mt 5:41-2; 10:8; Mk 4:24; Rom 5:15; 1Pet 4:10; Prov 18:16, 19:6. The parable of the *Wicked Husbandmen* (Lk 20:9-18) is a story of a man whose authority was mocked, so he sent the closest thing to himself—his own son—in an attempt to appeal to the tenants' sense of shame. He put *himself* into the hands of his tenants by giving his son. The parable reveals something profound about the *identification* between gift and giver. Gift-exchange exhibits similar features.

[21]A negative or silent response is sometimes the most eloquent statement of intention.

[22]Much more could be said of gift-exchange as a way to understand *commercium:* God's outpouring or self-giving, particularly in the Eucharist. There is a whole theology of the *admirabile commercium,* and Martin Luther contributed substantially to its development.

7. Strangers in the Place

[1]*Inculturation* here is synonymous with *contextualization.* Roman Catholics tend to use "Inculturation" to mean "the expression of one's faith through one's own culture" (Luzbetak, 1988). Protestants favor "contextualization," meaning "the dynamic reflection carried out by the particular church upon its own life in the light of the Word of God and historic Christian truth" (Gilliland, 1989). See James

Scherer and Stephen Bevans, *New Directions in Mission and Evangelization, 3* (Maryknoll, NY: Orbis, 1999): 5.

[2]Walter Kasper, "On The Church: A Friendly Reply to Cardinal Ratzinger," *America,* April 23-30 (2001): 8-14.

[3]"Oh wad some power the giftie gie us/ To see oursels as ithers see us!/ It wad frae monie a blunder free us/An' foolish notion." *To a Louse* (1786).

[4]For the early Greeks, hospitality was the primary social virtue. Every stranger should receive hospitality, because it might actually be Zeus in disguise.

[5]For this section we rely heavily on van Gennep, 1960/1977.

[6]See Alfred Schutz, 1944, 1945. Also Dunne, 1972: ix-x; Clasper, 1980: 122-135.

[7]Bernard-Antoine Joinet, 1972 and 1974, offers helpful advice.

[8]In psychology: "anxiety that results from simultaneously holding contradictory or otherwise incompatible attitudes, beliefs, or the like, as when one likes a person but disapproves strongly of one of his or her habits."

[9]The very basic notion of "culture shock" can be elaborated by any social or cultural anthropology text. An enlightening article in the present context is Nash, 1963: 149ff.

[10]In 1864, Fustel de Coulanges argued, in *The Ancient City,* that ancient cultures always strove to exclude strangers. He was wrong. Recent work clearly shows that strangers may in fact be necessary for a society to flourish. See Werbner, 1979.

[11]This will be explained below.

[12]Nash, 1963; Schutz, 1944, 1945; Simmel, 1950.

[13]See gift-exchange, in the previous chapter.

[14]van Gennep, 1960/1977: 26-38.

[15]Only in 1537 did a Papal Bull declare the inhabitants of the New World to be human. That meant they could be baptized. It also implied that they should be treated in a human fashion.

[16]One can accept that a stranger can be somewhat assimilated into another group. But this depends on several factors. It takes time (many incomers are named and treated as such for several generations, and at least until all who were alive when the incomer arrived are dead). It takes mutual willingness (an assimilated bride may have been socialized to accept a new identity within that group, which may accept incoming women as no longer strangers. Still that does not make them insiders but may keep them in an ambiguous and powerless situation. However, one group may traditionally receive wives from another group, so that incoming women are not complete strangers but encounter their own relatives). And it does not necessarily imply that the assimilated person has equal rights with the local people. See the next chapter, on Biblical Attitudes.

8. Missionary as Stranger

[1]Any good Bible dictionary will be a great start here. I recommend McKenzie, 1965: 847-9; or Stuhlmueller, 1996: 957-61.

[2]See Chapter Four.

[3]Brueggemann, 1979.

[4]The Greek has *paroikos* rather than the more common *xenos* of Matthew 25. It is used technically here, and refers to someone residing as an alien or stranger (see Gen 17:8; 26:2; Deut 5:14; Heb 11:9).

[5]Richard Gaillardetz, *Transforming Our Days: Spirituality, Community and Liturgy in a Technological Culture* (New York, NY: Crossroad, 2000): 39-45. *Friction* is "an essential qualit[y] that gives ordinary human existence texture—it is what makes our existence 'real.' It is precisely the 'rough fit,' the 'mixed bag,' of so many human interactions that brings freshness and vitality to our lives" (42). If such friction is an important component of our familiar domestic lives, it is surely even more so when our lives rub against an unfamiliar world.

[6]Perhaps the time has come for us to rework the familiar horticultural metaphor of *transplantation.* Cultures are more like organisms than gardens. We know enough about *organ transplantation* to accept that the immune system works *normally* by "rejecting" foreign tissues, unless it can be "persuaded" that they are necessary for its life. A culture's rejection of certain missionary approaches may not be pathological but a sign of a struggling rather than an unhealthy culture.

[7]Is Christianity so irrelevant today because Christians have failed to infect people with the living Spirit and the living words of Jesus, but have offered a set of rules or a dead text? We must constantly remember the priority of word over text, of gospel over bible, of spirit over letter.

[8]Gittins, 1984.

[9]Quasten and Plumpe (eds.), 1948.

Conclusion

[1]This was explained in the Introduction, but it might be more meaningful now, as we reach the end.

[2]Claude-Marie Barbour, "Seeking Justice and Shalom in the City," *International Review of Mission* (1984: 303-09), has developed this notion in theory and in practice. See also Gittins, 1993: 55-71.

[3]Barbour, 1984: 304.

[4]John Boberg, "The Missionary as Anti-Hero," *Missiology* 7 (1979): 418.

[5]Donal Dorr, *Mission in Today's World* (Maryknoll, NY: Orbis, 2000): 271.

[6]*Redemptoris Missio* (53), Encyclical Letter of Pope John Paul II, 1991, *On the Permanent Validity of the Church's Missionary Mandate*, in Burrows (ed.), 1993.

[7]T.S. Eliot, *Four Quartets,* "Little Gidding," pt. 5 (New York, NY: Harcourt, Brace, Jovanovich, 1971).

[8]Dorr, 2000: 269-285.

[9]Paul Clasper, *Eastern Paths and the Christian Way* (Maryknoll, NY: Orbis, 1980): 126-7.

[10]See reference at the beginning of Chapter One.

WORKS CITED

Achtemeier, Paul (ed.), 1985. *Harper Bible Dictionary.* New York, NY: HarperSanFrancisco.

Adler, Peter S., 1975. "The Transitional Experience: An Alternative View of Culture Shock." *Journal of Humanistic Psychology* 15, 4: 13-23.

Augsburger, David W., 1986. *Pastoral Counseling Across Cultures.* Philadelphia, PA: Westminster Press.

Austin, J.L., 1962. *How to Do Things with Words.* Cambridge, MA: Harvard University Press.

Bainton, Roland, 1950. *Here I Stand: A Biography of Martin Luther.* New York, NY: Abingdon Press.

Barbour, Claude-Marie, 1984. "Seeking Justice and Shalom in the City." *International Review of Mission* 73, 291: 303-9.

Barnard, Alan, and Jonathan Spencer (eds.), 1996. *Encyclopedia of Social and Cultural Anthropology.* London, UK, and New York, NY: Routledge.

Barnes, Barry, 1982. *T.S. Kuhn and Social Science.* London, UK: Macmillan.

Barrett, David, George T. Kurian, and Todd M. Johnson (eds.), 2001. *World Christian Encyclopedia: A Comparative Survey of Churches and Religions in the Modern World.* 2 vols. New York, NY: Oxford University Press.

Bausch, William, 1984. *Storytelling: Imagination and Faith.* Mystic, CT: Twenty-Third Publications.

Beattie, John, 1964. *Other Cultures.* London, UK: Cohen and West.

Berger, Peter, and Thomas Luckmann, 1967. *The Social Construction of Reality.* Garden City, NY: Anchor Books.

Bernard, Russell (ed.), 1998. *Handbook of Methods in Cultural Anthropology.* Walnut Creek, CA: Altamira/Sage.

Bevans, Stephen, 1991. "Seeing Mission Through Images." *Missiology* 19, 1: 45-57.

Boberg, John, 1979. "The Missionary as Anti-hero." *Missiology* 7, 4: 411-21.

Bohannan, Paul, 1959. "The Impact of Money on an Africa Subsistence Economy." *Journal of Economic History* 19, 4: 491-503.

Bosch, David, 1991. *Transforming Mission.* Maryknoll, NY: Orbis.

Brewer, E.C., 1988. *Dictionary of Phrase and Fable.* Leicester, UK: Galley Press.

Brewster, E. Thomas, and Elizabeth Brewster, 1982. "Language Learning *Is* Communication—*Is* Mission." *International Bulletin of Missionary Research,* October: 160-64; also published as booklet by Lingua House, 135 North Oakland, Box #114, Pasadena, CA, 1984.

Brown, Donald, 1991. *Cultural Universals.* Philadelphia, PA: Temple University Press.

Brueggemann, Walter, 1979. *The Land*. Minneapolis, MN: Fortress Press.

Burkert, Walter, 1996. *Creation of the Sacred: Tracks of Biology in Early Religions*. Cambridge, MA: Harvard University Press.

Burrows, William (ed.), 1993. *Redemption and Dialogue: Reading* Redemptoris Missio *and* Dialogue and Proclamation. Maryknoll, NY: Orbis.

Cardenal, Ernesto, 1982. *The Gospel in Solentiname*. 4 vols. Maryknoll, NY: Orbis.

Carrier, James, 1992. "The Gift in Theory and Practice in Melanesia." *Ethnology* 31, 2: 185-93.

Chomsky, Noam, 1957. *Syntactic Structures*. The Hague, Holland: Mouton.

Chomsky, Noam, 2000. *New Horizons in the Study of Language and Mind*. Cambridge, UK: Cambridge University Press.

Chupungco, Anscar, 1996. "Two Methods of Liturgical Inculturation." In S. Anita Stauffer (ed.), *LWF Studies: Christian Worship: Unity in Cultural Diversity*. Geneva: World Council of Churches: 77-93.

Clasper, Paul, 1980. *Eastern Paths and the Christian Way*. Maryknoll, NY: Orbis.

Cole, Michael, John Glick, et al., 1971. *The Cultural Context of Learning and Thinking*. New York, NY: Basic Books.

Cole, Michael, and Silvia Scribner, 1981. *The Psychology of Literacy*. Cambridge, MA: Harvard University Press.

Comblin, José, 1977. *The Meaning of Mission*. Maryknoll, NY: Orbis.

Dalby, David, 2000. *The Linguasphere: Register of the World's Languages and Speech Communities*. Hebron, UK: Linguasphere Press.

Dalton, George, 1965. "Primitive Money." *American Anthropologist* 1: 44-65.

Dominian, Jack, 1975. *Cycles of Affirmation*. London, UK: Darton, Longman & Todd.

Donovan, Vincent, 1979. *Christianity Rediscovered: An Epistle from the Maasai*. Maryknoll, NY: Orbis.

Dorr, Donal, 2000. *Mission in Today's World*. Maryknoll, NY: Orbis.

Duminuco, Vincent, 1999. *The Jesuit Ratio Studiorum of 1599: 400ᵗʰ Anniversary Perspectives*. Bronx, NY: Fordham University Press.

Dunne, John, 1972. *The Way of All the Earth: Experiments in Truth and Religion*. Notre Dame, IN: University of Notre Dame Press.

Duranti, Alessandro (ed.), 1999. *Language Matters in Anthropology: A Lexicon for the Millennium*. Journal of Linguistic Anthropology 9.

Eliot, T[homas] S[tearns], 1941/1971. "The Dry Salvages"; "Little Gidding." In *Four Quartets*. New York, NY: Harcourt, Brace, Jovanovich.

Ellis, Peter Berresford, 1994. *The Druids*. Grand Rapids, MI: Eerdmans.

Erchak, Gerald M., 1992. *The Anthropology of Self and Behavior*. New Brunswick, NJ: Rutgers University Press.

Flannery, Austin (ed.), 1996. *The Basic Sixteen Documents of Vatican Council II*. Northport, NY: Costello.

Foley, John M., 1995. *The Singer of Tales in Performance*. Bloomington, IN: Indiana University Press.

Fossion, André, 1980. "The Eucharist as an Act of Exchange." *Lumen Vitae* 35, 4: 409-16.

Foster, M.L., and L.J. Botscharow (eds.), 1990. *The Life of Symbols*. Boulder, CO: Westview Press.

Foucault, Michel, 1965. *Madness and Civilization*. New York, NY: Random House.

Gaillardetz, Richard, 2000. *Transforming Our Days: Spirituality, Community and Liturgy in a Technological Culture.* New York, NY: Crossroad.

Gallagher, Michael Paul, 1997. *Clashing Symbols: An Introduction to Faith and Culture.* London, UK: Darton, Longman and Todd.

Geertz, Clifford, 1973. *The Interpretation of Cultures: Essays in Interpretive Anthropology.* New York, NY: Basic Books.

Geertz, Clifford, 1983. *Local Knowledge: Further Essays in Interpretive Anthropology.* New York, NY: Basic Books.

Geertz, Clifford, 2000. *Available Light: Anthropological Reflections on Philosophical Topics.* Princeton, NJ: Princeton University Press.

Gilliland, Dean S. (ed.), 1989. *The World among Us: Contextualizing Theology for Mission Today.* Dallas, TX: Word Publishing.

Gittins, Anthony J., 1984. "Mission as Communication: A Marginal Note." *Review for Religious* 43, 4: 354-62.

Gittins, Anthony J., 1989a. *Gifts and Strangers: Meeting the Challenge of Inculturation.* Mahwah, NJ: Paulist Press.

Gittins, Anthony J., 1989b. "Belief and Faith, Assent and Dissent." *New Theology Review,* August: 65-85.

Gittins, Anthony J., 1989c. "When Behavior and Belief Don't Fit." *The Catholic World,* Nov.-Dec. 1989: 258-61.

Gittins, Anthony J., 1993. *Bread for the Journey: The Mission of Transformation and the Transformation of Mission.* Maryknoll, NY: Orbis.

Gittins, Anthony J., 1994. "Responding to Xenophobia." *The Month,* May: 185-90.

Gittins, Anthony J., 1996. "Stranger." In Stuhlmueller, 1996: 957-61.

Gittins, Anthony J., 1998. "Ethics, 'Hard Words,' and Liturgical Inculturation." In Hughes, 1998: 139-50.

Gittins, Anthony J. (ed.), 2000. *Life and Death Matters: The Practice of Inculturation in Africa.* Nettetal, West Germany: Steyler Verlag.

Gluckman, Max, 1963. "Gossip and Scandal." *Current Anthropology* 4: 307-16.

Godelier, Maurice, 1999. *The Enigma of the Gift.* Chicago, IL: University of Chicago Press.

Godelier, Maurice, and Marilyn Strathern (eds.), 1991. *Big Men and Great Men: Personifications of Power in Melanesia.* Cambridge, UK: Cambridge University Press.

Goody, Jack, 1968. *Literacy in Traditional Societies.* Cambridge, UK: Cambridge University Press.

Goody, Jack, 1986. *The Logic of Writing and the Organization of Society.* Cambridge, UK: Cambridge University Press.

Goody, Jack, 1987. *The Interface Between the Written and the Oral.* Cambridge, UK: Cambridge University Press.

Gregory, Christopher, 1980. "Gifts to Men and Gifts to God: Gift Exchange and Capital Accumulation in Contemporary Papua New Guinea." *Man* 15, 4: 626-52.

Hall, Douglas J., 1997. *The End of Christendom and the Future of Christianity.* Valley Forge, PA: Trinity Press International.

Hammersley, Martin, and Paul Atkinson, 1995. *Ethnography: Principles in Practice.* New York, NY: Routledge.

Harris, Marvin, 1977. *Cannibals and Kings.* Glasgow, UK: Fontana.

Haughton, Rosemary, 1973. *Tales from Eternity: The World of Fairy-Tales and the Spiritual Search*. New York, NY: Seabury Press.

Hawkes, Terence, 1977. *Structuralism and Semiotics*. Berkeley, CA: University of California Press.

Healey, Joseph, and Donald Sybertz, 1996. *Towards an African Narrative Theology*. Maryknoll, NY: Orbis.

Hick, John, and Paul Knitter (eds.), 1987. *The Myth of Christian Uniqueness*. Maryknoll, NY: Orbis.

Hiebert, Paul, 1976. *Cultural Anthropology*. Philadelphia, PA: J.B. Lippincott.

Hiebert, Paul, 1994. *Anthropological Reflections on Missiological Issues*. Grand Rapids, MI: Baker Book House.

Hill, Carol (ed.), 1975. *Symbols and Society*. Athens, GA: University of Georgia Press.

Hogbin, Ian, 1970. *The Island of Menstruating Men*. San Francisco, CA: Chandler.

Hollis, Martin, and Stephen Lukes (eds.), 1982. *Rationality and Relativism*. Oxford, UK: Blackwell.

Horton, Robin, 1970. "African Traditional Religion and Western Science." In Wilson, 1970: 131-71; also in Horton, 1993: 197-258.

Horton, Robin, 1993. *Patterns of Thought in Africa and the West*. Cambridge, UK: Cambridge University Press.

Hughes, Kathleen (ed.), 1998. *Finding Voice to Give God Praise*. Collegeville, MN: Liturgical Press.

Ingold, Tim (ed.), 1994. *Companion Encyclopedia of Anthropology*. London, UK, and New York, NY: Routledge.

Izard, Michel, and Pierre Smith (eds.), 1982. *Between Belief and Transgression*. Chicago, IL: University of Chicago Press.

Jackson, Michael, 1989. *Paths toward a Clearing: Radical Empiricism and Ethnographic Enquiry*. Bloomington, IN: Indiana University Press.

Joinet, Bernard-Antoine, 1972. "I Am a Stranger in My Father's House." *African Educational Review* 14, 3: 244-54.

Joinet, Bernard-Antoine, 1974. "I Speak in the House of My Hosts." *Lumen Vitae* 29, 4: 487-503.

Jorgensen, Danny, 1989. *Participant Observation*. Newbury Park, CA: Sage.

Judge, E.A., 1960. *The Social Patterns of Christian Groups in the First Century*. London, Tyndale.

Judge, E.A., 1986. "The Quest for Mercy in Late Antiquity." In O'Brien and Peterson, 1986: 107-21.

Kasper, Walter, 2001. "On the Church: A Friendly Reply to Cardinal Ratzinger." *America*, April 23-30: 8-14.

Kelber, Werner, 1983/1997. *The Oral and the Written Gospel*. Philadelphia, PA: Fortress Press.

Kingsolver, Barbara, 1999. *The Poisonwood Bible*. San Francisco, CA: HarperCollins.

Kirch, Patrick Vinton, 2001. *On the Road of the Winds: An Archaeological History of the Pacific Islands*. Berkeley, CA: University of California Press.

Klem, Herbert V., 1982. *Oral Communication of the Scriptures*. Pasadena, CA: Wm Carey Library.

Kopytoff, Igor, 1981. "Knowledge and Belief in Suku Thought." *Africa* 51, 3: 709-23.

Korse, Piet, 2000. "Baby Rituals, Ritual Baths, and Baptism—A Case from Congo." In Gittins, 2000: 119-34.

Kraft, Charles, 1979. *Christianity in Culture.* Maryknoll, NY: Orbis.

Kraft, Charles, 1996. *Anthropology for Christian Witness.* Maryknoll, NY: Orbis.

Kreider, Alan, 1999. *The Change of Conversion and the Origin of Christendom.* Harrisburg, PA: Trinity International.

Lakoff, Robin, 2000. *The Language War: The Politics of Meaning Making.* Berkeley, CA: University of California Press.

Lane, Harlan, 1979. *The Wild Boy of Aveyron.* London, UK: Paladin.

Lange, Kofi Ron, 2000. "Inculturation and Proverbs from Dagbani, Ghana." In Gittins, 2000: 135-44.

Lausanne Covenant, 1974. Lausanne International Congress on World Evangelization. See Scherer and Bevans, 1992.

LeCompte, Margaret, and Jean Schensul (eds.), 1999. *The Ethnographer's Toolkit.* 7 vols. Walnut Creek, CA: Altamira/Sage.

Lee, Jung Young, 1995. *Marginality: The Key to Multicultural Theology.* Minneapolis, MN: Fortress Press.

Levine, Donal N. (ed.), 1971. *Georg Simmel: Selected Writings on Individuality and Social Forms.* Chicago, IL: University of Chicago Press.

Lord, Albert B., 1960. *The Singer of Tales.* Cambridge, MA: Harvard University Press.

Lukes, Steven, 1970. "Some Problems about Rationality." In Wilson, 1970: 194-213.

Luzbetak, Louis, 1988. *The Church and Cultures: New Perspectives in Missionary Anthropology.* Maryknoll, NY: Orbis.

Malinowski, Bronislaw, 1922. *Argonauts of the Western Pacific.* London, UK: Routledge.

Manning, Frank, 1975. "The Prophecy and the Law: Symbolism and Social Action in Seventh Day Adventism." In Hill, 1975: 30-43.

Matthiessen, Peter, 1987. *At Play in the Fields of the Lord.* New York, NY: Vintage Books.

Mauss, Marcel, 1950/1970. *The Gift: Forms and Functions of Exchange in Archaic Societies.* London, UK: Cohen and West.

Maxwell, Kevin, 1983. *Bemba Myth and Ritual: The Impact of Literacy on an Oral Culture.* New York, NY, Frankfurt, Germany, and Berne, Switzerland: Peter Lang.

McKenzie, John (ed.), 1965. *Dictionary of the Bible.* New York, NY: Macmillan.

Menget, Patrick, 1982. "Time of Birth, Time of Being: The Couvade." In Izard and Smith, 1982: 193-209.

Meyer, Birgit, 1999. *Translating the Devil: Religion and Modernity among the Ewe in Ghana.* Edinburgh, UK: Edinburgh University Press.

Miles, Margaret, 1985. *Image as Insight: Visual Understanding in Western Christianity and Secular Culture.* Boston, MA: Beacon Press.

Nash, Denison, 1963. "The Ethnologist as Stranger." *South West Journal of Anthropology* 19: 149ff.

Nida, Eugene, and Charles R. Taber, 1969. *Theory and Practice of Translation.* Leiden, Holland: Brill.

O'Brien, P.T., and D.G. Peterson (eds.), 1986. *God Who Is Rich in Mercy: Essays Presented to D.B. Knox.* Sydney, NSW: Macquarie University Press.

Okpewho, Isidore, 1979. *The Epic in Africa*. New York, NY: Columbia University Press.

Okpewho, Isidore, 1992. *African Oral Literature: Background, Character, Continuity*. Bloomington, IN: Indiana University Press.

Oliver, Douglas, 1955. *A Solomon Islands Society: Kinship and Leadership among the Siuai of Bougainville*. Cambridge, MA: Harvard University Press.

Ong, Walter, 1981. *Orality and Literacy: The Technologizing of the Word*. New York, NY: Methuen.

Parry, Adam (ed.), 1971. *The Making of Homeric Verse: The Collected Papers of Milman Parry*. Oxford, UK: Clarendon Press.

Peterson, Nicholas, 1993. "Demand Sharing: Reciprocity and the Pressure for Generosity Among Foragers." *American Anthropologist*, December: 860-74.

Pinker, Steven, 1995. *The Language Instinct: How the Mind Creates Language*. New York, NY: HarperPerennial.

Quasten, Johannes, and Joseph Plumpe (eds.), 1948. *The Epistle to Diognetus*. In *Ancient Christian Writers: The Works of the Fathers in Translation*. Washington, DC: Catholic University of America, 6:135-47.

Reid, Barbara, 1999. *Parables for Preachers* (Year B). Collegeville, MN: Liturgical Press.

Reid, Barbara, 2000. *Parables for Preachers* (Year C). Collegeville, MN: Liturgical Press.

Reid, Barbara, 2001. *Parables for Preachers* (Year A). Collegeville, MN: Liturgical Press.

Rhoads, David, and Ian Michie, 1982. *Mark as Story:* Philadelphia, PA: Fortress Press.

Roxburgh, Alan J., 1997. *The Missionary Congregation, Leadership and Liminality*. Harrisburg, PA: Trinity Press International.

Sahlins, Marshall, 1963. "Poor Man, Rich Man, Big Man, Chief." *Comparative Studies in Society and History* 5: 285-303.

Sanneh, Lamin, 1989. *Translating the Message: The Missionary Impact on Culture*. Maryknoll, NY: Orbis.

Sardar, Ziauddin, 2000. *Thomas Kuhn and the Science Wars*. New York, NY: Totem Books.

Scherer, James, and Stephen Bevans (eds.), 1992. *New Directions in Mission and Evangelization, 1*. Maryknoll, NY: Orbis.

Scherer, James, and Stephen Bevans (eds.), 1995. *New Directions in Mission and Evangelization, 2*. Maryknoll, NY: Orbis.

Scherer, James, and Stephen Bevans (eds.), 1999. *New Directions in Mission and Evangelization, 3*. Maryknoll, NY: Orbis.

Schreiter, Robert, 1985. *Constructing Local Theologies*. Maryknoll, NY: Orbis.

Schreiter, Robert, 1993. "Defining Syncretism: An Interim Report." *International Bulletin of Missionary Research* 2: 50-53.

Schreiter, Robert, 1997. *The New Catholicity: The Church between the Local and the Global*. Maryknoll, NY: Orbis.

Schutz, Alfred, 1944. "The Stranger." *American Journal of Sociology* 49: 499.

Schutz, Alfred, 1945. "The Homecomer." *American Journal of Sociology* 50: 369-76.

Shenk, Wilbert, 1999. *Changing Frontiers of Mission*. Maryknoll, NY: Orbis.

Simmel. Georg, 1950. *The Stranger.* New York, NY: Free Press.

Simmel, Georg. See Levine, 1971.

Smith, Wilfred Cantwell, 1987. "Idolatry in Comparative Perspective." In Hick and Knitter, 1987: 53-68.

Spacks, Patricia, 1985. *Gossip.* Chicago, IL: University of Chicago Press.

Spradley, James, 1980. *Participant Observation.* New York, NY: Holt, Rinehart and Winston.

Stark, Rodney, 1996. *The Rise of Christianity: How the Obscure, Marginal Jesus Movement Became the Dominant Religious Force in the Western World in a Few Centuries.* Princeton, NJ: Princeton University Press.

Stock, Brian, 1983. *The Implications of Literacy.* Princeton, NJ: Princeton University Press.

Stock, Brian, 1990. *Listening for the Text: On the Uses of the Past.* Baltimore, MD: Johns Hopkins University Press.

Stuhlmueller, Carroll (ed.), 1996. *The Collegeville Pastoral Dictionary of Biblical Theology.* Collegeville, MN: Liturgical Press.

Szasz, Thomas, 1974. *The Myth of Mental Illness.* Revised edition. New York, NY: Harper and Row.

Titmus, Richard, 1971. *The Gift Relationship: From Human Blood to Social Policy.* London, UK: George Allen and Unwin.

van Gennep, Arnold, 1960/1977. *The Rites of Passage.* London, UK: Routledge and Kegan Paul.

Vries, Jan de, 1977. *Perspectives in the History of Religions.* Los Angeles, CA: University of California Press.

Waddell, Helen, 1927/1987. *The Wandering Scholars.* London, UK: Constable Co.

Walls, Andrew, 1997. "Old Athens and New Jerusalem: Some Signposts for Christian Scholarship in the Early History of Mission Studies." *International Bulletin of Missionary Research,* October: 146-53.

Walls, Andrew, 1999. "The Gospel as Prisoner and Liberator of Culture." In Scherer and Bevans, 1999: 17-28.

Warner, Marina, 1994. *The Beast and the Blonde: On Fairy Tales and Their Tellers.* New York, NY: Farrar, Straus and Giroux.

Warner, Marina, 1998. *No Go the Bogeyman: Scaring, Lulling and Making Mock.* London, UK: Chatto and Windus.

Weiner, Annette, 1992. *Inalienable Possessions: The Paradox of Keeping-While-Giving."* Berkeley, CA: University of California Press.

Werbner, Richard, 1979. "Totemism in History: The Ritual Passage of West African Strangers." *MAN* 14, 4: 663ff.

Wietzke, Walter R., 1988. *The Primacy of the Spoken Word.* Minneapolis, MN: Augsburg.

Wilson, Bryan (ed.), 1970. *Rationality.* Oxford, UK: Blackwell.

Wiredu, Kwasi, 1996. *Cultural Universals and Particulars: An African Perspective.* Bloomington, IN: Indiana University Press.

Yates, Frances S., 1984. *The Art of Memory.* ARK Edition. London, UK: Routledge and Kegan Paul.

Young, Michael, 1971. *Fighting with Food.* Cambridge, UK: Cambridge University Press.

INDEX

Of Related Interest

Other indispensable books on the intersection of culture, spirituality, and social justice

The Bible on Culture
Lucien Legrand
ISBN 1-57075-330-X-4

"Legrand displays a marvelous appreciation for the subtleties and complexities in the diverse ways faith expresses and encounters local cultures."
David Rhoads, Lutheran School of Theology at Chicago

African Earthkeepers: Wholistic Interfaith Mission
Marthinus L. Daneel
ISBN 1-57075-329-6

"If it is difficult to exaggerate the importance of environmental stewardship, it is equally difficult to imagine a more heartening and exemplary story than the one related in this book."
Jonathan J. Bonk, Overseas Minstries Study Center

The Divine Deli: Religious Identity in the North American Cultural Mosaic
John H. Berthrong
ISBN 1-57075-268-0

"John Berthrong speaks from his own experience of friendship with persons of different faiths. His book offers a real feast of religious pluralism in North American Society."
Julia Ching

Please support your local bookstore, or call us at 1-800-258-5838 or visit our website at www.orbisbooks.com. To purchase our books directly, visit us at www.maryknollmall.org

Thank you for reading Orbis Books.